Towards Zero-energy Architecture
New Solar Design

Towards Zero-energy Architecture
New Solar Design

Mary Guzowski

Laurence King Publishing

With love and appreciation to
John and James Lindbeck
and the next generation of ecological designers.

LAURENCE KING

First published in Great Britain in 2010
This paperback edition published in 2012 by
Laurence King Publishing Ltd
361–373 City Road
London EC1V 1LR
United Kingdom
Tel: + 44 20 7841 6900
Fax: + 44 20 7841 6910
e-mail: enquiries@laurenceking.com
www.laurenceking.com

A catalogue record for this book is available
from the British Library

ISBN: 978-1-78067-026-3
Design: Godfrey Design
Printed in China

Contents

Introduction

"Solar radiation is the primary source of renewable energy. Besides offering a direct source of energy, it drives the Earth's climate creating opportunities to draw energy from wind, waves, tidal (together with the moon) and a host of biological sources… Since the sun drives every aspect of the climate it is logical to describe the techniques adopted in buildings to take advantage of this fact as 'solar design'."[1]
Peter F. Smith, *Architecture in a Climate of Change*

Humans continue to adapt to the rhythms of light and darkness in the eternal cycle of night and day as the sun rises and sets, season after season, millennium upon millennium. We find ways to harness the forces of the sun and wind to sustain our lives, and these forces have shaped the built environment. Our ancestors used simple and ingenious strategies to create dwellings, neighborhoods, public spaces, villages, and even sophisticated solar cities. The forces of the sun and wind have inspired architectural design at all scales, from building form to plan, section, materials, and detailing. We have always relied on the sun and wind to meet seasonal needs for lighting, heating, and cooling; always celebrating our relationships with the varied places and climates of the world.

Not until the mid-twentieth century, with the widespread construction of roads, distribution of fossil fuels, and manufacture of mechanical systems were we able to turn our backs on the sun and wind as providers of light, heat, and air. As a consequence, in just a few decades we have witnessed an exponential growth in the consumption of resources, production of pollution and waste, and alienation from the natural world. Fortunately, in response to this grim trajectory, architects and designers from around the world are joining a movement to create buildings that mitigate global warming and climate change. Zero-energy and carbon-

neutral architecture has emerged as a top priority, although low-energy and low-carbon design is often more readily achieved.

A true architecture of the sun and wind is more than the sum of passive strategies, technological systems, and ecological engineering. Buildings that are shaped by the sun and wind promote social and ecological values by revealing how our lives can be powered by renewable resources; and just as importantly, they also promote aesthetic values by creating relationships with place and site that are based on the form-giving and poetic attributes of these forces. The new solar architecture has a thin profile that optimizes light and air; it employs an ecological envelope that is responsive to the site and environmental forces; it reduces or eliminates dependence on fossil fuels, is renewable, and strives for little or no carbon-based energy consumption.

Above all, a true architecture of the sun and wind is beautiful and fosters health, well-being, and a connection to the local site and ecosystems. As architect Sim Van der Ryn explains in *Design for Life*: "Architecture is 're-membering'— putting back together our collective dreams… The building should tell a story about place and people and be a pathway to understanding ourselves within nature."[2] This new generation of architecture uses the sun and wind not only to address energy and resource consumption but

also to awaken, or "re-member," our ecological relationship to the world and to express an ecological aesthetic.

The growing interest in zero-energy and carbon-neutral architecture is generating an evolution in design processes, strategies, and protocols. Evidence of this transition is found in recent legislation, revisions to green standards and guidelines, new evaluative tools, and in design firms that are striving to learn more about the issues. It is a hopeful sign that a great number of projects are in the development stage. In the next few years there will be many more precedents to help designers understand the architectural opportunities and challenges of reducing or eliminating fossil fuel consumption and greenhouse gas emissions.

The firms that have designed the ten architectural projects featured in this book are leading the way into a new and more sustainable future. Differing in size, location, and scope, these projects can be viewed as pilot studies, in some cases even experimental endeavors, that explore and expand the role of the sun and wind in reducing or eliminating our dependence on fossil fuels. The ten case studies reveal that there is no single strategic approach to low- and zero-energy architecture. Formal, aesthetic, and expressive responses are as varied as are the individual architects and design firms. Yet, a common thread in all of the projects is a deep

commitment by the design teams to harvest the sun, wind, and other sources of on-site renewable energy to heat, light, and cool the buildings. Spanning the range of these architectural expressions we also find approaches to solar design that integrate ancient lessons of passive and climate-responsive design with state-of-the art technologies and new, innovative approaches to high-performance and responsive building envelopes. Working within essential solar and climate-responsive parameters, we find seemingly unlimited formal, stylistic, and expressive design opportunities.

Five broad themes emerged from the study of these pioneering works. First, the projects inspire change. They strive to go beyond incremental improvements to energy codes and instead respond to the design problems with deeper ecological solutions. Second, the projects respond to place. The works are clearly informed by the environmental forces of their immediate site in addition to the surrounding landscapes. Passive strategies that are essential in reducing energy consumption are coupled with renewable-energy technologies to take advantage of the particular diurnal and seasonal attributes of sun and wind in each location. Third, the projects tend to be modest in size and scope. The architects eliminate excess and seek multiple pathways toward efficiency and ecological effectiveness. The projects find ways to do more with less without compromising design integrity.

Above left
Detail of the terraces and hanging gardens at the Sino-Italian Ecological and Energy Efficient Building (SIEEB) at Tsinghua University, Beijing, China. Photovoltaic shading devices provide thermal and luminous control while generating electricity. A terraced building form was selected to block northern winter winds and admit winter sun, while providing solar control and shading to the south during summer months.

Above right
Aerial view of the observation tower and landscape at the Steinhude Sea Recreational Facility, Germany. The building is sited to minimize ecological impacts and to protect a neighboring bird sanctuary as well as to take advantage of northern views over the Steinhude Meer while harvesting on-site solar energy.

North facade of the west bedroom pavilion at the Rozak House on Lake Bennett in Australia's Northern Territory. The building envelope creates a minimal boundary and plays a critical role in achieving zero-energy and low-carbon emission goals. Porches, screened walls and floors, jalousie windows, and solar louvers enclose spaces while creating dynamic and adjustable connections.

Fourth, the projects focus on design of the envelope as a means to create a responsive skin that enhances building performance, ecological response, and connections to the site. And last but not least, the projects are beautiful. They demonstrate that design excellence is as important as is ecological performance. These five themes guide us through the thoughtful and elegant ways in which the architects have approached the new solar architecture to achieve ecological effectiveness within aesthetically beautiful designs.

Each case study includes an overview of the design intentions, climate and site responses, daylighting and thermal strategies, energy systems, lessons for the next generation of sustainable design thinking and practice, and a profile summarizing design strategies. Basic solar analyses are provided for each case study using the Ecotect Solar Tool to illustrate the varied diurnal and seasonal conditions for solar access at the site scale. The solar studies are illustrated for the solstices and equinoxes (December 21, March/September 21, and June 21) at 9:00 a.m., noon, and 3:00 p.m. In addition, each case study includes a summary of climate data which was developed with the Ecotect Weather Tool (using the Energy-Plus weather data from the US Department of Energy) to provide a general introduction to the seasonal averages in temperature, relative humidity, solar radiation, wind speed, and prevailing wind direction. The

solar studies and climate data are intended to provide the reader with a general overview of the context and prevailing bioclimatic conditions that informed the architectural design and are not intended for design or engineering purposes.

The following case studies may be useful in inspiring a broader understanding of the potential of the sun and wind to shape the next generation of sustainable architecture. The pioneering architects and projects featured in the case studies reveal the promise of a new solar architecture that responds deeply to the ecological challenges of our day, while recognizing that when our buildings delight our senses, architecture can help inspire us to dwell more lightly on our beautiful Earth.

Endnotes:

1 Peter F. Smith, *Architecture in a Climate of Change* (Oxford: Architectural Press, 2001), 33, 45.
2 Sim Van der Ryn, *Design for Life* (Layton, Utah: Gibbs Smith, Publisher, 2005).

Chapter 1

Fostering an ecological vision

"We are now experiencing a moment of significance far beyond what any of us can imagine. What can be said is that the foundations of a new historical period, the Ecozoic Era, have been established in every realm of human affairs. The mythic vision has been set into place. The distorted dream of an industrial technological paradise is being replaced by the more viable dream of a mutually enhancing human presence within an ever-renewing organic-based Earth community… In the larger cultural context the dream becomes the myth that both guides and drives the action."[1]
THOMAS BERRY, theologian and historian,
The Great Work: Our Way into the Future

"Solar power: All energy is solar energy, stored in different forms. Every two minutes the sun gives the earth more energy than is used annually world-wide. It is the only renewable resource with the capacity to provide all the energy we need on a global level."[2]
BRUCE MAU, *Massive Change*

To reach the next level of sustainable design we will need more than just the best ecological design strategies, principles, and performance indicators; we will also need a new vision to inspire our imaginations. As Thomas Berry explains in *The Great Work*, the challenge of our day is to envision a new ecological era: "History is governed by those overarching movements that give shape and meaning to life by relating the human venture to the larger destinies of the universe. Creating such a movement might be called the Great Work of a people... The Great Work now, as we move into a new millennium, is to carry out the transition from a period of human devastation of the Earth to a period when humans would be present to the planet in a mutually beneficial manner... This is our Great Work and the work of our children..."[3] This vision will come into being when we design not only to make a profound ecological difference, but also to guide new ways of living on Earth. David Orr, Professor of Environmental Studies at Oberlin College in the USA, argues that we— *homo sapiens sapiens*—are the design challenge: "The greatest impediment to

an ecological design revolution is not, however, technological or scientific, but rather human... A real design revolution will have to transform human intentions and the larger political, economic, and institutional structure that permitted ecological degradation in the first place..."[4]

During the past decade there has been significant progress in mainstreaming ecological principles into architectural practice. A variety of voluntary sustainable design guidelines and standards such as the US Green Building Council's Leadership in Environmental Design, the UK's Code for Sustainable Homes, and the International Organization for Standards (ISO 21930:2007) have been established around the world. Although we have seen expectations for ecological performance raised through such regulatory codes and building standards, the scope and breadth of the current ecological challenges require an even greater level of leadership from the design communities. We need innovative designers to imagine ever-deeper ecological visions of the future. This will

require more than the incremental, yet slow, changes we have seen over the past several decades.

In considering the panoply of emerging trends and responses to the design challenges occurring throughout the world, Bruce Mau from the Institute Without Boundaries, cites the wisdom of former US president John F. Kennedy, whose words are as relevant today as they were four decades ago: "The problems of the world cannot possibly be solved by skeptics or cynics whose horizons are limited by the obvious realities. We need people who can dream of things that never were."[5] Over the past several years, we have seen new visions and depths of innovation emerging as designers reconsider the interrelated design consequences of fossil fuel consumption and greenhouse gas emissions. This has led to a growing focus on zero-energy, zero-emission, and carbon-neutral design; as well as explorations into plus-energy and carbon-sequestering approaches that promote the healing principles of regenerative and restorative design. To reach zero and go beyond, designers

View of the kitchen, dining area, and outdoor garden spaces in the First LivingHome in Santa Monica, California, USA. Large floor-to-ceiling sliding doors enable the inhabitants to extend the house into the gardens as the seasons change.

are looking with renewed interest and commitment to the abundant and renewable resources of sun and wind. Nearly 30 years ago, legendary innovator and visionary R. Buckminster Fuller encouraged designers to look to nature, and specifically the sun, for answers to our ecological design challenges: "Nature as the omni-informed and omni-concerned, omni-considerate cosmic designer discovered and heeded the fact that human organisms and their absolutely essential ecological support complex could not operate safely at a distance of less than ninety-two million miles away from the nearest atomic-energy plant—the sun—and all the latter's lethal radiation involvements. The would-be exploiters of atomic energy on board our planet Earth will in due course discover there is no way for them to solve atomic-energy-radiation waste-disposal problems save by rocketing it all back into the sun, where it belongs. Humans will then have to learn how to keep all humans and their ecological support system operating successfully on our vastly adequate daily income of solar atomic energy."[6] As authors Sophia

and Stefan Behling explain in *Solar Power*, the sun is the giver of all life and all energy on Earth: "The sun is the Earth's only energy source… Solar energy is far more than just radiation… Solar energy reaches the atmosphere in various forms. The sun is a non-polluting source of renewable energy and is essential in the formation of wind, clouds, thunderstorms, rain, and other weather conditions, some of which can be converted into usable energy."[7]

The new ecological designers have developed fresh and effective ways to integrate both passive design and active systems into projects that combine the lessons of ancient climatic-design traditions with the most brilliant state-of-the-art technologies. In responding to the forces of the sun (and the related dynamics of the wind, climate, place, and the seasonal cycles and the rhythms of day and night) these projects address our ecological concerns while also speaking to our deepest design and aesthetic aspirations. While the ecological challenges of our day may not be completely new, we are certainly facing an unprecedented

scale of concern and rate of change. The elevated sense of urgency has given rise to a new spirit of design innovation and exploration, and a commitment to redouble efforts for deeper ecological response. Today, perhaps more than ever, we need to return to our essential source of life—the sun—to design our way into a more sustainable future.

Can architecture address serious ecological concerns and also people that we can live comfortably and elegantly at a new level of sustainability? To go beyond the current limits of "best practice," the profession must reframe the fundamental questions that inform design thinking. Designers need to push beyond current design thinking to take architectural design—and the people who inhabit buildings—to the next generation of sustainability. Inspiration and vision are needed to move design beyond mandates and regulations. David Orr reminds us that we need to find ways to elicit new human behaviors and values. Orr suggests that ecological design is a vehicle for profound and transformative ecological education: "The ultimate object of

ecological design is not the things we make but rather the human mind and specifically its capacity for wonder and appreciation... If it is not to become simply a more efficient way to do the same old things, ecological design must become a kind of public pedagogy built into the structure of daily life... The goal is to calibrate human behavior with ecology, which requires a public that understands ecological possibilities and limits. To that end we must begin to see our houses, buildings, farms, businesses, energy technologies, transportation, landscapes, and communities in much the same way that we regard classrooms... ecological design becomes a way to expand our awareness of nature and our ecological competence.[8]

The two case studies that follow reveal a new level of design inspiration and provide a glimpse of the next generation of sustainable design thinking and practice. A fresh and expanded approach to solar design for the twenty-first century lies at the heart of the projects. As the sun gives shape to the environmental forces of climate, weather, wind, and seasonal cycles so also does it deeply shape the works of architect Ray Kappe and developer Steve Glenn in the First LivingHome, and Sheppard Robson in the Lighthouse. Both projects challenge, reframe, and redefine the questions for the next generation of sustainable architecture: In what ways can architecture contribute to a more sustainable future? Can design inspire people to live more ecologically? Can architecture help to create a new ecological ethos? What are the roles of the sun and wind in creating the next generation of sustainable architecture? Both projects raise the bar for ecological performance and, more importantly, they reframe the goals in ecologically expansive and visionary ways. The projects and architects take on the difficult challenges of zero energy and carbon neutrality while integrating the highest degree of design excellence. Ray Kappe Architects and Sheppard Robson present prototypes for living that are resilient and responsive to the ever-changing conditions of climate change. In these projects we see the poetic and the pragmatic integrated in ways that embody both a new solar aesthetic and a new level of solar performance. In so doing, the First LivingHome and the Lighthouse provide insights into two diverse paths to the next generation of sustainable architecture.

Left
Detail of the west-facing louvered shading device made for the Lighthouse in Watford, UK. As an extension of the south-facing roof and facade, the slatted eaves provide shade for the west facade while creating a dappled quality of light and a glimpse of the sky.

Right
West facade of the Lighthouse. Wood shutters and slatted eaves on the south facade provide solar control.

Endnotes:

1 Thomas Berry, *The Great Work: Our Way into the Future* (New York: Bell Towers, 1999), 201.
2 Bruce Mau, *Massive Change* (New York: Phaidon Press Inc., 2004), 79.
3 Thomas Berry, 1, 8.
4 David Orr, *The Nature of Design: Ecology, Culture, and Human Intention* (Oxford: Oxford University Press, 2002), 23–24.
5 Bruce Mau, 71.
6 R. Buckminster Fuller, *Critical Path* (New York: St. Martin's Press, 1901), 346.
7 Sophia and Stefan Behling, *Solar Power: The Evolution of Sustainable Architecture* (Munich: Prestel, 2000), 27–29.
8 David Orr, 4, 30–32.

Project:
Location:
Architect:

First LivingHome Model Home
Santa Monica, California, USA
Ray Kappe Architects/Planners and
LivingHomes (owner/developer)

"Solar is just good design. Integrate solar and focus on spatial quality and seasonal benefits. Solar does more than one thing."
Ray Kappe, Fellow of the American Institute of Architects

"The drama is in the cascade of shifting levels, ceiling heights, sight lines, and the light that pours in, even on a gloomy gray day… In short, this is a signature Kappe house."
Greg Goldin, *The Architect's Newspaper*, May 2, 2007

View of the east entry and upper-level south and east balconies at sunset. High-performance energy-efficient electric lighting is used for site and interior illumination. The house steps up the sloping site from the southern underground parking to the northern retaining wall. Ecological and climate-responsive gardens are integrated throughout the landscape design.

Design intentions
The next generation of sustainable design must reconsider the physical attributes of architecture to help us reduce our impact on the environment while challenging us to live more ecologically on a day-to-day basis. To achieve this, the design profession must fundamentally reconsider project goals. An exemplary building that defines a new standard for sustainable living is found in the first LEED (Leadership in Environmental Design) Platinum-rated residence in the US. Formerly known as the Z6 House, the First LivingHome in Santa Monica, California, was designed as a model of sustainable prefabricated housing by Ray Kappe Architects with owner and developer Steve Glenn of LivingHomes. The team established robust goals, with "six zeros" as the performance targets: zero waste, zero energy, zero water, zero carbon, zero emissions, and zero ignorance. The First LivingHome was designed to produce a dramatically reduced ecological footprint, with the residents actively participating in the process of meeting the goals. Steve Glenn explains the design priorities and role of solar: "The company is targeting consumers who exist, people who value design, health, and sustainability. There are always three things we consider that are not separate: 1) form and function, 2) health, sustainability, and the ecological footprint, and 3) the price and value. We have sixteen different homes, with five standard models with Ray Kappe and

five standard models with Kieran Timberlake. Fifty percent are custom and fifty percent are standard. Architects design a 'line' of homes. Solar is a standard part of every project."

The First LivingHome defines a new standard of sustainable design excellence for both prefabricated and standardized housing. Rather than striving to incrementally change standard performance goals and energy codes, the team challenges the fundamental paradigm of housing design by elevating all of the performance goals to zero. Setting the "zero goals" in the earliest phase of design established an ambitious ecological commitment for the project. GreenBiz highlights the accomplishments of the First LivingHome: "Since the LEED program's inception in 2000, 550 buildings have been certified and only 20 have achieved Platinum… No residences have received a Platinum rating to date, making LivingHomes the first homebuilder in the United States to reach such a level of environmental achievement. Through careful design, rigorous testing, and thorough integration of comprehensive environmental systems, LivingHomes has set the benchmark high for sustainable residential design."[1] The First LivingHome was constructed of prefabricated factory-built modules, while the foundation was constructed on site. As a modular construction, the 230m^2 (2,480 sq ft) house is designed to allow for disassembly,

thereby enabling the owner to move it to another site.

Climate and site

Designed for the temperate coastal climate of Santa Monica, the First LivingHome is responsive to the sun, wind, and changing qualities of the site and climate. With an average low temperature in January of 5°C (41°F) and an average high temperature in July of 32°C (90°F), the climate in Santa Monica is well suited to passive solar strategies for heating and cooling. Average summer temperatures range from 21–24°C (70–75°F) from June through September, which enables the house to be naturally ventilated and seasonally opened to the site and climate. As LivingHomes explains: "The design maximizes the opportunities of the mild, marine climate with a passive cooling strategy using cross-ventilation and a thermal chimney."

A 2.4-kilowatt photovoltaic array and a solar hot-water collector take advantage of the sunny location, as does the daylighting strategy for the interior.[2] In discussing the site response, architect Ray Kappe and LivingHomes emphasize that they created ecological opportunities at the site scale: "The project is a single-family residence that was added to a multifamily-zoned lot with an existing duplex. Prior to construction, this portion of the site was covered in hardscape and lawn. To recreate the open feeling of the space prior to construction, the

project team incorporated a green roof with plantings of native species, mostly sedums, native grasses, and rushes. The site also includes a small vegetable and herb garden. The landscaping around the house consists of newly planted native groundcover, shrubs, and trees… Rainwater collected from the roof, combined with stormwater diverted from site drains and swales, is stored in a cistern and used to irrigate the gardens."[3]

To achieve many of the "zero" goals, including zero energy, zero emissions, and zero carbon, it was necessary to harvest free energy and renewable resources from the site. Solar design is essential to reduce energy consumption and enhance design quality. Given his lifelong fascination with prefabricated housing and sensitivity to bioregional and climate-responsive design for California, Ray Kappe (founder and former dean of the Southern California Institute of Architecture) was happy to accept the challenge of designing a prefabricated house that responded to the particulars of place. Known for designing homes with elegant and sophisticated spatial qualities, Kappe brought his sensitivity for space, climate, and human experience to the First LivingHome prototype: "The large doors, large glazed openings, and multiple exterior decks and terraces connect the interior to the site and allow the living space to expand to the outdoors. This flexible relationship between indoor and outdoor living spaces is traditional in southern California

Interior view looking southwest over the kitchen, dining area, and adjacent gardens. Exterior overhangs and louvers on the south and west facades are designed to respond to changing seasonal needs for shading or direct sunlight.

Night view from the second floor looking south and west. Upper and lower levels are integrated through a series of elegant double-story spaces that support the movement of air, borrowed light, and connection to the expansive views.

architecture."[4] The two-story house, with four bedrooms, two bathrooms and a separate toilet, is a series of intersecting horizontal platforms, balconies, and connecting terraces that create diverse spatial qualities and break down the boundaries between inside and outside. Daylighting weaves together the site and interior spaces through changing views and qualities of light through time. Ray Kappe has designed a prefabricated house that is still intimately and dramatically shaped by the particularities of site, sun, and wind.

Daylighting and thermal design

The goal of "six zeros" inspired and shaped the sustainable performance as well as the design and spatial experience of the First LivingHome. While a great variety of ecological design strategies and concepts are used in the house, the response to sun and wind is essential to reaching the zero-energy, zero-emissions, and zero-carbon goals. Compared to a standard house in the US, the overall energy loads were dramatically reduced through programming, site design, passive design, and high-performance systems. The building reduces energy loads by harvesting passive heating, and through daylighting and natural ventilation. LivingHomes explains their seasonal response to passive strategies that use the sun and wind: "The home is oriented 45 degrees from a north–south axis. There are operable windows and doors on the southwest, southeast, and northeast faces

that provide natural ventilation. The design incorporates an open-plan and two-story volume that ventilates the entire house. A whole-house fan located at the top of the stair tower leading to the roof helps to draw hot air out of the building. The chimney effect is in evidence on warm days. Each of the southwest, southeast, and northeast facades also has large deck overhangs to prevent solar heat gain from the summer sun. In the winter, the southeast glazing admits direct sunlight, which heats up the concrete floors at the first level thereby warming the house into early evening on a sunny day. Glass ceilings in the upstairs bathrooms capture heat from the sun in the winter and shading devices divert the heat in the summer months."[5]

The house is designed so that the residents can intentionally interact with the environment to experience the moods and changing qualities of the site, sun, and wind. The house invites occupants to migrate through different rooms according to the time of day and season to follow the sun, shade, or wind and to tune the envelope to adjust light and air in response to thermal and luminous comfort needs. The building section, high ceilings, and window, skylight, and clerestory locations optimize daylight as well as cross and stack ventilation. Material details and finishes are designed to ensure daylight reflection and penetration, solar control, and proper airflow, which results in full daylighting and natural ventilation throughout

Opposite
View looking east into the guest room. Multi-lateral sidelighting provides views to the east, south, and west. Trellised shading and adjustable envelopes allow the inhabitant to modify natural ventilation, solar control, and passive heating on a seasonal basis. The space can be opened onto the balcony.

Above left
View of bathroom showing bilateral daylighting, including sidelighting and toplighting. Operable windows and solar shading provide privacy as well as thermal and luminous control.

Above right
Detail of the east entry. Translucent glazing adjacent to the entry provides illumination while controlling privacy.

the living spaces. Natural ventilation is designed to significantly reduce summer cooling loads and eliminate the need for air conditioning. The envelope of the house is 73 percent glazing, which is constructed of high-performance double-pane low-E glass panels and 25 mm (1 in) thick polycarbonate glazing. Interior walls are movable so that the spaces can be reconfigured for future uses and changing family needs. Solar studies and energy analyses enabled Kappe to provide solar control through exterior balconies, overhangs, and trellises, while admitting direct sunlight during the heating season. In an interview, he emphasized the intersection of pragmatic and poetic concerns: "Forms come out of rational decisions; this includes the solar elements such as overhangs, shading devices, and the form and section."

While the design consciously optimizes passive strategies to meet explicit performance goals for heating and cooling, the quality of the space and human experience are equally important. Kappe's exceptional spatial skills are celebrated through the house's changing levels and sloping site. Architectural critic Greg Goldin emphasizes the exceptional spatial qualities in an essay on the house: "The residence basically inverts its steep lot by cutting into the slope to form one level, then stepping back up to the original grade to create another platform. This maneuver allows dramatic changes in ceiling heights, which in turn define a succession of spaces, from living

room to dining room to kitchen to study. Floating above is the second floor, which remains almost completely open to the ground floor. The drama is in the cascade of shifting levels, ceiling heights, sight lines, and the light that pours in, even on a gloomy gray day, through the walls of thermally efficient glass and Polygal. In short, this is a signature Kappe house."[6]

Energy systems
LivingHomes' Steve Glenn explains that load-reduction was a critical energy strategy: "We focus on energy. It is the single most important resource to ration and think through. Buildings use far more energy over the useful life than the materials to create a house. It is more critical to make the house energy efficient and to reduce the demand to generate what is needed with solar photovoltaics or geothermal. Energy is always on the agenda, including passive and active solar. There are many other issues, solar is just one." Passive and active solar systems work in tandem to meet winter heating loads. In addition to direct solar gain, an active solar radiant floor heating system supplements the passive heating. A gas-fired boiler is used as a back-up system, while an evacuated tube solar collector heats domestic hot water and the radiant floor. The First LivingHome has come close to meeting its ambitious zero-energy, zero-emissions, and zero-carbon goals. According to LivingHomes: "The home is projected to be 80 percent more energy efficient than a conventional

residence of similar size and was produced with 75 percent less construction waste compared to traditional home constructions…"[7]

LivingHomes explain how they dramatically reduced energy consumption by integrating passive design and active systems: "The Z6 House [First LivingHome] has a very low energy profile in part because it has no forced-air heating or cooling. The building takes advantage of natural ventilation from the prevailing breezes, with an open plan and a whole-house fan drawing air up through the top of the home. The house was designed to optimize passive solar heating, with glazing to admit winter sun and balconies placed to shade the house from summer sun. A radiant floor heating system is powered by a solar hot-water collector. All of the appliances are Energy Star rated and the lighting system is a low energy usage LED system that is controlled by an integrated home automation system. A 2.4-kilowatt photovoltaic (PV) array above the roof acts as a shade canopy for the roof stair access. The PV array was designed to provide 60–75 percent of the home's energy usage, and includes battery storage. This, and the operable windows and doors in every room, will make the house habitable during a blackout. Most daytime lighting is handled with natural light from skylights and floor-to-ceiling glass."[8] A monitoring system continuously evaluates energy and water consumption as well as the performance of the systems. Ray Kappe explains

that the monitoring system is part of the "zero ignorance goal," which encourages the residents to monitor energy consumption and adjust their lifestyles accordingly.

Next-generation thinking

The First LivingHome provides a new housing prototype that inspires homebuilders, architects, and design professionals to have higher ecological expectations. As a model for prefabricated sustainable housing, the First LivingHome sets a standard for sustainable living that strives for zero waste, zero energy, zero water, zero carbon, zero emissions, and zero ignorance. This new vision for housing actively engages the occupants through the goal of "zero ignorance," which emphasizes the importance of educating the occupants and enabling them to participate in creating an ecological future.

To achieve new results, designers must challenge the most basic premises of program and activity along with the notion of how we live in our homes. The LivingHome combines low-technology passive strategies with highly efficient active systems and a monitoring system that enables the occupants to visualize the ecological impacts of their lifestyle decisions. If we are able to visualize our ecological footprints we are more likely to take actions to reduce our impacts. An ecological architecture enables us to engage with the environment in our day-to-day lives, as David Orr explains in *The Nature of Design*:

Above left
View from the upper level towards the north and east. Adjustable walls facilitate the movement of light and air while creating a sense of spaciousness and connection to the site and environmental forces.

Above right
View into the guest bedroom. Multilateral sidelighting provides views to the site and living areas below. Adjustable walls allow the inhabitants to expand or contract the space and to adjust the spatial connection to the living spaces on the first and second floors.

Above left
Exterior view of the southwest corner of the house, including the south-facing photovoltaic array, west-facing evacuated tube solar hot-water system, and the upper-level balconies. The facades are carefully designed with roof overhangs and louvered shading devices.

Above right
Detail of the upper-level photovoltaic array, which generates electricity while providing solar control and shading to the rooftop balcony. To the southwest is a distant view of the adjacent neighborhood.

"Ecological design is the art that reconnects us as sensuous creatures evolved over millions of years to a beautiful world. That world does not need to be remade but rather revealed."[9] As Ray Kappe explains: "Solar is just good design. Integrate solar and focus on spatial quality and seasonal benefits. Solar does more than one thing." The sun and environmental forces are celebrated in the First LivingHome as a means to awaken our ecological connection to place and beauty, as well as a means to meet new and ever more ambitious levels of sustainable design performance.

Plans, sections, drawings

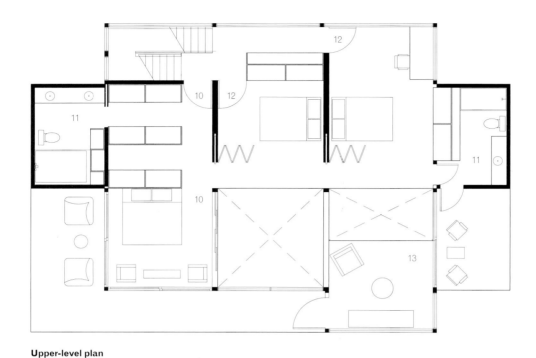

1. Kitchen
2. Entry/gallery
3. Living area
4. Dining
5. Study
6. Toilet
7. Laundry/pantry
8. Media
9. Upper living
10. Master bedroom
11. Bathroom
12. Bedroom
13. Guest bedroom

Upper-level plan

Lower-level plan

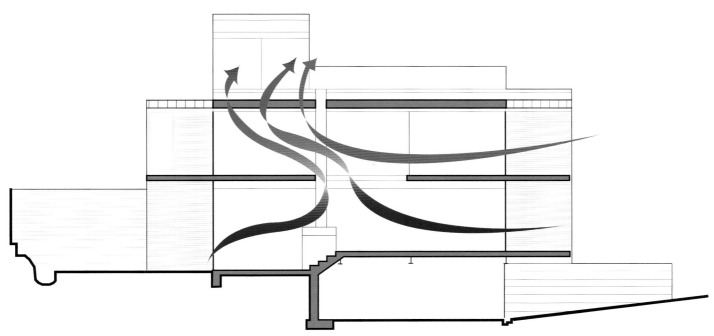

Section illustrating natural ventilation and solar shading

East elevation

North elevation

West elevation

South elevation

Wind studies

Fostering an ecological vision: First LivingHome Model Home

Project location:
**Santa Monica,
CA, USA**

Wind data location:
**Santa Monica,
CA, USA**

Prevailing winds
March
Wind frequency (hours)
Location: Santa Monica Municipal
Airport, USA (34.0°, -118.4°)
Time: 00:00–24:00

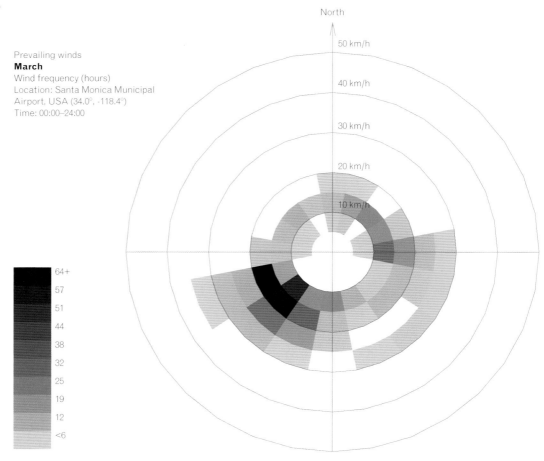

North
50 km/h
40 km/h
30 km/h
20 km/h
10 km/h

64+
57
51
44
38
32
25
19
12
<6

Prevailing winds
September
Wind frequency (hours)
Location: Santa Monica Municipal
Airport, USA (34.0°, -118.4°)
Time: 00:00–24:00

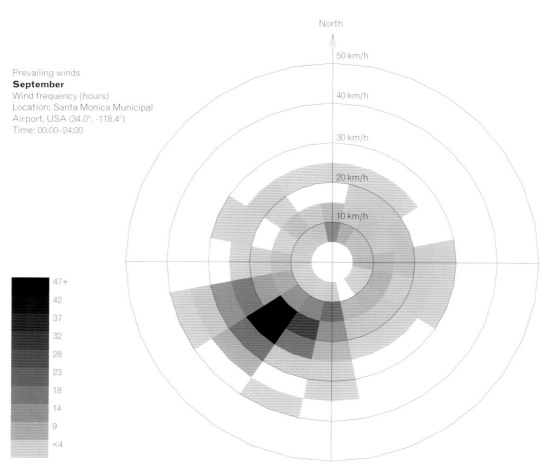

North
50 km/h
40 km/h
30 km/h
20 km/h
10 km/h

47+
42
37
32
28
23
18
14
9
<4

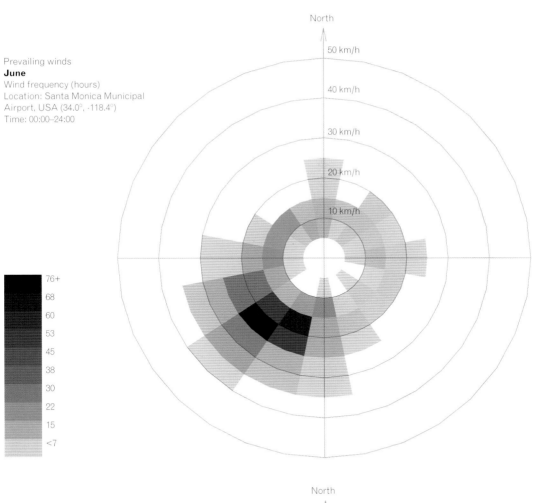

Prevailing winds
June
Wind frequency (hours)
Location: Santa Monica Municipal
Airport, USA (34.0°, -118.4°)
Time: 00:00–24:00

North

50 km/h
40 km/h
30 km/h
20 km/h
10 km/h

76+
68
60
53
45
38
30
22
15
<7

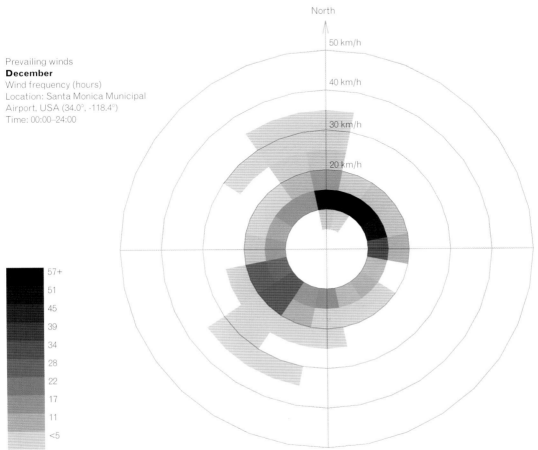

Prevailing winds
December
Wind frequency (hours)
Location: Santa Monica Municipal
Airport, USA (34.0°, -118.4°)
Time: 00:00–24:00

North

50 km/h
40 km/h
30 km/h
20 km/h

57+
51
45
39
34
28
22
17
11
<5

Sunpath case studies

Project location:
**Santa Monica,
CA, USA
Latitude: 34° NL**

December

09:00

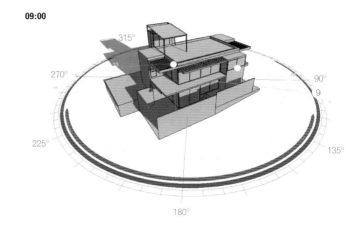

March/September

09:00

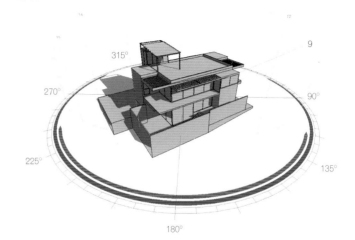

June

09:00

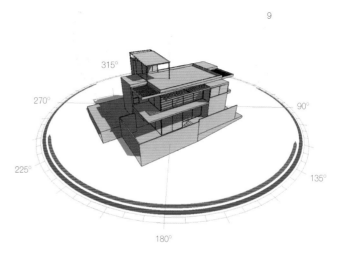

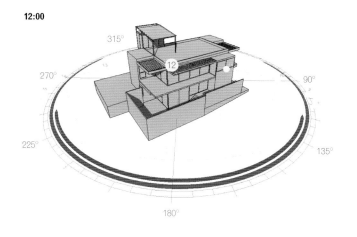

12:00

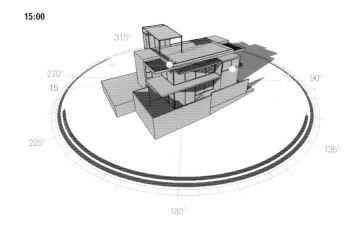

15:00

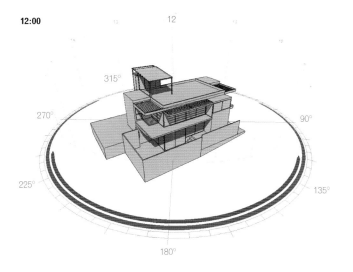

12:00

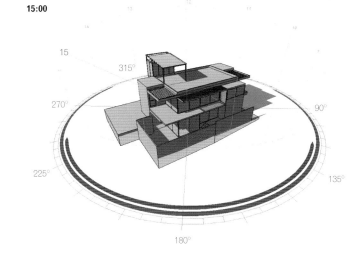

15:00

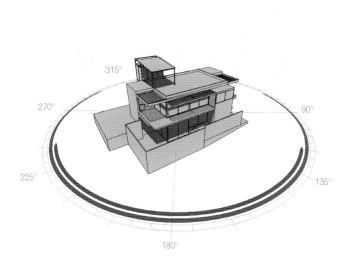

12:00

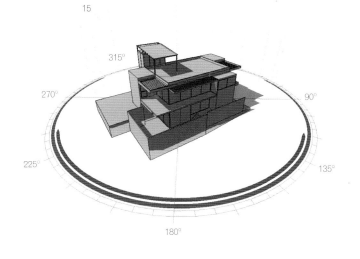

15:00

Climate data

Project location:
Santa Monica, CA, USA

Climate data location:
Santa Monica, CA, USA

Diurnal average temperatures

24 Hrs.

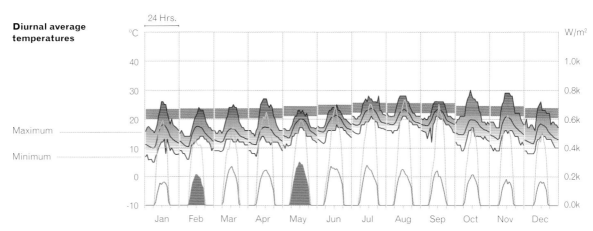

Maximum

Minimum

Dry bulb temperatures 1 Jan to 31 Dec

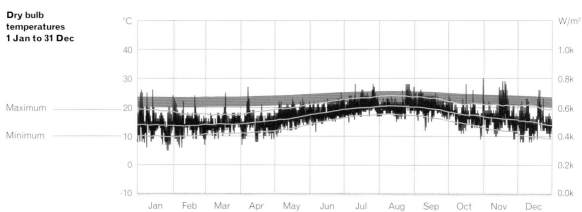

Maximum

Minimum

Direct radiation 1 Jan to 31 Dec

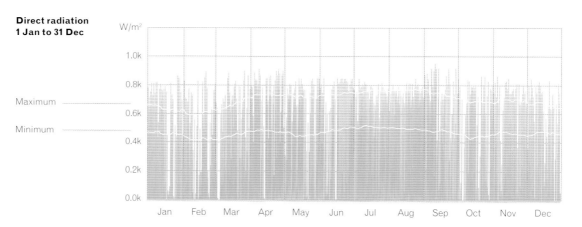

Maximum

Minimum

Relative humidity 1 Jan to 31 Dec

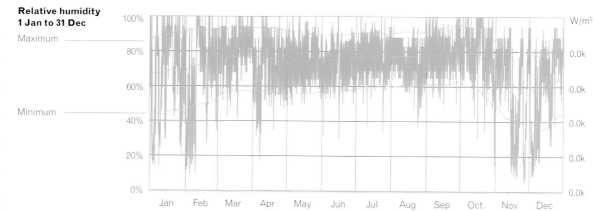

Maximum

Minimum

Temperature (°C)

Relative humidity (%)

Wind speed (W/m²)

Direct solar (W/m²)

Diffuse solar (W/m²)

Cloud cover (%)

Thermal neutrality

Design profile

Building Profile	Building name:	**First LivingHome Model Home (formerly the Z6 House)**
	Architect:	Ray Kappe Architects/Planners, Pacific Palisades, California, USA for LivingHomes (owner/developer), Santa Monica, California, USA; www.livinghomes.net
	Location:	Santa Monica, California, USA
	Building type:	Residential
	Square meters/feet:	230 m² (2,480 sq ft)
Solar Design Profile	Latitude:	34° NL
	Heating Degree Days:	865 heating degree days °C (1,696 heating degree days °F) (18°C and 65°F base temperature; average 3 years)
	Cooling Degree Days:	490 cooling degree days °C (798 cooling degree days °F)
	Conservation strategies:	Flexible space planning to adapt to future needs and uses, designed to be thermally comfortable without air conditioning
	Passive solar strategies:	Daylighting, operable windows, cross and stack ventilation, direct gain passive solar, exterior shading
	Active solar strategies:	Photovoltaic system, solar hot water thermal system for radiant floor heating and domestic hot water
	Other renewable energy strategies:	None
	High-performance strategies:	Energy Star appliances, LED lighting, automated control system, whole-house fan for night cooling, high-performance glazing and envelope
Performance Profile [10] [11]	Total annual building energy consumption:	44 kWh/m² (14 kBtu/sq ft) estimated
	Total annual on-site energy produced:	60 percent on-site renewable energy, 9.6 percent grid-supplied renewable energy
	Size of photovoltaic system:	2.4-kW photovoltaic system (designed to meet 60–75 percent of electrical needs)
	Size of solar thermal system:	Evacuated tube solar hot-water heating for radiant floor heating and domestic hot water
	Carbon dioxide emissions:	Not available

Endnotes:
First LivingHome Model Home

1 GreenBiz Staff, "USGBC Awards LivingHomes First-Ever Platinum Rating in Residential Design," GreenBiz (August 16, 2006); http://www.greenerbuildings.com/news/2006/08/16/usgbc-awards-livinghomes-first-ever-platinum-rating-residential-design.
2 LivingHomes, "Z6 House" (Santa Monica, CA: no date), 2.
3 American Institute of Architects Committee on the Environment

(AIA COTE), "Z6 House," AIA COTE Top Ten Green Projects, (2007 Awards Program); http://www.aiatopten.org.
4 LivingHomes, "Z6 House" (Santa Monica, CA: no date), 2–3.
5 Ibid.
6 Greg Goldin, "Kappe House," The Architect's Newpaper (May 2, 2007); www.archpaper.com.
7 RE News, "Built Green," Solar Today (Nov./Dec. 2006), 38.
8 LivingHomes, "Z6 House" (Santa

Monica, CA: no date), 8.
9 David Orr, The Nature of Design (Oxford: Oxford University Press, 2002), 31–32.
10 American Institute of Architects Committee on the Environment.
11 LivingHomes, "Z6 House" (Santa Monica, CA: no date), 8.

Project: **Kingspan Lighthouse**
Location: **Building Research Establishment Ltd. (BRE)**
                Innovation Park, Watford, Hertfordshire, UK
Architect: **Alan Shingler and Martin Rose, Sheppard Robson**

"We have to make sure we are not designing something that cannot be built or that is too complicated. If we are going to live in the house, it has to be intuitive. It has to respect the local environment. With passive energy, occupants have to be able to intuitively adjust the house. Active systems need to be low tech with simple controls. Design can encourage behavioral changes."
Alan Shingler, Architect, Sheppard Robson

"This super insulated, airtight building has been designed to provide a way of living that encourages lifestyles that are inherently 'light' on the world's resources. It includes effective solar control, together with integrated building services, which are based around a platform of renewable and sustainable technologies, water efficiency techniques, and passive cooling and ventilation." [1]
Kingspan

West facade of the Lighthouse, the first net zero-carbon house in the UK. The primary living spaces are located on the second floor. The glazing on the west facade and the balcony are shaded by the slatted extension of the south facade, a vertical fin, and adjustable shutters. The glazed balcony railing provides views and admits daylight.

Design intentions

As the name suggests, the "Lighthouse" poetically illustrates that high style and high performance are compatible in the next generation of sustainable housing. Shaped by light, wind, and place, the Lighthouse is located in the Building Research Establishment's (BRE) Innovation Park in Watford, in the United Kingdom. As the first net zero-carbon house in the UK, it meets Level 6, which is the highest standard in the Code for Sustainable Homes. The Innovation Park includes a community of low-carbon demonstration homes, highlighting innovative sustainable design strategies and technologies as well as new code standards. As explained in the code: "The Code for Sustainable Homes has been introduced to drive a step-change in sustainable home building practice… It will form the basis for future developments of the Building Regulations in relation to carbon emissions from, and energy use in, homes, therefore offering greater regulatory certainty to developers."[2] The Lighthouse provides a place- and climate-specific solution for net zero-carbon housing while at the same time promoting design excellence. In an interview, architect Alan Shingler of Sheppard Robson explained that from the beginning the design team focused on the integration of design and energy performance: "Homes are for people to live in. We did not allow the 'Code for Sustainable Homes' to compromise lifestyle

and architecture." The quality of space, relationship to place, thermal and luminous comfort as well as the experience of light were thoughtfully reconciled with the strictest of standards for zero-energy and net zero-carbon design.

Climate and site

Located in a maritime temperate climate at 51°NL, the thermal comfort requirements for the Lighthouse include winter heating, modest summer cooling, and varied responses to seasonal transitions that may require either heating or cooling. With an average low temperate of 5°C (41°F) in January and an average high of 23°C (73°F) in July, the moderate climate, when coupled with the predominantly overcast skies in the winter, posed a challenge for traditional passive solar design. Alan Shingler explains that the Lighthouse solution is unique to the particular site and microclimate in England: "There is not one answer to solar design. How to use microclimate depends on the specific location, not just the geographical location, but the actual location and the impact of surrounding land and buildings." As a demonstration project that is intended to be replicated across other sites throughout the UK, the Lighthouse could be sited in a great variety of communities with the same temperate and overcast climatic profile. The design response to the site and integration of passive solar design strategies would be

profoundly different in a sunnier geographic and microclimatic location.

The only definitive solar site constraint inherent in the design is the necessity to have access to direct sunlight on the roof surface, which restricts the height of adjacent buildings and the site orientation to optimize solar gain. The long axis of the building is optimally oriented on the east–west axis, with the solar roof facing due south. Alan Shingler explains that the Level 6 criteria require on-site electric energy generation, which restricts building form and orientation. Because the electricity is generated on site for all the appliances, lighting, fans, and cooking, the roof has to orient south to accommodate the photovoltaic array and the solar water collectors. Shingler explains: "If we did not need such a high level of criteria for zero carbon we might have done things differently. We may not have all roofs facing south." The necessity for direct solar access also suggests a road and community organization with a north–south street configuration to safeguard entry, views, sunlight, and cross ventilation through the east and west facades. While the main entry is on the east facade and the secondary entry is on the west, the plan (but not the roof orientation) could easily be rotated to accommodate entry from either direction.

Minimal apertures are located on the north and south facades, which allows for a fairly dense neighborhood configuration. A design challenge for any prototype house is to provide sufficient

flexibility in the design to enable the prototype to be constructed in a variety of other possible site and geographic locations. Architect Dan Burr, as quoted in Sandra Andrea O'Connell's article "Light Years Ahead" in *Architecture Ireland*, explains that the Lighthouse can be configured in a variety of ways at the building and community scales: "… the design is 'modular and can be adapted to suit bigger space needs by adding a home office, separate apartment (for elderly relatives or young teenagers), or a garage space.' The house module can also be grouped as semi-ds [semi-detached houses], terraced [row] houses, and clustered around courtyards for larger housing developments."[3] Despite the solar access restrictions, the site layout and proximity between adjacent buildings remains flexible and adaptable to a variety of different site conditions.

Daylighting and thermal design

A particular challenge for the Lighthouse was to meet the strict standards for net zero carbon for "heating, lighting, hot water, and all other energy uses in the home," while also creating a meaningful home environment and experience. When coupled with the overcast climate of England, the Level 6 standards for net zero carbon create challenging design constraints, especially for passive solar integration. Alan Shingler emphasizes that the Lighthouse is a solution based on a particular location and the design criteria of the sustainable house code:

Above left
Stairs to the upper-level mezzanine. Open risers and glazed railings afford daylight to the lower level. Abundant daylight is admitted to the dining area beyond from the east and south facades.

Above right
Interior view of the living area looking west. Solar controls protect the expansive west glazing, utilizing the extended eaves of the south facade, double-story vertical fin, and adjustable solid shutters. A small balcony with a glazed railing provides physical and visual access to the site.

Opposite
Detail of the shading elements on the upper levels of the west facade, including the slatted eaves of the south facade, the double-story vertical fin, and operable shutters.

"With solar design, the solution is also different depending one whether one uses the criteria for Level 6 [a net zero carbon target] in the 'Code for Sustainable Homes' which requires a highly insulated airtight envelope with reduced glazing." Shingler underscores that at Level 6, a mandatory heat-loss parameter requires a high U-value for windows and walls. In the Lighthouse this leads to triple-glazed gas-filled windows and a glazing area of 18 percent in lieu of the typical glazing area of 25–30 percent.[4] The smaller glazing area and the highly insulated and airtight envelope reduce the heating season to four months.

In contrast to the more traditional approach to passive solar design in the UK, which often includes the use of buffer spaces (like a "woolly jumper [sweater]" according to Shingler), the Lighthouse combines passive and active strategies with systems that operate differently on a seasonal basis. The hybrid thermal design shifts from a predominantly passive mode for cooling and ventilation in the summer and transitional months to an active mode for heating and ventilation in the winter. Regarding the integration of passive solar design, Alan Shingler explains that there is not just a single set of rules to consider, but also the client's brief and the particular location. From these three issues (passive solar, client brief, and location) one can work backward to a design solution. Shingler cautions that the Lighthouse should not be viewed as a design solution that will work in other

locales. He argues that the particulars of place matter, and that the design has to be assessed for different microclimates and sites.

The Level 6 requirements fo a highly insulated envelope and reduced glazing area led to several design decisions that affected the form and massing of the Lighthouse. Given the reduced glazing area and the concern for high-quality living spaces with abundant daylight, the team chose to locate the sleeping spaces on the lower level and the living spaces on the upper level where there is greater access to daylight, air, and views. The first floor includes the entry, stairway, utility room, bathroom, and two bedrooms. Daylight is borrowed through the stairwell to mark the vertical passage to the living area above. Open risers and a glass balustrade provide visual and luminous connections between the two floors. High clerestory windows in the lower-level bedrooms ensure privacy and security, while enabling soft indirect daylight to wash across the white ceilings and provide illumination throughout the rooms. The upper-level living space contains the main living area, centrally located kitchen, and the dining area. A third-level mezzanine overlooks the living space. Windows and skylights are located throughout the upper levels to optimize a sense of spaciousness, brightness, and connection to the site. View windows are provided in the dining room, clerestories in the kitchen, and large sliding glass doors in the

View to the east and south in the dining area and kitchen. Operable windows provide cross ventilation while fostering views and bilateral illumination. Simple interior blinds enable inhabitants to control direct sunlight on diurnal and seasonal bases.

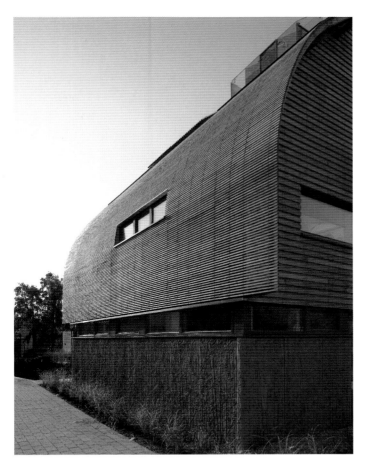

Above left
In contrast to a passive solar house, the solid south facade is juxtaposed with the transparent east and west facades. The concrete base of the house is complemented by the sweet chestnut wood-cladding on the upper levels. Clerestory windows provide security and privacy while admitting daylight and air to the lower-level bedrooms. The photovoltaic array, evacuated tube hot-water system, and wind catcher/light funnel are located at the pinnacle of the south facade.

Above right
Detail of the east facade showing the glazed door of the balcony on the upper mezzanine and the kitchen windows below. The slatted eaves create a dynamic play of light and shadow on the east facade.

living room. A stacked row of vertical windows on the west facade washes daylight along the north wall. Two sidelight windows are located on the north wall at the bottom and top of the stair linking the living area and the mezzanine. A daylight factor of 1.5–2.0 percent is provided throughout the house to ensure a high-quality luminous environment.

An ingenious "wind catcher/light funnel" is located at the heart of the house to provide toplighting, passive cooling, and natural ventilation. The ventilation device creates a stack effect by admitting cooler outside air to displace warmer inside air. Operable windows can be coupled with the wind catcher to provide additional cross ventilation, connection to the site, or to flush air through the house during overheated periods. Small exterior balconies on the west and east facades extend the living area and the mezzanine workspace to the outside. Even the glass rails around the balconies have been designed to admit daylight into the house. Solar control is provided on the west facade by extending the roof plane into slatted eaves to create a shaded south enclosure around the balcony and glazing. Sliding wooden shutters can be adjusted seasonally and diurnally to shade the western vertical windows.

Alan Shingler explains that as the Lighthouse is not a traditional passive solar building Sheppard Robson approached the notion of

thermal mass differently: "Thermal mass is provided by a wax polymer board [BASF phase-change material plasterboard] that changes from a solid to liquid state at 20°C (68°F). The mass helps to stabilize the temperatures seasonally." This innovative material, which looks similar to fiberboard, is located in the ceiling plane. A timber frame carries the structural loads to the lower level, with the walls and roofs constructed from structural insulated panels (SIPs).[5] A sense of enclosure and privacy is created on the first floor by the high clerestory windows. The upper floor is clad in sweet chestnut, which contrasts with the solidity of the concrete finish on the lower level. The upper portion of the house has a sense of openness due to the carefully located glazing and abundant direct and reflected daylight. Based on a 40-degree angle, the roof form is shaped to optimize the performance of the photovoltaic panels and solar thermal collectors. Daylighting, shading, ventilation, and passive cooling are adjusted seasonally to create the desired quality and character of thermal and luminous comfort for the home owner.

Energy systems
Passive architectural design strategies are combined with active systems in the Lighthouse to meet varying seasonal needs for heating and cooling. Design strategies were the first line of action to reduce the energy demand and to set a

Above left
High clerestories are complemented by floor-to-ceiling windows on the west facade. Positioned adjacent to light-colored interior walls, the vertical window allows daylight to reflect deeply into the room while also allowing a glimpse of the site. Solar control is provided by the balcony above.

Opposite and below right
Night and day views of the west facade.

Above right
Daylight is reflected from the ceiling to provide illumination, while maintaining privacy and security for the lower-level bedrooms. Dynamic patterns of sunlight provide visual interest, and foster connections with the site and environmental forces as the seasons change.

low energy budget that could be met with high-performance systems and appliances as well as renewable energy systems.

The design team worked with engineers at Arup to integrate the energy systems and achieve an overall energy consumption estimated at 83 kWh/m²/yr (26 kBtu/sq ft). The operating costs for the Lighthouse are modest, with the following estimate based on the energy analyses: "The energy cost of running the Kingspan Lighthouse would be about £31 per year for the wood pellets, assuming wood pellets cost 1.8p/kWh. The electricity is free, from the sun! A house of the same size and shape but built to 2006 Building Regulations standards would cost about £500 [$800] a year in energy bills."[6] Solar hot-water heating, a 4.7 kW grid-tied photovoltaic array, mechanical ventilation with heat recovery, a biomass boiler, and efficient electric lighting meet demands throughout the year for hot water, electricity, space heating, and lighting. Energy consumption is estimated to be: 35 percent for domestic hot water, 24 percent electricity use, 19 percent for space heating, 11 percent catering, 5 percent lighting, 4 percent mechanical ventilation and heat recovery fans, and 2 percent other fans and pumps.[7] Water-use reductions are achieved with low volume and efficient appliances and fixtures, including a graywater system that captures water from the bath for toilet flushing.

Design strategies and systems are integrated to facilitate ease of use and promote ecologically

responsive behavior in the homeowner. As Alan Shingler explains: "We wanted the home owner to have flexibility and control and to make sure it was not too complicated. Occupants adjust the house intuitively."

Next-generation thinking

As the Department for Communities and Local Government explain in the Code for Sustainable Homes, there is an urgent need to respond to climate change through architectural design: "In 2004, more than a quarter of the UK's carbon dioxide emissions—a major cause of climate change—came from the energy we use to heat, light, and run our homes. So it's vital to ensure that homes are built in a way that minimizes the use of energy and reduces these harmful emissions."[8] Carbon dioxide emissions and climate change were both considered in the design of the Lighthouse. Annual carbon dioxide emissions produced by the Lighthouse are estimated at 45 kg (99 lb) CO_2/yr, which are offset by producing electricity from a renewable energy source to result in a net zero-carbon home.[9] Additional electricity generated by the photovoltaic system is exported to the grid.

A unique aspect of the Lighthouse is that the design team also assessed how the house could respond to future increases in annual temperature due to climate change. The building itself—the passive means of cooling, ventilating, illuminating, and controlling solar gain—provides the ways

Above left
Detail of the west facade at the intersection of the glazed balcony railing and the slatted eaves of the south facade.

Above right
Detail of the slatted eaves of the south facade with a view to the living space beyond.

Detail of the active and passive solar systems on the south-facing roof, including the photovoltaic array, evacuated tube solar hot-water systems, and the combined wind catcher/light funnel that provides passive cooling and natural daylight to the interior of the house.

to respond to them. Six strategies are used to adapt to climate change and minimize summer overheating: large secure ventilation openings, modest-sized windows, solar shading (adaptable with future upgrades), low-energy appliances (low heat-emitting), "thermally heavyweight" room surfaces to absorb daytime heat, and purge ventilation (to remove heat at night).[10] As Shingler explains: "We designed for adaptation to climate change, with predicted increases in temperature of 2.5°C (4.5°F)—hotter than record summer temperatures. We did not design the Lighthouse to be retrofitted with air conditioning if ambient air temperatures increase. Instead, the temperatures can be stabilized by cutting out solar gains with the retractable shutters on the west and opening the wind catcher on the roof. This is coupled with the thermal mass in the fabric of the house, which uses a wax polymer board in the ceiling to cool the space overnight and to stabilize temperatures internally." A "smart metering" environmental control system monitors the energy consumption of the house so that home owners can make informed decisions on a day-to-day basis and modify their lifestyles or adjust the house (including the shading, ventilation, and daylighting systems) to meet energy and comfort needs.

On considering the lessons of the project, Shingler concludes: "We used a rigorous process. Now that model can be replicated in similar microclimates. We have to make sure we are not designing something that cannot be built or

that is too complicated. If we are going to live in the house, it has to be intuitive. It has to respect the local environment. With passive energy, occupants have to be able to intuitively adjust the house. Active systems need to be low tech with simple controls. Design can encourage behavioral changes."

As the name suggests, the Lighthouse is an elegant light-filled home that can adapt and change to both future climate conditions and contemporary family needs. It provides an example of the thoughtful integration of contemporary design and state-of-the-art systems and technologies to support the highest standards of performance, design excellence, and quality of living.

Plans, sections, drawings

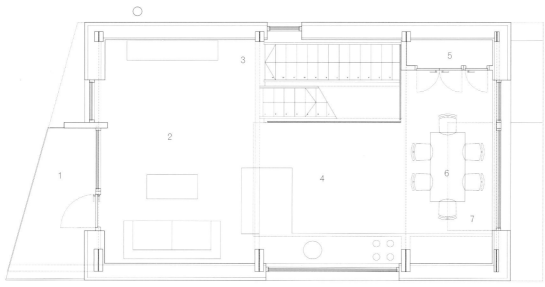

Level 2 plan

1. Balcony
2. Living room
3. Landing
4. Kitchen
5. Mechanical ventilation and heat recovery (MVHR)
6. Dining room
7. Void

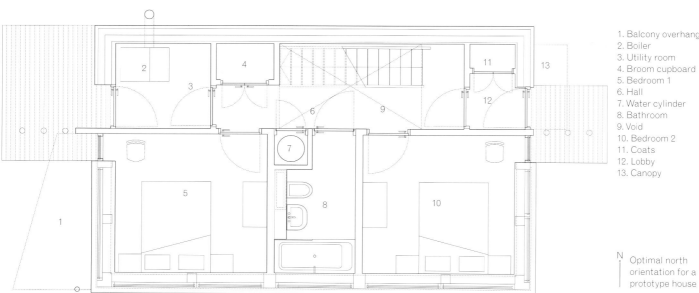

Level 1 plan

1. Balcony overhang
2. Boiler
3. Utility room
4. Broom cupboard
5. Bedroom 1
6. Hall
7. Water cylinder
8. Bathroom
9. Void
10. Bedroom 2
11. Coats
12. Lobby
13. Canopy

N
Optimal north orientation for a prototype house

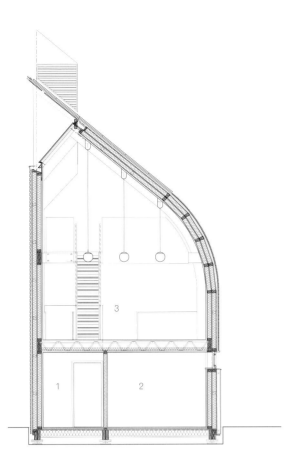
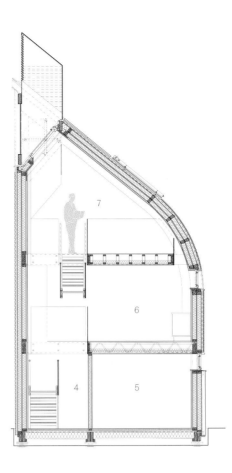

1. Utility
2. Bedroom
3. Living room
4. Hall
5. Bathroom
6. Kitchen
7. Mezzanine

Cross sections

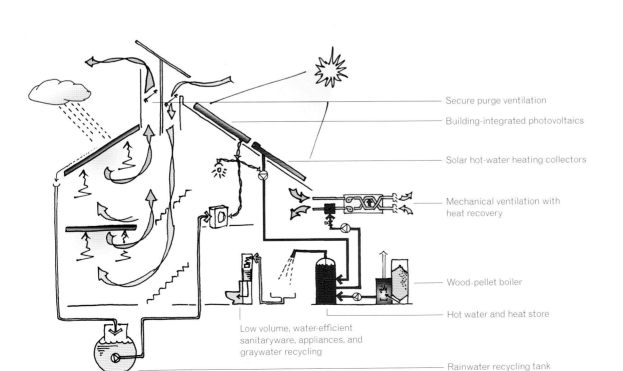

Secure purge ventilation

Building-integrated photovoltaics

Solar hot-water heating collectors

Mechanical ventilation with heat recovery

Wood-pellet boiler

Hot water and heat store

Low volume, water-efficient sanitaryware, appliances, and graywater recycling

Rainwater recycling tank

Section concept diagram showing the integration of the passive and active energy systems, including the passive wind catcher/light funnel that provides light and air to the core of the house; the roof-mounted south-facing active photovoltaic array and evacuated tube solar hot-water system; and the wood-pellet heating system.

Wind studies

Project location:
**Watford,
Hertfordshire, UK**

Wind data location:
London, UK

Fostering an ecological vision: Kingspan Lighthouse

Prevailing winds
March
Wind frequency (hours)
Location: London, UK (51.4°, 0.0°)
Time: 00:00–24:00

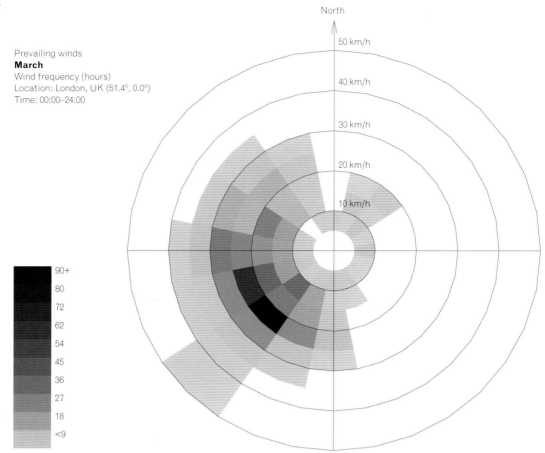

Prevailing winds
September
Wind frequency (hours)
Location: London, UK (51.4°, 0.0°)
Time: 00:00–24:00

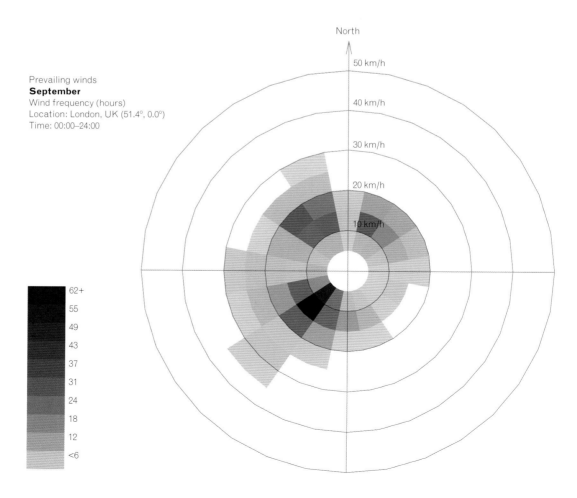

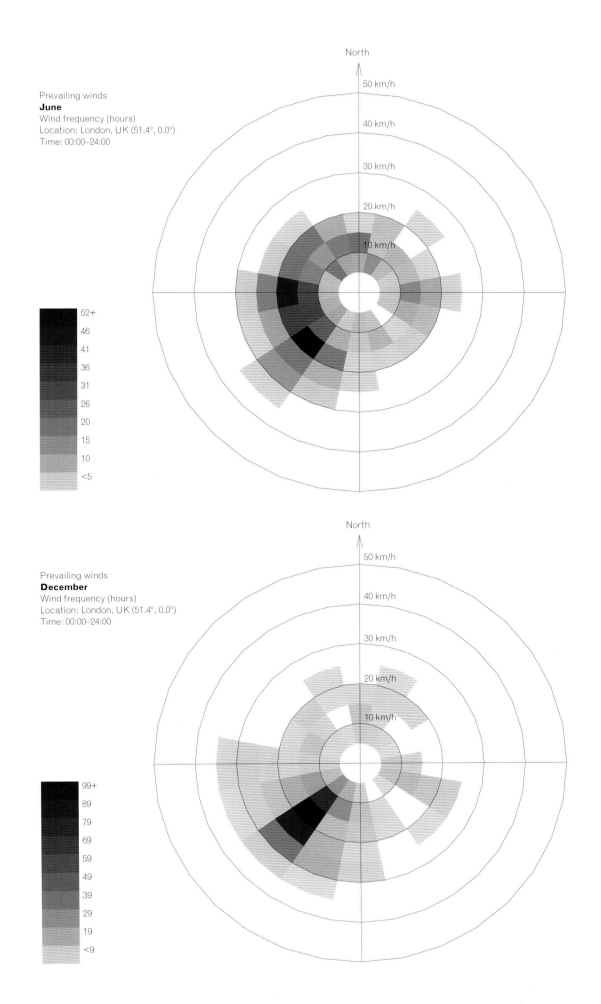

Prevailing winds
June
Wind frequency (hours)
Location: London, UK (51.4°, 0.0°)
Time: 00:00–24:00

North
50 km/h
40 km/h
30 km/h
20 km/h
10 km/h

52+
46
41
36
31
26
20
15
10
<5

Prevailing winds
December
Wind frequency (hours)
Location: London, UK (51.4°, 0.0°)
Time: 00:00–24:00

North
50 km/h
40 km/h
30 km/h
20 km/h
10 km/h

99+
89
79
69
59
49
39
29
19
<9

Sunpath case studies

Fostering an ecological vision: Kingspan Lighthouse

Project location:
**Watford,
Hertfordshire, UK
Latitude: 51° NL**

December

09:00

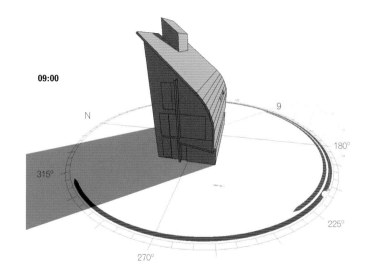

March/September

09:00

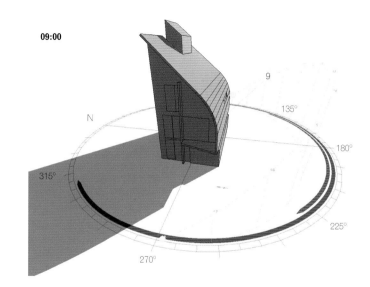

June

09:00

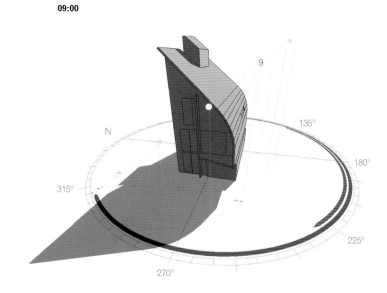

12:00

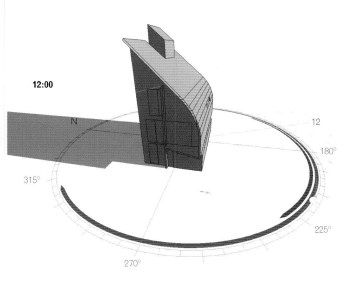

15:00

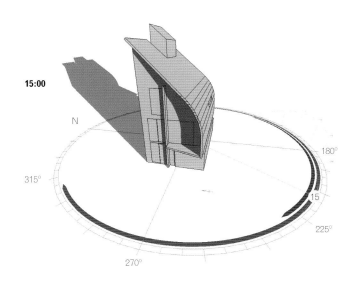

12:00

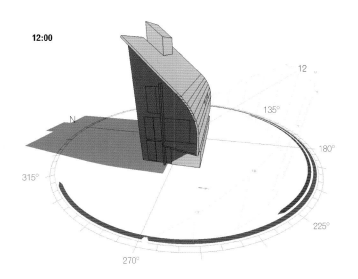

15:00

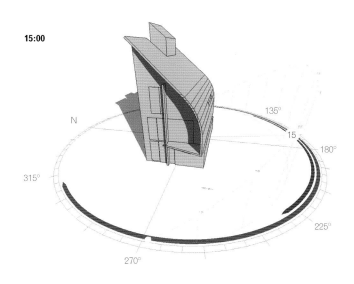

12:00

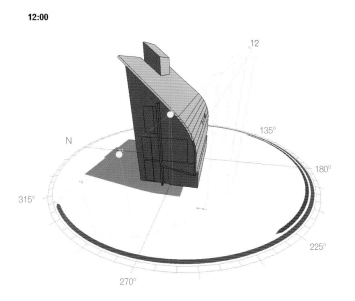

15:00

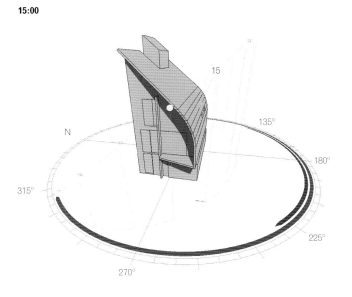

Climate data

Project location:
**Watford,
Hertfordshire, UK**

Climate data location:
London, UK

Fostering an ecological vision: Kingspan Lighthouse

**Diurnal average
temperatures**

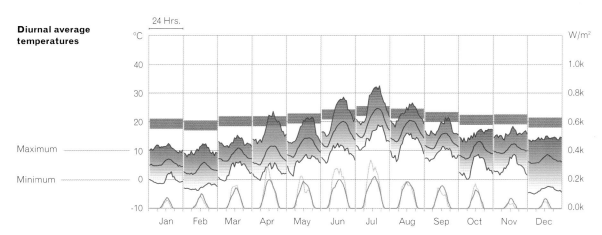

**Dry bulb
temperatures
1 Jan to 31 Dec**

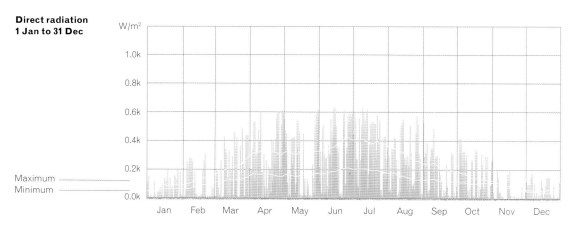

**Direct radiation
1 Jan to 31 Dec**

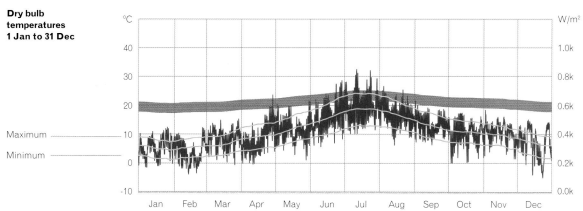

**Relative humidity
1 Jan to 31 Dec**

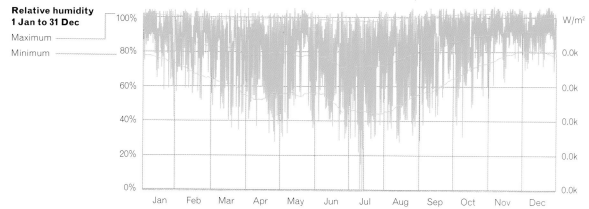

Temperature (°C)

Relative humidity (%)

Wind speed (W/m²)

Direct solar (W/m²)

Diffuse solar (W/m²)

Cloud cover (%)

Thermal neutrality

Design profile

Building Profile	Building name:	**Kingspan Lighthouse**
	Architect:	Sheppard Robson, Alan Shingler and Martin Rose, London, UK; www.sheppardrobson.com
	Location:	Building Research Establishment Ltd. (BRE) Innovation Park, Watford, Hertfordshire, UK
	Building type:	Residential
	Square meters/feet:	93.3 m² (104 sq ft)
Solar Design Profile	Latitude:	51° NL
	Heating Degree Days:	2,258 heating degree days °C (4,787 heating degree days °F) (18°C and 65°F base temperature; average 5 years)
	Cooling Degree Days:	211 cooling degree days °C (345 cooling degree days °F)
	Conservation strategies:	Reduced floor plan, no mechanical air conditioning, flexible space planning to adapt to future needs and uses
	Passive solar strategies:	Daylighting, operable windows, cross ventilation, solar chimney, solar shading, designed to respond to future increases in temperature of 2.5°C (4.5°F) due to climate change
	Active solar strategies:	Photovoltaic system, solar hot water thermal system
	Other renewable energy strategies:	None
	High-performance strategies:	High-performance mechanical systems and low heat-emitting appliances, mechanical ventilation with heat recovery, biomass boiler, efficient electric lighting, thermal mass with phase-change materials, high-performance glazing and envelope, highly insulated envelope
Performance Profile [11] [12]	Total annual building energy consumption:	83 kWh/m² (26 kBtu/sq ft); space heating: 19 kWh/m² (6 kBtu/sq ft); hot water: 29 kWh/m² (9.19 kBtu/sq ft)
	Total annual on-site energy produced:	Not available
	Size of photovoltaic system:	4.7 kW, 46 m² (495 sq ft) photovoltaics
	Size of solar thermal system:	2,940 kWh/yr solar thermal
	Carbon dioxide emissions:	Space heating and hot water: 45 kg (99lb)CO_2/yr (offset by photovoltaic energy exported to the grid)

Endnotes:
Kingspan Lighthouse

1 Kingspan, "Lighthouse," http://www.kingspanlighthouse.com/.
2 Department for Communities and Local Government, Code for Sustainable Homes (London: Department for Communities and Local Government, 2006), 2.
3 Sandra Andrea O'Connell, "Light Years Ahead – Kingspan Century's Lighthouse," *Architecture Ireland* (September 2007), 89.
4 Sheppard Robson, "Kingspan Lighthouse" (London: Sheppard Robson, no date), 1.
5 Potton, "Lighthouse by Potton" http://www.lighthousebypotton.co.uk/Press/LighthouseBrochure.pdf, 3.
6 Kingspan, http://www.kingspanlighthouse.com/energy.htm.
7 Potton, "Lighthouse by Potton," 12.
8 Department for Communities and Local Government, 2.
9 Kingspan Lighthouse, Energy, http://www.kingspanlighthouse.com/energy.htm.
10 Kingspan, http://www.kingspanlighthouse.com/accomodating_climate_change.htm.
11 Kingspan Lighthouse, Energy, http://www.kingspanlighthouse.com/energy.htm.
12 Potton, 13.

Chapter 2

Prioritizing passive design

"Ecological design is the art that reconnects us as sensuous creatures evolved over millions of years to a beautiful world. That world does not need to be remade but rather revealed. To do that, we do not need research as much as the rediscovery of old and forgotten things."[1]
DAVID ORR, *The Nature of Design*

"… this will be the path to sustainable, energy-efficient solar architecture. It begins with passive solar use, is easy to implement, and is reliable… It is controllable through intelligent, self-regulating control technologies— smart control. Finally it combines passive and active solar systems… Keywords in this field are hybrid solar systems, microclimatic building skins, and self-regulating facades. The development of smart solar architecture will give rise to new technologies, and to an eagerly anticipated new architecture."[2]
MANFRED HEGGER, *Solar Architecture*

Place matters. As influential on our daily lives as is gravity, the bioclimatic forces of sun, wind, weather, and site have shaped architecture and our experience of place throughout history. Designs that respond to place also tend to provide a connection to nature that reveals and celebrates the essence of a site and a region. David Orr, Professor of Environmental Studies at Oberlin College in the USA, argues that humans have an essential need to connect with nature: "… quite possibly we have certain dispositions toward the environment that have been hardwired in us over the course of our evolution. EO Wilson, for example, suggests that we possess what he calls 'biophilia,' meaning an innate 'urge to affiliate with other forms of life'… The growing evidence supporting the biophilia hypothesis suggests that we fit better in environments that have more, not less, nature. We do better with sunlight, contact with animals, and in settings that include trees, flowers, flowing water, birds, and natural processes than in their absence. We are sensuous creatures who develop emotional attachments to particular landscapes. The implication is that we need to create communities and places that resonate with our evolutionary past and for which we have deep affection."[3]

We come to know the places we inhabit by engaging the rhythms of the day through the shifting seasons and ever-changing weather. Simple interactions such as adjusting a window for the breeze, dropping a blind to control the afternoon heat, or migrating to a different part of the home to experience a sunset demonstrate how architecture can help us reconnect with nature. By gaining a more intimate knowledge and understanding of a place, we might also come to love and care more deeply for each other and the world in which we live. Ralph Knowles, architect and professor emeritus at the University of Southern California, suggests that humans have an urgent need to rediscover nature: "Understanding how the elements affect our lives is more vital than ever. High-energy enclosed building systems have cut us off from nature, but we can reconnect to our landscapes and to humanity through buildings that honor ecological balance, personal choice, and creativity. By engaging nature in our designs, we can create shelters that are unique to their climate, their region, and their relationship to the sun."[4]

If architects focus on place-based design, then the forces of sun and wind are sure to inspire at all scales; from massing and plan to section and details. David Miller, architect and professor at the University of Washington, underscores the importance of using a regional approach to solve ecological problems in an aesthetic manner: "For a greater part of the twentieth century and now into the twenty-first, architects have engaged in an ongoing debate on the apparent contradiction between the universal and the particular… Architects need to work toward a rational and timeless architecture that sustains the qualities of place. The imperative question then becomes 'How does a designer determine the overall conception and realization of architectural form that captures the spirit and quality of place and at the same time addresses the compelling issue of our day—the world's ecological dysfunction?'…

West elevation of the Sonnenschiff (Solarship) in Freiburg, Germany, revealing the juxtaposition of commercial spaces, upper-level living units, and gardens. The horizontal rhythm of the commercial spaces is punctuated by alternating windows and colorful ventilation slots. Glazed stairways link the lower and upper levels. Living units are shaped and oriented to optimize passive strategies for heating, cooling, and daylighting, as well as active solar strategies for hot-water and electric-energy generation.

A designer must contend with these global concerns by connecting design to the spirit and natural conditions of a specific region."[5] A place-based architecture responsive to the forces of sun, wind, and site inevitably leads to an expression that embodies the qualities and character of a given region. The design, experiential, and ecological opportunities of place-based architecture are boundless.

In his book *Architecture in a Climate of Change*, architect and professor Peter Smith emphasizes that: "Solar radiation is the primary source of renewable energy. Besides offering a direct source of energy, it drives the earth's climate creating opportunities to draw energy from wind, waves, tidal (together with the moon), and a host of biological sources… Since the sun drives every aspect of the climate it is logical to describe the techniques adopted in buildings to take advantage of this fact as 'solar design'."[6] Despite the abundance of solar energy and renewable resources on almost every site, the transition to an ecological architecture that fully embraces solar design (and related

renewable design options) is still emerging. As Christian Schittich, architect and editor of inDETAIL explains: "The energy potential, which the sun places at our disposal on a daily basis, seems inexhaustible. The incident radiation on the landmasses of the earth alone is 3,000 times greater than the worldwide demands. Yet we continue to meet these demands almost exclusively with nonrenewable energies generated primarily from fossil fuels…"[7] The often crude solar designs of the 1960s and 1970s caution us to be aware that design integrity is essential to establish a fresh and vital twenty-first century approach to solar architecture.

How will solar architecture and renewable energy design be expressed in the twenty-first century? The first priority will be passive design, which uses the architecture itself to harvest energy. The second priority will be renewable technologies to supplement the design solutions. Bill Bordass of the Usable Building Trust in London explains: "We say: keep it simple, do it well, and only then be clever. Unfortunately, our

POE [post-occupancy evaluation] work tells us that we often try to be clever before we get the basics right. So you find $1m of PV on top of a 50,000sq ft building reducing its carbon footprint by 10 percent, while you could have saved the same amount merely by ensuring the building was properly airtight and the heating was controlled better… Prevention is better than cure!"[8] Without focusing first on the architectural and ecological opportunities of passive design, it will be difficult, if not impossible, to reach low- and zero-energy goals.

Christian Schittich emphasizes the need for a holistic approach to solar design: "… solar architecture cannot be reduced to isolated measures such as collectors or photovoltaic installations on the roof. Rather, a building must be understood as a complex configuration—a total energy concept—that makes the best possible use of locally available natural resources such as solar energy, wind, and geothermal energy for a variety of requirements. Passive and active measures complement

Site view looking southwest to the surrounding forest at the Aldo Leopold Legacy Center in Baraboo, Wisconsin, USA. In response to the extreme temperature variations and cold climate, the building is oriented and shaped to optimize passive design strategies and active solar systems.

one another in this approach, from the orientation and division of the building to the integration of systems for the generation of warm water or power. Flexible envelopes, regulated by intelligent control systems and capable of reacting to varying influences and weather conditions are making increasingly important contributions…"[9] A hybrid approach that integrates passive design and active systems at the earliest phases of design conception and planning is evident in the leading examples of new solar architecture. As Manfred Hegger explains in his essay "From Passive Utilization to Smart Solar Architecture": "While passive use of solar energy was the only option available prior to the beginning of the fossil [fuel] age… fossil heating sources and the technologies derived from them allow for active temperature control today, completely independent of conditions in the environment, and the form and materials of our homes. The stages of first passive and then active energy supply in buildings are being overtaken by interactive or smart building concepts, which adopt certain passive systems and complement them with intelligent components."[10]

The following case studies explore buildings that respond to the moods and rhythms of place and in so doing help the occupants learn to live differently on the land, experience the cycles of time and season, and reduce their ecological footprints. As David Orr suggests: "Ecological design is the art that reconnects us as sensuous creatures evolved over millions of years to a beautiful world. That world does not need to be remade but rather revealed. To do that, we do not need research as much as the rediscovery of old and forgotten things."[11] The Solarsiedlung am Schlierberg (Solar Community at Schlierberg) by Rolf Disch Architects and the Aldo Leopold Legacy Center by Kubala Washatko Architects use simple architectural design strategies coupled with high-performance and renewable energy technologies to harvest solar and wind energy for heating, lighting, and cooling. The projects illustrate how a hybrid approach that combines passive design and active technologies can enable new levels of ecological performance. While the design strategies and technologies are straightforward and commonly available, it is their holistic design integration that enables the buildings to harvest and produce energy on site while dramatically reducing carbon emissions.

The Solar Community and Aldo Leopold Legacy Center demonstrate principles of regenerative design that go beyond zero-energy targets and actually produce energy. By deeply responding to the forces of place, sun, wind, and site, these projects give form to an architecture that is good for the Earth and good for us. As David Miller emphasizes: "The core of sustainable design lies in responding to a 'spirit of place.' Architecture that heals the heart, our biological systems, and the environment is sustainable. It needs to be shaped by and for a region's conditions. The green past has relevance for the future."[12] At the Solar Community and Aldo Leopold Legacy Center, we find that architecture thoughtfully integrated with solar and renewable energy design really can change our ecological impact and the way in which we live.

Aerial view of the Solarsiedlung (Solar Community) in Freiburg, Germany. Residential units are located east of the mixed-use Sonnenschiff (Solarship). Each multistory row house has a ground-level terrace, upper-level balcony, and garden space. All units are oriented and shaped to optimize the integration of solar strategies and foster connections to the site and environment.

Endnotes:

1 David Orr, *The Nature of Design: Ecology, Culture, and Human Intention* (Oxford: Oxford University Press, 2002), 32.
2 Manfred Hegger, "From Passive Utilization to Smart Solar Architecture," *Solar Architecture*, edited by Christian Schittich (Basel: Birkhäuser, 2003), 24.
3 David Orr, 25–26.
4 Ralph Knowles, *Ritual House* (Washington, DC: Island Press, 2006); www.islandpress.org/bookstore/details.php?isbn=9781597260503).
5 David E. Miller, *Toward a New Regionalism* (Seattle: University of Washington Press, 2005), xv.
6 Peter F. Smith, *Architecture in a Climate of Change: A Guide to Sustainable Design* (Oxford: Architectural Press, 2001), 33, 45.
7 Christian Schittich, ed., *Solar Architecture* (Basel: Birkhäuser, 2003), 9.
8 Bill Bordass, Society of Building Science Educators Listserver, December 4, 2008.
9 Christian Schittich, 9.
10 Manfred Hegger, 24.
11 David Orr, 32.
12 David E. Miller, xi.

Project: **Solarsiedlung am Schlierberg**
Location: **Freiburg, Germany**
Architect: **Rolf Disch Architects**

"Children and the sun…
what an inexhaustible power!"
Visitor at Solarsiedlung am Schlierberg[1]

"When you build a house… you have a
responsibility for the whole society… It's not a
question of the Technik [technology]. We have the
Technik. Of course, the Technik can develop more
and more. But it's a question of the mind, and
[doing] it. We have a problem [doing] it. We have
no technical problems anymore."[2]
Rolf Disch Architects

Design intentions

The Solarsiedlung am Schlierberg (Solar
Community at Schlierberg) was designed by
architect Rolf Disch. The community is located
in the Vauban district of Freiburg, Germany, a
new ecological suburb that has emerged as a
model for sustainable living. The city of Freiburg
is considered to be the solar capital of Europe;
it exemplifies the integration of innovative
renewable energy design from the level of public
policy and urban planning down to the details
of architectural form and technologies. This
status is due, in part, to leadership from the
Freiburg City Council, which has provided policies
that promote sustainable urban planning and
architectural design.

Dr. Dieter Wörner, director of the
Environmental Protection Agency of the City
of Freiburg, explains the important role of city
policies: "Freiburg's energy policy has three
pillars: energy conservation, the use of new
technologies such as combined heat and power,
and the use of renewable energy sources such
as solar to meet new demand, instead of fossil
fuels, with the goal of realizing an ecologically
oriented energy supply. Behind this, there lies
a deeper goal to create sustainable regional
development for the area as a whole. In 1996,
this was strengthened by a city resolution to
reduce Freiburg's CO_2 emissions to 25 percent
below the 1992 level by 2010, which calls for
initiatives in the areas of transportation,

waste, and industrial production, as well as
energy."[3] Leaders and community members
in the Vauban district decided to go beyond
these goals. They established community-scale
sustainability plans to promote renewable
energy lifestyles that minimize or even
eliminate dependence on fossil fuels. One
vision of this lifestyle is embodied in the Solar
Community. As a flagship project in Vauban,
the complex includes two major components, a
commercial and residential mixed-use building
called the Sonnenschiff (or Solarship) and
the Solarsiedlung (or Solar Community) row
houses, which include various models of a
modular structure called the Plusenergie®haus
(Plus-Energy House). The complex is an
example of social and ecological sustainability
that supports sustainable lifestyles while
generating more energy than is consumed by
its businesses and residents.

Climate and site

The Vauban district was created in 1990 after
the fall of the Berlin Wall. Located southwest
of the historic city center of Freiburg, Vauban
was formerly part of a compound used by the
French military. Architectural critic Chris Turner
elaborates on the history of the community:
"Vauban was not, however, a singular vision,
which may be one of the keys to its success.
Early in the planning stages, a group called
Forum Vauban was started, to direct community
participation. From its deliberations, there

emerged a grander scheme, most of which is not manifest: a district made up of mixed-income, mixed-use units that are hyper-efficient and (mostly) sustainably powered… they demonstrate how different low-rise condominiums might look if they were built to the specifications of the people who live in them, instead of profit-focused developers who never will."[4] While the desired diversity of this urban vision has yet to be fully realized, the complex provides a model for ecological living that inspires designers from around the world to reconsider the social and ecological roles of sustainable solar design.

Freiburg is located in a beautiful region of Germany, surrounded by mountains and the Black Forest. The region is known as the sunbelt of Germany, with a relatively mild climate and uniquely clear skies. The average low temperature is 2°C (35°F) in January and the average high is 20°C (69°F) in July. The climate and location allow for the efficient use of both passive and active solar design. Although winter heating is required, summer temperatures are sufficiently moderate for there to be no need for air conditioning when ventilation and passive cooling are properly designed. Guidelines in the solar district of Freiburg require southerly orientations to ensure that all homes and commercial spaces have appropriate solar access for seasonal heating and daylighting. The site design also celebrates the movement of sunlight through the landscape,

creating outdoor spaces and gardens that foster community and social connections while supporting a sustainable and healthy lifestyle.

Rolf Disch Architects describe the Solarship (the commercial portion of the project) as the most modern solar mixed-use building in Europe. Extending for 125 m (410 ft) along Merzhauser Strasse, the linear building runs on a north–south axis with retail spaces at street level, offices on the second and third floors, and eight south-facing multistory penthouses with roof gardens on the upper levels. The residential area designated as the Solar Community includes 50 family row houses that are located to the east, behind the visually and acoustically sheltering Solarship. The row houses extend perpendicular to the retail building, with five fingerlike rows of family housing oriented on an east–west axis. Pedestrians and bicycles have access to the residential areas through entries along the commercial street. Woodlands provide a natural buffer along the eastern edge of the community, while a combination of private and community gardens, walkways, and bike paths weaves throughout the row housing. Outside spaces are designed to extend the interior living spaces into the landscape, with storage rooms, fences, and layers of gardens distinguishing private from communal spaces.

Despite the density of the complex, an abundance of landscaped areas, including

Aerial view of the commercial Solarship, which is oriented on the north–south axis along the street. The solar row houses in the Solar Community can be seen beyond the commercial building. Oriented on an east-west axis, the row houses are designed to optimize passive and active solar strategies.

personalized balconies, vegetable and flower gardens, terraces, public pathways, gardens, and play areas ensures that the public areas feel spacious and dynamic: "Forum Vauban decided that the spaces between the townhouses would be for people, so there are no cars, not even roads, just laneways and green space laced with walking paths and dotted with park benches and playground equipment. For those who own cars, there's a parking garage, its roof carpeted in PV panels. But because parking spaces are pricey and the area is amply served by Freiburg's extensive transit network, about 40 percent of the residents live car-free."[5] Careful site planning, which included the appropriate spacing and scale of dwelling units, ensured that interior and exterior areas receive solar access and air throughout the year. By integrating the living areas and garden spaces, the design enhances awareness of diurnal and seasonal cycles and fosters a connection to the site and gardens. Architect Rolf Disch optimized seasonal sun angles and solar insolation at the site scale while simultaneously enhancing the qualitative experiences of sunlight and air movement throughout the individual and communal living spaces.

Daylighting and thermal design

Passive design strategies shape the ecological performance and experiential qualities of the complex. Rolf Disch Architects emphasize that: "The function determines the aesthetics. This is true of the whole configuration. It also becomes apparent in the ventilation components that are integrated into the facade and which serve the purpose of heat recovery in the winter and of cooling the building units at nighttime in the summer, as well as in the components for heat insulation, soundproofing, and sunshading. These protruding construction units, the colors of which are gradated according to the harmonious color design of the Berlin artist Erich Wiesner—called 'the dyer'—in coordination with the Solarsiedlung, animate the facade and give the Sonnenschiff a very special touch."[6] The lower-level commercial and office spaces at the Solarship are not passively oriented (they follow the north–south axis of the street) and therefore the commercial building is designed to reduce energy consumption through daylighting and natural ventilation. Abundant bilateral daylight is admitted on the east and west facades and natural ventilation slots are integrated along the perimeter of the three-dimensional ventilation boxes that alternate colorfully with the windows on the western and eastern facades. The thin plan and section maximize daylighting and natural ventilation to reduce energy consumption.

The eight two-story penthouses on top of the Solarship are based on the Plus-Energy House design. The adjacent residential area also uses Plus-Energy houses that are configured as multistory row houses. Each house is shaped in orientation, plan, and section to harvest heat,

light, and air from the site. Modular construction facilitates a variety of configurations that can easily accommodate differing lifestyle and space needs. A basic plan includes a first-floor living area and dining space oriented to the south with a kitchen, bathroom, and work niche to the north. The living area can be opened onto an adjacent southern terrace and garden space as the seasons dictate. A typical second-floor plan includes bedrooms on the south, a centrally located stair, and a bath and work niche on the north. A narrow balcony overlooks the southern garden and public walkways. A third-floor balcony, tucked behind the south-sloping photovoltaic roof, has a view to neighboring gardens. The open floor plan gathers heat, light, and air from the fully glazed and operable south facade. Apertures on the north facade provide cross ventilation and bilateral daylighting. The transparency of the south facade contrasts with the solidity and modestly sized openings on the north. South shading and solar control are provided by a large overhanging photovoltaic roof and a variety of simple, operable fabric shading devices at the ground-level gardens. To balance the uniform orientation and building massing, the row houses are animated by materials and textures made vibrant by alternating cladding, colors, shading devices, vertical screens, landscaping, and climbing vegetation.

In addition to passive solar design, which reduces overall energy demand, the "plus-energy" goal of generating more energy than the residents

consume requires that energy be generated on site. To accomplish this, a photovoltaic array covers the entire roof area of the housing units. The roof form is defined by a southern orientation, a 22-degree angle that is optimal for photovoltaic performance, and shading criteria to moderate solar gain. The extensive photovoltaic roof array may suggest that the Solar Community relies on a technological approach, but in fact the housing units are primarily shaped by passive architectural strategies.

Energy systems

With a goal of energy independence, the complex is powered by renewable energy sources from the sun, wind, and biomass. Given site constraints and building orientation, the Solarship has less passive solar potential than the row house portion of the community, and consequently depends on energy from other sources, as Rolf Disch Architects explain: "On balance, the Sonnenschiff will gain its power demand entirely from regenerative kinds of energy. Heating, power supply, and water heating will be based exclusively on the energy sources sun and wood. The heat supply of the Sonnenschiff is gained through local heat from a woodchip block heat and power plant. Thus, the building falls altogether far below the legal requirements of the energy-saving regulations, by even more than the factor 10."[7]

The Solarship is designed to reduce energy demand through ecological programming, space planning, and architectural design. Rolf

Above left
West and north facade of multistory row houses. Larger four-story units are sited in the northern section of the community to ensure solar access to the lower three-story row houses. Ground-level terraces and upper-level balconies on the south and north facades provide inhabitants with a variety of thermal and luminous experiences that vary with the seasons and times of day.

Above right
South facade of multistory row houses. North and south facades are designed to respond to the prevailing wind conditions and passive and active solar strategies for heating, cooling, and daylighting as well as hot-water and electric-energy generation.

Interior view of ground-floor living space, looking south toward the terrace and exterior garden. The colorful north facade of a neighboring row house can be seen in the background. Simple living spaces are animated by patterns of sunlight, air, and garden views that change with the seasons.

Disch Architects emphasize the importance of construction and architectural detailing to optimize energy performance in the Solarship: "As far as its energy efficiency is concerned, the Sonnenschiff largely meets the Plusenergie®-haus standard of the Solarsiedlung… The lack of south orientation is compensated by the compactness of the Sonnenschiff. Computer simulations show that a heating energy demand of yearly 10 to 20 kWh per m² [3.2–6.3 kBtu/sq ft] effective area is to be expected—depending on the usage, the position, and the proportion of the units' exterior surfaces. The heating energy demand is kept at such a low level due to the highly heat-insulated outer casing, the decentralized ventilation system with a highly efficient heat recovery, and the passive-solar use of solar energy with a three-pane heat insulation thermopane glazing."[8] While reducing the energy demand is the first order of design, the plus-energy goal is ultimately met by electricity produced by the 112-kW grid-tied photovoltaic system on the penthouse roofs of the Solarship.

Units are designed to meet an energy goal of 10–15 kWh/m² (3.2–4.8 kBtu/sq ft) for Plus-Energy housing, which is approximately one-tenth the energy consumption of conventional housing. Super-insulation, a U-value of 0.12 for exterior walls and ceilings, and windproof construction minimize infiltration and heat loss. Energy systems include heat pumps, a heat recovery system, solar hot-water collectors (on the Solarship), and photovoltaics. Each house has its own photovoltaic system to generate electricity. Based on the size and needs of the housing unit, the photovoltaic systems have outputs that vary from 3.0 to 12.0 kW (for a total of 333 kW for the row houses). High-performance triple glazing and solar shading work in tandem to optimize winter and summer solar benefits for both heating and cooling. Andrew Purvis, in the *Observer*, confirms the low energy consumption and costs in an interview with resident Meinhard Hansen: "It is 6°C [43°F] outside, and a dusting of snow can be seen on the Schauinsland… In Meinhard Hansen's apartment, however, it is perpetual summer; the sun streams in through tall, south-facing windows and a gauge on the wall reads '24°C [75°F]'. Next to it, the words 'Heizung 0' appear in a small glass window. 'Heating, zero,' Meinhard translates. 'In fact, we haven't switched the heating on for weeks.' While a typical home in Germany (or Britain, for that matter) squanders 220 kilowatt hours of energy a year for each square metre of floor space, this one wastes 15 kWh/m² [4.8 kBtu/sq ft] a year."[9]

Paul Gipe, an energy expert from *Windworks*, analyzed the energy performance of the commercial and residential areas in an essay on the Solar Community. He found that the commercial Solarship, at 6,034 m² (64,949 sq ft) is a net energy producer that consumes 17 kWh/m² (5.3 kBtu/sq ft) per year, and produces 18 kWh/m² (5.7 kBtu/sq ft) per year. Fifty Plus-Energy houses,

with a total of 6,745 m² (72,602 sq ft), annually consume 2,200 kWh per house, while generating 6,280 kWh per house. The total photovoltaic output for the Solar Community is 455 kW, including 333 kW from the row houses and 112 kW from the Solarship.[10] Gipe summarizes: "… the average electricity consumption for the homes is only 2,200 kWh/year. That's one-third the average of the typical California home, one-fifth that of the typical Ontario house, and one-sixth that of the typical Texan. The rooftop solar panels produce (almost) 6,300 kWh/home per year or three times more than each home consumes.[11]

Next-generation thinking

In an essay for PV Upscale, architect Dr. Ingo Hagemann from Architekturbüro Hagemann summarizes the findings of a report on the experience of living in the Solar Community: "Occupants report that they enjoy living in the Solarsiedlung am Schlierberg. They experience a variety of benefits compared to occupants of conventional settlements. For example: enjoying living in a solar home and contributing to a resource-efficient life style; benefits from the good innercity location; easy and short access to public transport facilities nearby; an infrastructure appropriate for children (no cars etc.); less illness due to a healthy indoor climate/air quality; finding the social environment they are looking for…"[12]

The Solar Community at Schlierberg demonstrates that it is possible to achieve

not only a zero-energy (or even "plus-energy") design, but Rolf Disch Architects also focused on the intersection of energy and human health at the scales of design details, systems, and material specifications: "A de-central ventilation system based on the principle of heat recovery makes sure the air quality is constantly good: the house is breathing. Timber or linoleum floors further contribute to the good quality of the indoor air as textiles, adhesives, PVC, formaldehyde, and solvents are being avoided and the relative air humidity is kept in balance thanks to the material timber, the windproof properties of the building and the ventilation with heat and humidity recovery."

The project illustrates that solar design is as much about a way of living as it is about energy performance. The Solar Community demonstrates that we can live a high-quality life that also gives back to the environment.

Detail of the south-facing photovoltaic array. The roof extends beyond the south facade to seasonally shade the living spaces below. Glimpses of the sky can be seen between the photovoltaic cells and structure, creating changing patterns of sun and shadow on the south facade.

Above
West and south facades of a row house at the Solar Community. Solar units of varying sizes and configurations are available in the community.

Right
View looking east to the adjacent woodland. The repetition of the row houses is relieved by varied colors and different types of cladding, landscaping, and personalization of the units and outdoor spaces.

Plans, sections, diagrams

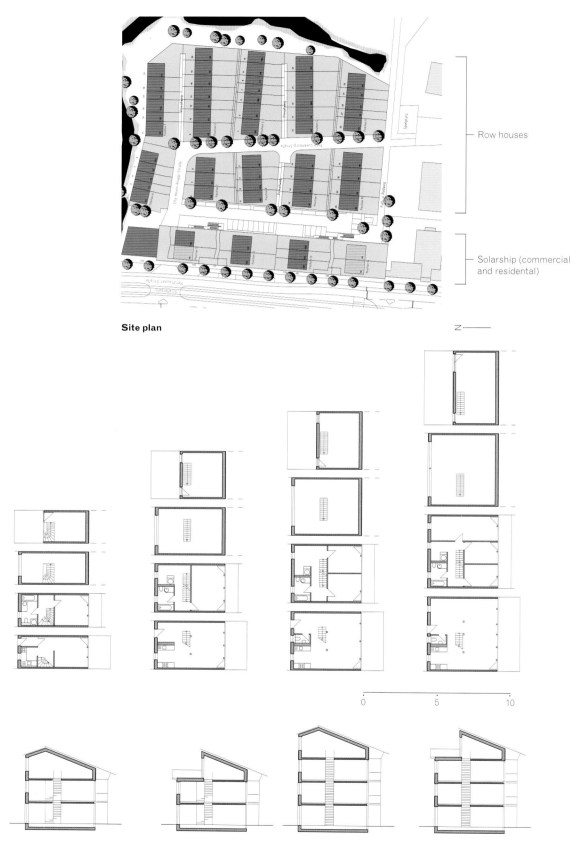

Site plan

Row houses

Solarship (commercial and residental)

Sample floor plans and sections of row houses

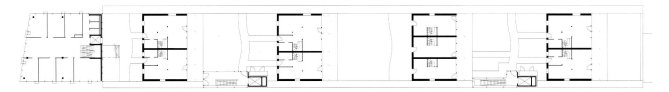

Penthouse-floor plan

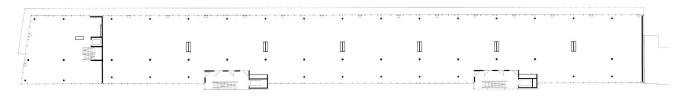

Second- and third-floor plan

Ground-floor plan

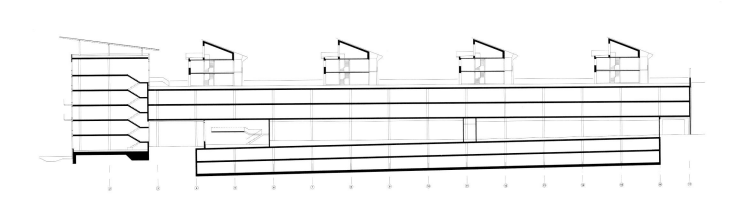

Solarship section looking east

Wind studies

Project location:
Freiburg, Germany

Wind data location:
Freiburg, Germany

Prevailing winds
March
Wind frequency (hours)
Location: Freiburg, Germany (48.0°, 7.8°)
Time: 00:00–24:00

Prevailing winds
September
Wind frequency (hours)
Location: Freiburg, Germany (48.0°, 7.8°)
Time: 00:00–24:00

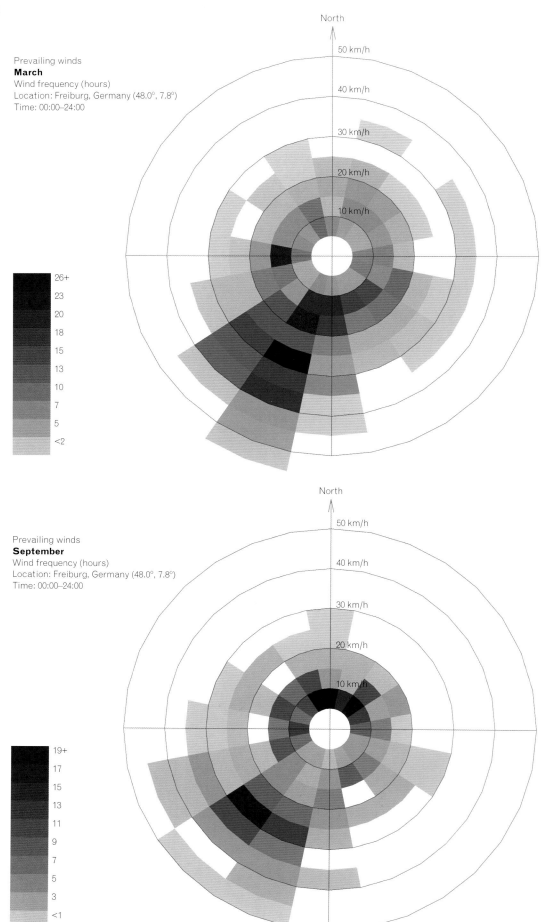

26+
23
20
18
15
13
10
7
5
<2

19+
17
15
13
11
9
7
5
3
<1

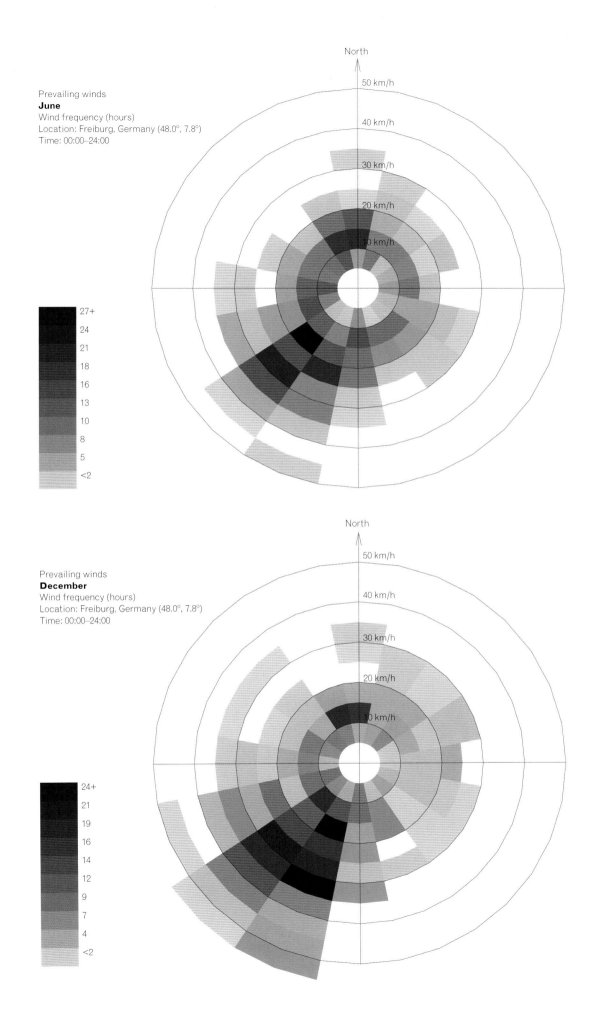

North

50 km/h
40 km/h
30 km/h
20 km/h
10 km/h

Prevailing winds
June
Wind frequency (hours)
Location: Freiburg, Germany (48.0°, 7.8°)
Time: 00:00–24:00

27+
24
21
18
16
13
10
8
5
<2

North

50 km/h
40 km/h
30 km/h
20 km/h
10 km/h

Prevailing winds
December
Wind frequency (hours)
Location: Freiburg, Germany (48.0°, 7.8°)
Time: 00:00–24:00

24+
21
19
16
14
12
9
7
4
<2

Sunpath case studies

Project location:
Freiburg, Germany
Latitude: 48° NL

December

09:00

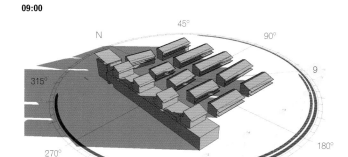

March/September

09:00

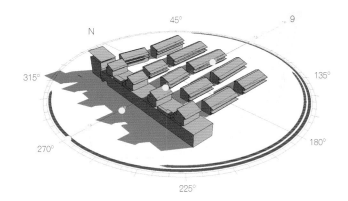

June

09:00

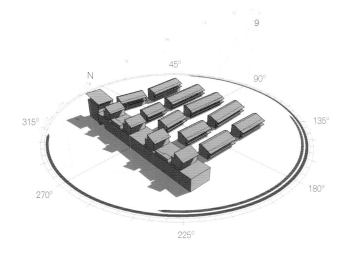

12:00

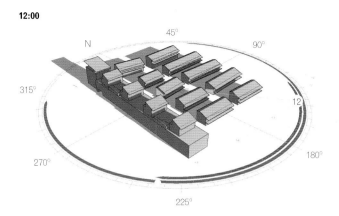

15:00

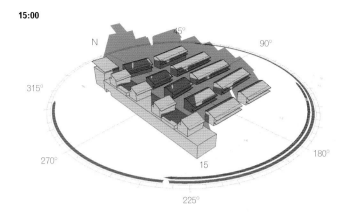

12:00

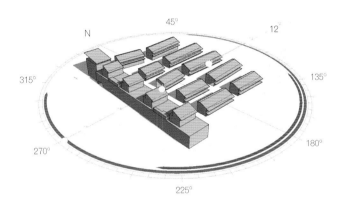

15:00

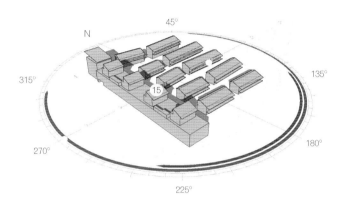

12:00

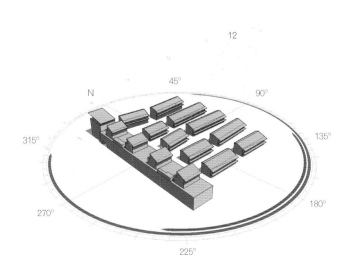

15:00

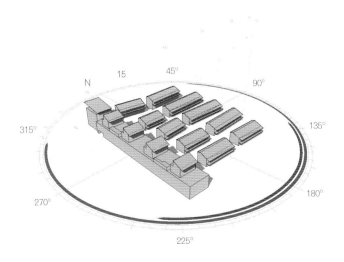

Climate data

Project location:
Freiburg, Germany

Climate data location:
Freiburg, Germany

Diurnal average temperatures

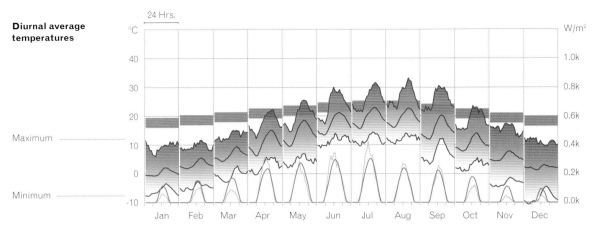

**Dry bulb temperatures
1 Jan to 31 Dec**

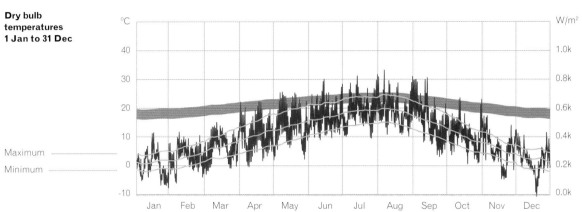

**Direct radiation
1 Jan to 31 Dec**

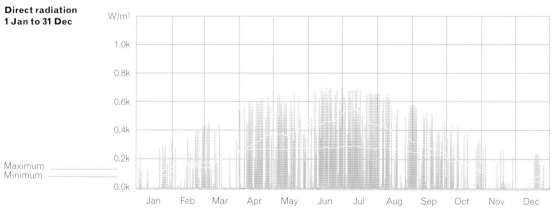

**Relative humidity
1 Jan to 31 Dec**

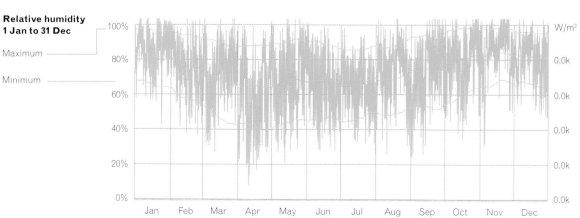

Temperature (°C)

Relative humidity (%)

Wind apeed (W/m²)

Direct aolar (W/m²)

Diffuse aolar (W/m²)

Cloud cover (%)

Thermal neutrality

Design profile

Building profile	Building name:	**Solarsiedlung am Schlierberg (Solar Community at Schlierberg)**
	Architect:	Rolf Disch Architects, Freiburg, Germany; www.rolf-disch.de
	Location:	Freiburg, Germany
	Building type:	Residential
	Square meters/feet:[13]	Sonnenschiff: 6,034 m² (64,949 sq ft); 50 Plusenergie®haus: 6,745 m² (72,602 sq ft)

Solar design profile	Latitude:	48° NL
	Heating Degree Days:	3,660 heating degree days °C (6,775 heating degree days °F) (18°C and 65°F base temperature; average 5 years)
	Cooling Degree Days:	227 cooling degree days °C (375 cooling degree days °F)
	Conservation strategies:	Modest-sized units; thermal and luminous zoning PDi
	Passive solar strategies: solar shading	Direct solar gain, daylighting, operable windows, cross ventilation,
	Active solar strategies:	Photovoltaic system, solar hot-water thermal system
	Other renewable energy strategies:	None
	High-performance strategies:	High-performance building envelope, triple glazing, heat recovery from facade-integrated ventilation components, high-performance ventilation system, energy-efficient appliances and lighting systems, neighborhood woodchip heat and power plant

Performance profile [14]	Total annual building energy consumption:	Sonnenschiff: estimated 10–20 kWh/m²/yr (3.2–6.3 kBtu/sq ft) Plusenergie®haus: estimated 10–15 kWh/m²/yr (3.2–4.8 kBtu/sq ft)
	Total annual on-site energy produced:	Not available
	Size of photovoltaic system:	Estimated total: 455 kW (112 kW for Sonnenschiff; 333 kW for 50 Plusenergie®haus)[15]
	Size of solar thermal system:	evacuated tube solar hot-water heating for domestic hot water (size not available)
	Carbon dioxide emissions:	Not available

Endnotes:
Solarsiedlung am Schlierberg
(Solar Community at Schlierberg)

1 Rolf Disch Architects, www.rolfdisch.de.
2 Chris Turner, "Solar Settlement," *Azure*, v. 23, issue 175 (May 2007), 63.
3 Dieter Wörner, "Sustainable City Freiburg," *Freiburg Fair* (Madison, WI: Office of the Mayor, August 2005); www.madisonfreiburg.org/sustainablecity.htm.
4 Chris Turner, 65.
5 Ibid, 66.
6 Rolf Disch Architects,

www.rolfdisch.de.
7 Rolf Disch Architects, www.rolfdisch.de.
8 Ibid.
9 Andrew Purvis, "Is This the Greenest City in the World?," *Observer*, Sunday, March 23, 2008; www.guardian.co.uk/environment/2008/mar/23/freiburg.germany.greenest.city.
10 Paul Gipe, "Freiburg's Solar Siedlung," *Windworks*, (April 7, 2007).

11 Ibid.
12 Ingo B. Hagemann, "Solarsiedlung am Schlierberg, Freiburg (Breisgau), Germany," PV Upscale; www.pvupscale.org/IMG/pdf/Schlierberg.pdf.
13 Paul Gipe.
14 Rolf Disch Architects, www.rolfdisch.de.
15 Paul Gipe.

Project: **Aldo Leopold Legacy Center**
Location: **Baraboo, Wisconsin, USA**
Architect: **The Kubala Washatko Architects**

"A land ethic, then, reflects the existence of an ecological conscience, and this in turn reflects a conviction of individual responsibility for the health of the land. Health is the capacity of the land for self-renewal. Conservation is our effort to understand and preserve this capacity." [1]
Aldo Leopold, *A Sand County Almanac*

South facade of the centrally located main building, which includes the public entry, information area, restrooms, staff areas, and museum. The building design responds to cold-climate temperature extremes with integrated strategies for passive heating and cooling as well as active solar hot-water and electric-energy generation.

Design intentions

The Aldo Leopold Legacy Center is lauded as the first contemporary carbon-neutral building in the United States. The goal of the center is to build on the ecological teachings, conservation research, and land stewardship of Aldo Leopold (1887–1948). As a forester, ecologist, educator, and leading proponent of wildlife conservation, Aldo Leopold had a profound influence on the development of environmental ethics in the early and mid twentieth century. The Legacy Center is located on land that Leopold owned and transformed into a living experiment in wildlife conservation and management. According to information provided by the Legacy Center, when Leopold purchased the land in the winter of 1935 it was an abandoned and desolate farmstead. He and his family "… embraced the farm as a new kind of workshop or laboratory—a place to tinker and experiment with restoring health to an ailing piece of land…" The Leopold family gradually converted the land into a home away from home, where they "… tended a garden, cut firewood, and planted trees—eventually, some 40,000… Thousands of pines and other plantings eventually thrived, transforming the landscape into a mosaic of conifers, hardwoods, and prairie."[2] The 60 ha (150 acres) belonging to the Leopold family are now part of the 600-ha (1,500-acre) Leopold Memorial Reserve, which is dedicated to continuing his land-stewardship efforts by preserving and restoring the native oak savanna, woodland, prairie, and riparian ecological communities.

Leopold's teachings provide guidance toward seeing the land as an ecological community rather than as a commodity. As Leopold explains in his foreword to *A Sand County Almanac*: "We abuse land because we regard it as a commodity belonging to us. When we see land as a community to which we belong, we may begin to use it with love and respect… That land is a community is the basic concept of ecology, but that land is to be loved and respected is an extension of ethics. That land yields a cultural harvest is a fact long known, but latterly often forgotten."[3] Leopold goes on to explain, "A land ethic, then, reflects the existence of an ecological conscience, and this in turn reflects a conviction of individual responsibility for the health of the land. Health is the capacity of the land for self-renewal. Conservation is our effort to understand and preserve this capacity."[4]

Leopold's land ethic also reflects the ecological and ethical philosophies that Kubala Washatko Architects applied to the design project. In an interview, Tom Kubala underscored that the land ethic informed the broad design goals for the Legacy Center, which were to "strive for wholeness" and to "see the interconnectedness" as an ecological basis for the project. Kubala and associates developed an "ecological pattern language" (a sustainable design variation of Christopher Alexander's architectural pattern language) to inform their design and decision-making processes. Kubala explains: "The

pattern language becomes the medium to direct unfolding of building design, from a larger scale to a smaller scale. The patterns are used to solve issues at the large scale and prepare the ground to solve more issues downstream." Kubala continues: "At heart, the Legacy Center attempts to answer the essential question: 'How can we ensure both people and the land will prosper in the long run?' Leopold defined conservation as a way of life in which land does well for its inhabitants, citizens do well by their land, and both end up better by reason of partnership… The Legacy Center not only meets the highest standards of the US Green Building Council [the Leadership in Environmental Design—LEED—Platinum Standards], but also sustains the health, wildness, and productivity of the land, locally and globally. It is a place to learn about Leopold's intimate, lifelong relationship with the American landscape and see his ideas put into practice."[5] From the outset, carbon neutrality and energy independence were primary goals for the Legacy Center. The design team also worked to integrate Leopold's land ethic into the design and operation of the center so that it will demonstrate how the built environment can play a role in healing the entire biotic community.

Climate and site
Located at 43° NL in rural Baraboo, Wisconsin, the Legacy Center experiences the extreme seasonal temperature variations of a cold–temperate climate. The average low is -17°C (1°F)

in January and the average high is 28°C (82°F) in July. This northern site experiences distinct seasons with ever-changing temperatures, wind patterns, day lengths, microclimates, and types of precipitation (including rain, sleet, snow, and fog). The design of the Legacy Center celebrates the seasonal moods through its relationship with the land and by the integration of year-round passive heating and cooling. To honor the land ethic, the designers sought to integrate the building into the surrounding landscape with the goal of promoting the well-being of the entire ecological community. As Leopold explained: "The land ethic simply enlarges the boundaries of the community to include soils, waters, plants, and animals, or collectively: the land."[6]

The Legacy Center provides a gateway into a living landscape of educational facilities and gardens. There are four buildings and three gardens that serve as outdoor classrooms. To provide shelter from the harsh climate and extreme winter conditions, the building compound runs from east to west and opens to the south. The main building is centrally located and includes the public entry, information area, public restrooms, staff areas, and the exhibition space. To the west is located a conference building, while a three-season hall and workshop are sited on the southeast side of the main facility, bracketing and sheltering the gardens. This simple site design provides access to the sun and wind for daylighting, passive heating, and natural ventilation; the forces necessary to

Panoramic view of the building cluster that surrounds the central outdoor space. The south-facing main building is flanked on the west by the conference wing and on the east by the three-season hall and workshop. The center expands and contracts seasonally as portions of the facility are closed off in the winter months. Pine trees planted by Aldo Leopold in 1938 were used for many parts of the building, including trusses, columns, beams, and interior finishes.

meet the goals of carbon neutrality and zero-energy design. Visual and physical access to the garden spaces and the thin building massing provide diurnal and seasonal connections to the landscape.

Daylighting and thermal design

The Legacy Center experiences 16 hours of sunlight in June versus only nine in December and has an average summer to winter temperature shift of 27°C (80°F). Because of these conditions, the facility has a dominant heating load, which increased the challenge of using passive solar to reach the goal of zero energy and carbon neutrality. Many of the ecological design patterns used to guide the design process therefore addressed solar and climatic conditions. Patterns of particular interest at the building scale include: "window to the sun," "fresh air naturally," "the electric roof," and "positive outdoor space." These patterns emphasize the importance of harvesting the sun and wind for daylight, ventilation, and passive heating.

The architects focused on the power of the sun and wind not only to heat and cool; they also placed considerable emphasis on using these forces to shape the luminous and thermal experience, foster comfort, and connect the facility with the site. Two ecological design patterns used toward these ends—"don't turn on that light!" and "never too far from outdoors"—illustrate the design philosophy of involving occupants in operating the buildings

and keeping them connected to the greater site area. Additional patterns focused on window placement, interior finishes, the positions of workstations, and other details to make the best use of daylight, reduce glare, and maximize natural ventilation. Tom Kubala explains that the team took a holistic approach that brought together human experience and energy performance: "We always organize around wholeness-based design. It is antithetical to think of sun as a separate issue. The sun is there for more than energy. More important is the experiential influence of the sun on participants and as a spiritual metaphor. Solar energy is the happy byproduct."

The Legacy Center used a variety of planning and design strategies to reach the goal of zero energy and carbon neutrality. Early in the planning process the designers decided to heat and cool the buildings and spaces selectively. The main building with staff and exhibition spaces are conditioned throughout the year but the conference room is heated only when occupied. The three-season hall and workshop spaces have no mechanical heating and cooling systems, although a wood stove in the hall provides supplemental heating during the coldest periods. The main building consumes the greatest amount of energy and therefore it is oriented east–west to optimize solar gains in the winter. During the heating season, a "thermal flux zone" on the south gathers and stores direct solar gains that

Opposite
Interior view looking
east in the main
building. A centrally
located social space
includes a staff
kitchen and gathering
area. Private offices
are located to the
north, while an open
office area is located
at the eastern end
of the room. Indirect
daylight is provided
by a clerestory in
the north facade,
while direct sunlight
animates the space
through a large
south-facing skylight
monitor. The south
wall can be opened
and closed to mediate
heating, cooling, and
illumination from the
thermal flux zone.

Above left and right
View looking east
along the thermal
flux zone. The staff
area is located to the
north. Sliding doors
and operable windows
allow the staff to
modify the quality and
quantity of heat, light,
and air borrowed from
the thermal flux zone.

are borrowed through large sliding doors and windows into the staff work area. During the cooling season, a simple roof overhang prevents direct sunlight from entering the flux zone. Shading adjacent to the flux zone was sized to admit midday sunlight fully during the months of November to January and to block the midday sun fully from May to July. Operable windows allow cross ventilation to be admitted through the southern facade and "borrowed" into the spaces beyond. An open kitchen is strategically located at the center of the staff area, illuminated from above by a large south-facing clerestory window.

Abundant sunlight creates a vibrant social gathering space at the heart of the main building. A north-facing clerestory runs the length of the central staff area and the northernmost work niches have operable windows that provide direct views and physical connections to the site. The staff area is bathed by soft indirect northern daylight, reflected in part from the ceiling of the south-sloping roof on which an extensive photovoltaic array generates on-site electricity. On cold winter days, direct sunlight is welcomed into the kitchen through a south-facing skylight monitor and large double sliding doors that open out into the thermal flux zone. The exhibition area is sheltered from direct sunlight and instead uses a northern clerestory to provide indirect illumination.

Architectural design strategies used to harvest on-site solar and wind energy for the

main building include the narrow building form, abundant windows and clerestories, shading, reflective interior finishes, and a high-performance envelope. Kubala Washatko used high-performance glazing, windows, doors, and detailing to reduce infiltration and the insulation throughout the building produces a thermal quality of 0.009 $Btu/h/m^2$ (0.1062 Btu/h/sq ft), as compared to the ASHRAE (American Society of Heating, Refrigerating and Air-Conditioning Engineers) requirement of 0.021 $Btu/h/m^2$ (0.2350 Btu/h/sq ft).[7] Distinct thermal zones can be separated or joined, depending upon whether the work area needs to be heated or cooled. These simple passive design strategies are coupled with renewable energy and mechanical systems to meet the year-round heating, cooling, ventilation, and illumination needs at the Legacy Center, demonstrating that buildings in northern climates can achieve zero energy and carbon neutrality.

Energy systems
Tom Kubala explains that solar design is the foundation for a net zero-energy goal: "The sun shapes the project. You do have to feel the sun and climate. Then you can address the more technical issues… Everything starts with setting the solar budget. This energy budget determines what is available; what you can glean from the sun. Then you design the building in that energy budget." Only after designing the building with passive strategies does the team integrate heating, cooling, ventilation, water heating, and

photovoltaic systems. According to information provided by the Legacy Center: "To make the Aldo Leopold Legacy Center carbon-neutral in its operation, it first needed to be built as a net zero-energy building. The design team studied nine existing high-performance buildings to develop performance standards for the Legacy Center… [They] set 5 kWh per square foot floor per year [54kWh/m^2;17 kBtu/sq ft] as an energy-performance goal for the Aldo Leopold Legacy Center. Given that goal, roughly 280 m^2 [3,000 sq ft] of photovoltaic panels would be needed to produce the energy the building would require, leading to a zero-energy building."[8]

On-site solar energy was harvested through three strategies that include the previously discussed passive solar design, as well as an active hot-water system and a photovoltaic array. Geothermal and wood heat were coupled with the solar strategies to reduce the energy budget to 582 kWh/m^2 (6.27 kWh/sq ft) per year in the main space (829.8 m^2; 8,932 sq ft). The heating and cooling systems include a ground-source heat pump to warm and cool the floor slab. A separate displacement ventilation system brings 100 percent outside air at 0.018 cfm/m^2 (0.2 cfm/sq ft) into the building through earth tubes to heat or cool the air. Solar hot-water heating systems meet the hot water needs, while a 39.6-kW grid-tied photovoltaic array supplies 61,250 kWh of electricity per year.[9] Supplemental heat is provided by a

fireplace in a "mud room" that links the staff and exhibition areas, and also by a wood stove in the conference building and three-season hall. All wood is harvested selectively and sustainably on site.

Professor Michael Utzinger of the University of Wisconsin-Milwaukee and Helios Design established a carbon protocol for the Legacy Center based on the Greenhouse Gas Protocol from World Resources Institute. Total annual carbon dioxide emissions of 45.3 metric tons at the facility are counterbalanced by 49.9 metric tons of carbon dioxide offsets. According to Kubala Washatko, carbon dioxide emissions include: 19.9 metric tons of direct emissions (direct combustion and vehicles); 20.8 metric tons of indirect emissions from electricity generation (green power contract and site solar generation); and 25.4 metric tons of indirect emissions from organizational activities (employee commuting, travel, and solid waste removal). Carbon dioxide offsets are achieved through 29.1 metric tons of carbon sequestered in a managed forest, 10.6 metric tons through green power purchased from a local utility, and 10.2 metric tons offset through on-site solar generation.[10]

Next-generation thinking
The Legacy Center website summarizes a possible future for ecological design: "Energy conservation can easily demonstrate cost savings and short- or long-term financial

Preceding pages
View to the northwest from the three-season hall. This space is used seasonally for varied educational activities. Closed during the winter months, the room opens to the west and north to connect with the outdoor spaces and to provide a cool sheltered refuge in the summer months.

Above
Exhibition area looking west. North and south clerestory windows provide bilateral daylighting.

Construction view of the earth tubes used to pretreat ventilation air. The heating and cooling systems include a ground-source heat pump to warm and cool the floor slab. A separate displacement ventilation system brings 100 per cent outside air through the earth tubes into the building to heat or cool the air.

paybacks. Less obvious benefits to the community have not been documented as thoroughly, but using less energy would mean less stress on our few remaining wild places and many rural landscapes and communities, less danger of polluting fresh water and the oceans, as well as the atmosphere. These benefits will accrue to society and future generations in the form of healthier lands, which provide not only space for wild things but the foundation of prosperous and sustainable communities."[11]

Aldo Leopold would surely commend the Legacy Center and the design team for taking on the still emerging and complex equation of carbon emissions and carbon budgets, which challenge all of us to look more deeply at how we live in relation to other species and the natural and built environments. Buddy Huffacker, executive director of the Aldo Leopold Foundation, reminds us of our great challenge in meeting Leopold's vision: "Drawing on his lifelong study of ecology, land use, history, and ethics, Aldo Leopold concluded that the highest task of civilization was to figure out how 'to live on a piece of land without spoiling it.' It's an ideal articulated by one of the greatest thinkers of the 20th century, an ideal we must embrace in this one."[12]

This small facility in a rural part of the northern United States reminds us that a series of modest yet thoughtful design strategies can achieve both net zero energy and carbon neutrality. In honor of Aldo Leopold, the design profession should take these lessons to heart and expand them into everyday architectural practice.

Plans, sections, drawings

The facility includes the conference wing, main staff building (which includes the administration wing and exhibition space), three-season hall, and workshop.

1. Conference wing
2. Thermal flux zone
3. Administration wing
4. Mudroom
5. Exhibition area
6. Workshop
7. Three-season hall
8. Forward garden
9. Welcome garden
10. Prairie
11. Rain garden

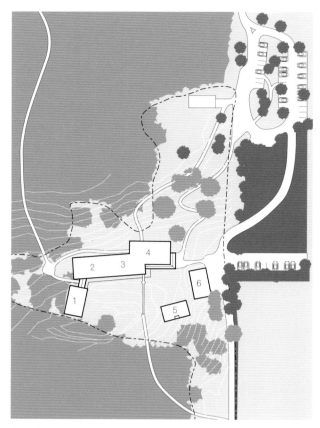

The Legacy Center comprises a cluster of buildings to incorporate interior and exterior spaces for the staff and educational programs.

1. The outlook and conference wing
2. The upshot research and administration wing
3. Mighty fortress foyer
4. Great processions interpretive wing
5. Home range hall
6. Axe-in-hand restoration workshop

Site plan

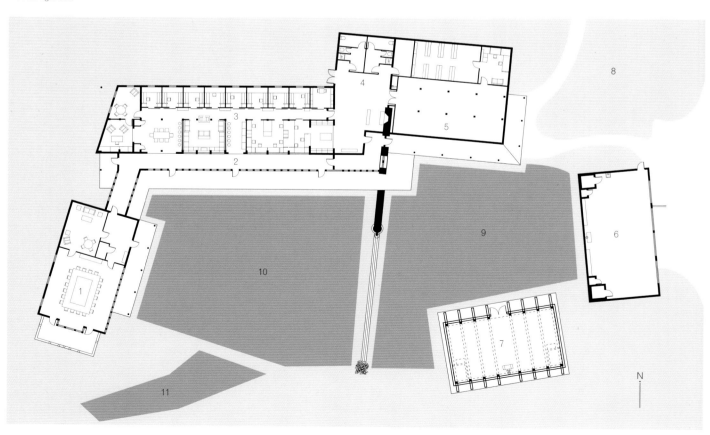

Ground-floor plan

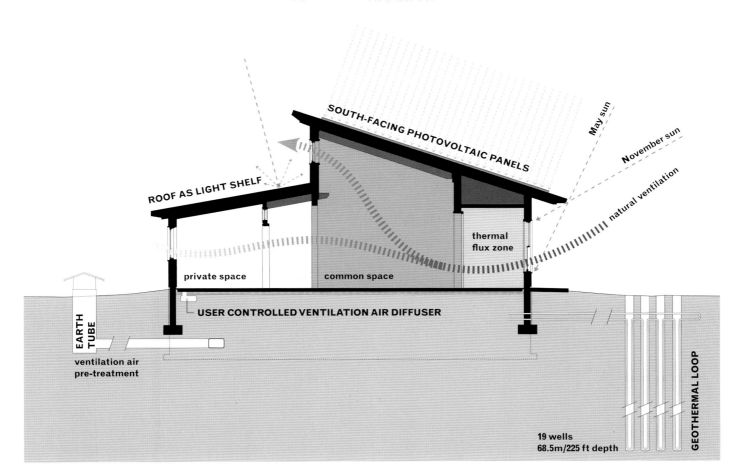

SOUTH-FACING PHOTOVOLTAIC PANELS

May sun

November sun

natural ventilation

ROOF AS LIGHT SHELF

thermal flux zone

private space

common space

USER CONTROLLED VENTILATION AIR DIFFUSER

EARTH TUBE

ventilation air pre-treatment

19 wells
68.5m/225 ft depth

GEOTHERMAL LOOP

Section looking east

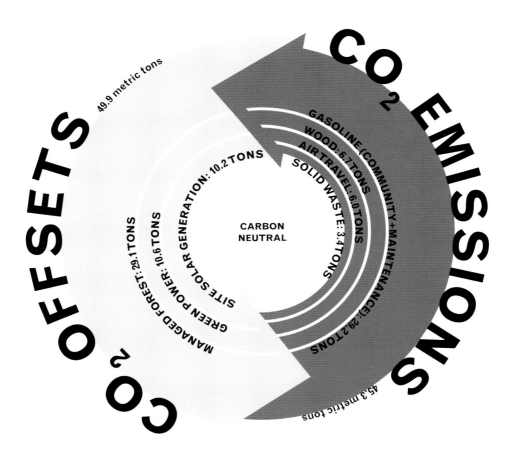

CO² OFFSETS

49.9 metric tons

MANAGED FOREST: 29.1 TONS

GREEN POWER: 10.6 TONS

SITE SOLAR GENERATION: 10.2 TONS

CARBON NEUTRAL

CO² EMISSIONS

GASOLINE (COMMUNITY+MAINTENANCE): 29.2 TONS

WOOD: 6.7 TONS

AIR TRAVEL: 6.0 TONS

SOLID WASTE: 3.4 TONS

45.3 metric tons

CO² diagram indicating the estimated balance of emissions and offsets. All data is given in metric tons.

Wind studies

Project location:
Baraboo, WI, USA

Wind data location:
Madison, WI, USA

Prevailing winds
March
Wind frequency (hours)
Location: Madison, USA (43.1°, -89.3°)
Time: 00:00–24:00

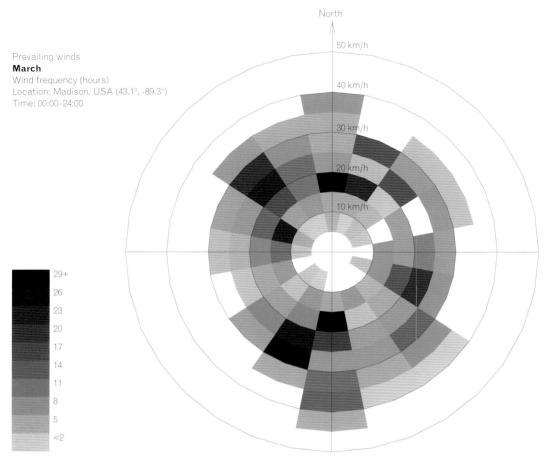

Prevailing winds
September
Wind frequency (hours)
Location: Madison, USA (43.1°, -89.3°)
Time: 00:00–24:00

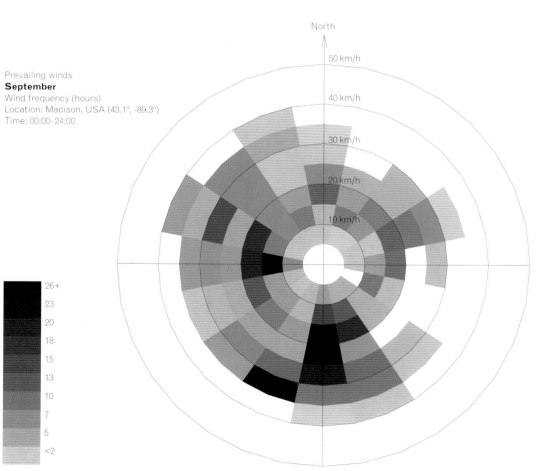

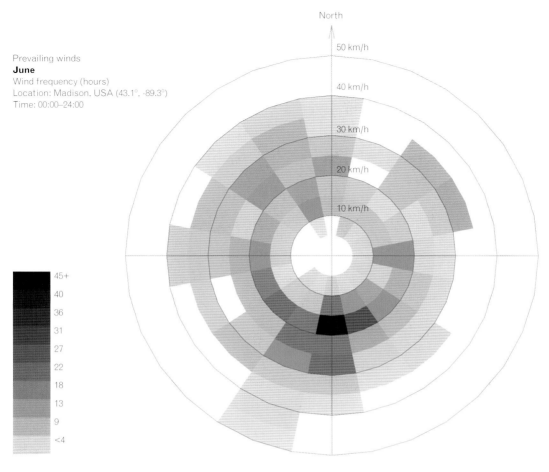

North

50 km/h
40 km/h
30 km/h
20 km/h
10 km/h

Prevailing winds
June
Wind frequency (hours)
Location: Madison, USA (43.1°, -89.3°)
Time: 00:00–24:00

45+
40
36
31
27
22
18
13
9
<4

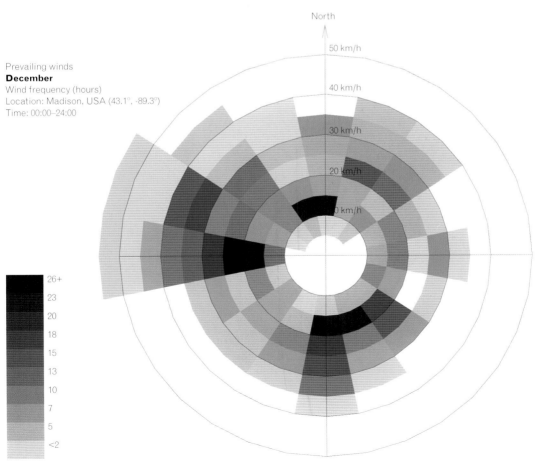

North

50 km/h
40 km/h
30 km/h
20 km/h
10 km/h

Prevailing winds
December
Wind frequency (hours)
Location: Madison, USA (43.1°, -89.3°)
Time: 00:00–24:00

North

26+
23
20
18
15
13
10
7
5
<2

Sunpath case studies

Prioritizing passive design: Aldo Leopold Legacy Center

Project location:
Baraboo, WI, USA
Latitude: 43° NL

December

09:00

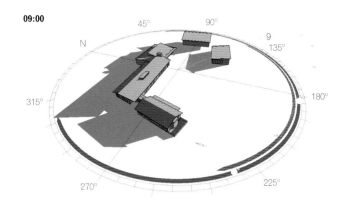

March/September

09:00

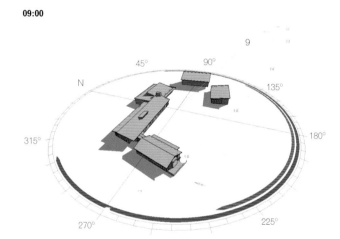

June

09:00

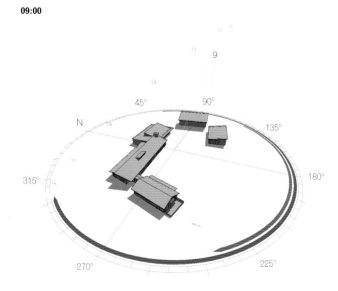

12:00

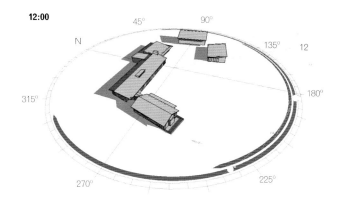

15:00

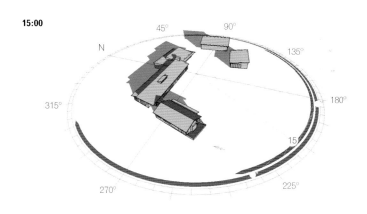

12:00

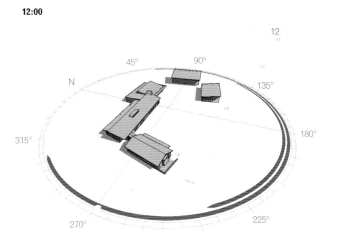

15:00

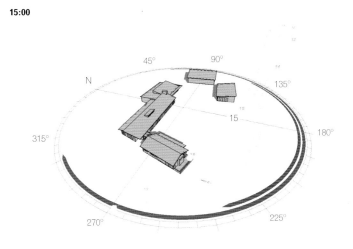

12:00

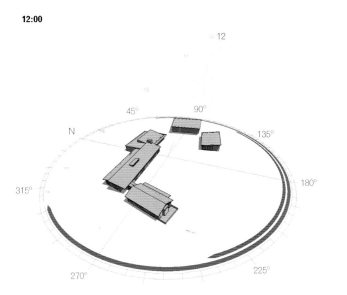

15:00

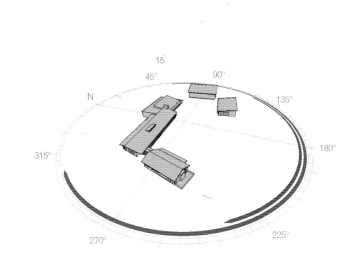

Climate data

Project location:
Baraboo, WI, USA

Climate data location:
Madison, WI, USA

Diurnal average temperatures

Dry bulb temperatures 1 Jan to 31 Dec

Direct radiation 1 Jan to 31 Dec

Relative humidity 1 Jan to 31 Dec

Temperature (°C)

Relative humidity (%)

Wind speed (W/m²)

Direct solar (W/m²)

Diffuse solar (W/m²)

Cloud cover (%)

Thermal neutrality

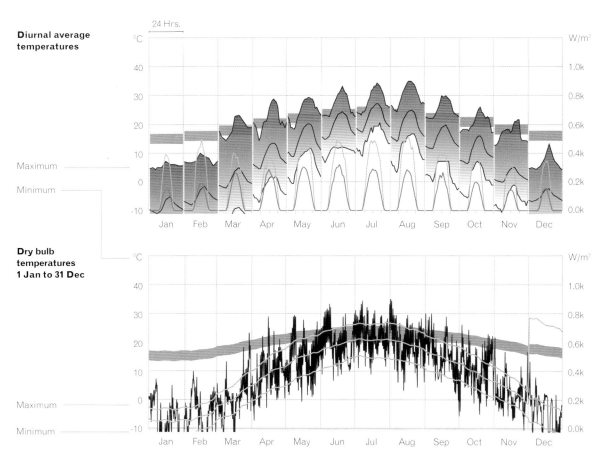

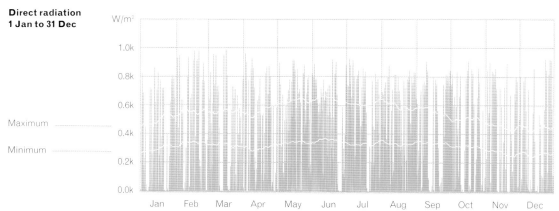

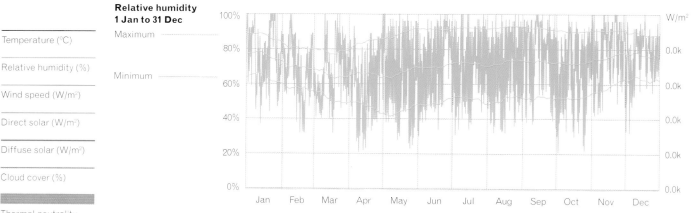

Design profile

Building profile	Building name:	**Aldo Leopold Legacy Center**
	Architect:	The Kubala Washatko Architects, Milwaukee, Wisconsin, USA; www.tkwa.com/
	Location:	Baraboo, Wisconsin, USA
	Building type:	Educational
	Square footage:	1,115 m² (12,000 sq ft)
Solar design profile	Latitude:	43° NL
	Heating Degree Days:	3,955 heating degree days °C (7,281 heating degree days °F) (18°C and 65°F base temperature; average 5 years)
	Cooling Degree Days:	466 cooling degree days °C (786 cooling degree days °F)
	Conservation strategies:	Separation and zoning of program activities; year-round heating and cooling in the main staff and museum spaces only
	Passive solar strategies:	Direct solar gain, thermal flux space, daylighting, cross ventilation, shading
	Active solar strategies:	Photovoltaic system, solar hot-water thermal system
	Other renewable energy strategies:	Earth tubes and ground-source heat pump
	High-performance strategies:	High-performance envelope, glazing, lighting, and systems
Performance profile [13] [14] [15]	Total annual building energy consumption:	Estimated total: 48 kWh/m² (15.6kBtu/sq ft); estimated purchased: 6.4 kWh/m² (-2.02 kBtu/sq ft); estimated on-site renewable: 56 kWh/m² (17.6 kBtu/sq ft)
	Total annual on-site energy produced:	Estimated 56 kWh/m² (17.6 kBtu/sq ft)
	Size of photovoltaic system:	39.6-kW grid-tied photovoltaic array supplies 61,250 kWh
	Size of solar thermal system:	Solar hot-water system, size not available
	Carbon dioxide emissions:	-4.6 metric tons of CO_2; 45.3 metric tons of CO_2 emissions are outweighed by 49.9 metric tons of CO_2 offsets

Endnotes:
Aldo Leopold Legacy Center

1 Aldo Leopold, *A Sand County Almanac* (London: Oxford University Press, 1949), 203–204.
2 Aldo Leopold Legacy Center, website, www.aldoleopold.org/legacycenter.
3 Leopold, *A Sand County Almanac*, viii.
4 Ibid., 203–204.
5 Aldo Leopold Legacy Center, www.aldoleopold.org/legacycenter.
6 Leopold, *A Sand County Almanac*, 203–204.
7 Kubala Washatko, "The Greenest Building in the World?," Living Futures 2008 Conference, 2008, 35.
8 Aldo Leopold Legacy Center, www.aldoleopold.org/legacycenter.
9 American Institute of Architects Committee on the Environment, Top Ten Projects, American Institute of Architects; www.aiatopten.org.
10 Kubala Washatko, 53–55.
11 Aldo Leopold Legacy Center, www.aldoleopold.org/legacycenter.
12 Ibid.
13 American Institute of Architects Committee on the Environment, www.aiatopten.org.
14 Kubala Washatko, 50, 53–55, 75–76.
15 American Institute of Architects Committee on the Environment.

Chapter 3

Defining an ethic of enough

"Loving our limits can set the stage for our life. As we recognize that we only have one Earth—which has finite capacity to support life—becoming comfortable with limits will open our minds and hearts for the work of taming the appetite. Global living doesn't attempt to impose limits on others… It seeks to inspire our creativity, our ability to see that there are infinite satisfying lifestyle packages compatible with living on a finite, equitable share of nature. Global living seeks to give you the tools to be the architect."[1]
JIM MERKEL, *Radical Simplicity*

"The larger design challenge is to transform a wasteful society into one that meets human needs with elegant simplicity. Designing ecologically requires a revolution in our thinking that changes the kinds of questions we ask from how can we do the same old things more efficiently? to deeper questions such as: Do we need it? Is it ethical? What impact does it have on the community?… The quality of design, in other words, is measured by the elegance with which we join means and worthy ends."[2]
DAVID ORR, *The Nature of Design*

It is vital that we learn to live and design more modestly, that we learn to see the opportunities of working within the energy and resource limits of a finite planet. Decades ago, economist E.F. Schumacher argued in his seminal book *Small is Beautiful* that we need to live more resourcefully if we are to achieve universal prosperity: "The question with which to start my investigation is obviously this: Is there enough to go round? Immediately we encounter a serious difficulty: What is 'enough'? Who can tell us? Certainly not the economist who pursues 'economic growth' as the highest of all values, and therefore has no concept of 'enough.' There are poor societies which have too little; but where is the rich society that says: 'Halt! We have enough'? There is none…"[3] We must still heed Schumacher's plea, for we have yet to define "how much is enough?" How much energy? How many resources? How much space? How do we define prosperity?

Assessments of the Earth's carrying capacity and the global footprints of countries around the world suggest that the current rate of resource

consumption is unsustainable.[4] Professor William Rees of the University of British Columbia, co-author of the ecological footprint analysis method, describes some of the global challenges created by current rates of resource consumption: "This situation is, of course, largely attributable to consumption by that wealthy quarter of the world's population who use 75 percent of global resources. The WCED's [World Commission on Environment and Development] 'five- to ten-fold increase in industrial output' was deemed necessary to address this obvious inequity while accommodating a much larger population. However, since the world is already ecologically full, sustainable growth on this scale using present technology would require at [least] five to ten additional planets."[5]

To shift away from our current trajectory that is endangering the Earth's carrying capacity, we must learn to "do more with less," to be more resourceful and thoughtful in our consumption, and to live differently. In the *The Nature of Design*, Professor David Orr of Oberlin College suggests that we need to

reframe our questions about resource consumption and waste: "The larger design challenge is to transform a wasteful society into one that meets human needs with elegant simplicity. Designing ecologically requires a revolution in our thinking that changes the kinds of questions we ask…"[6] Professor Orr goes on to explain: "The larger design challenge is to transform a wasteful society into one that meets human needs with elegant simplicity. Designing ecologically requires a revolution in our thinking that changes the kinds of questions we ask from how can we do the same old things more efficiently? to deeper questions such as: Do we need it? Is it ethical? What impact does it have on the community? Is it safe to make and use? Is it fair? Can it be repaired or reused? What is the full cost over its expected lifetime? Is there a better way to do it? The quality of design, in other words, is measured by the elegance with which we join means and worthy ends."[7]

Designing for the limits of a finite planet does not mean that we need to live a life of hardship and constraints, nor

Detail of the exhibition space at the Tim and Karen Hixon (Government Canyon) Visitor Center in Helotes, Texas, USA. This modest building with an elegantly simple envelope can be adjusted to manage the forces of sun and wind.

does it suggest that there should be no growth. In *Cradle to Cradle*, architect William McDonough and chemist Michael Braungart discuss the concept of "good growth": "... unquestionably there are things we all want to grow, and things we don't want to grow. We wish to grow education and not ignorance, health and not sickness, prosperity and not destitution, clean water and not poisoned water. We wish to improve the quality of life. The key is not to make human industries and systems smaller, as efficiency advocates propound, but to design them to get bigger and better in ways that replenish, restore, and nourish the rest of the world. Thus the 'right things'... to do are those that lead to good growth—more niches, health, nourishment, diversity, intelligence, and abundance—for this generation of inhabitants on the planet and for generations to come."[8]

McDonough and Braungart suggest that designers should shift away from the often narrow concept of "eco-efficiency" and instead adopt the more expansive concept of "eco-effectiveness": "Eco-efficiency is an outwardly admirable, even noble, concept, but it is not a strategy for success over the long term, because it does not reach deep enough... It presents little more than an illusion of change... Plainly put, eco-efficiency only works to make the old, destructive system a bit less so... Last but not least, efficiency isn't much fun. In a world dominated by efficiency, each development would serve only narrow and practical purposes. Beauty, creativity, fantasy, enjoyment, inspiration, and poetry would fall by the wayside, creating an unappealing world indeed..."[9] Eco-effectiveness, on the other hand, represents a conceptual shift in which "... designers expand their vision from the primary purpose of a product or system and consider the whole. What are its goals and potential effects, both immediate and wide-ranging, with respect to both time and place? What is the entire system—cultural, commercial, ecological—of which this made thing, and way of making things, will be a part?"[10]

Environmentalist and journalist Paul Hawken suggests that design plays a key role in moving to a zero-waste society:

"Today, the creation of a zero-waste society is a global movement carried out by thousands of organizations. The ostensible purpose is to institute cyclical systems that eliminate waste by design, not by management at end-of-pipe."[11] How can designers see modesty and resourcefulness as design opportunities rather than design constraints? What is "enough" in architectural terms? What new questions arise when we begin to conceive of modesty and voluntary limits as being integral to the planning, design, construction, and inhabiting of architecture? While simplicity is a key factor in taking a more modest approach to design, it is a deceptively challenging concept. Achieving an "elegant simplicity" requires a thoughtful integration of often complex issues, ideas, and considerations. What may appear "elegantly simple," may actually embody a synthesis of seemingly disparate, yet interrelated, ecological design issues.

The Tim and Karen Hixon (Government Canyon) Visitor Center by Lake | Flato Architects and the SOLTAG Energy Housing by Nielsen and Rubow et al. and Velux Danmark demonstrate a

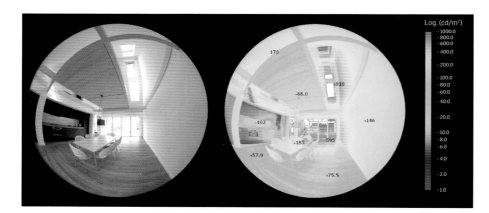

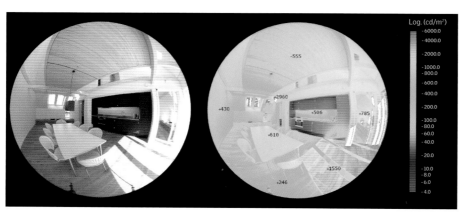

variety of design strategies that embrace an "ethic of enough." These projects practice restraint and modesty from the scale of the site to final detailing yet they do not compromise the quality and richness of the architectural experience. Both projects set out to demonstrate that it is possible to maintain a high-quality lifestyle within the constraints of a finite resource base. They start by identifying the optimal size needed to fully meet client needs, using the concepts of "right sizing" and "reduced sizing" to decrease the conditioned building footprint. The question of scale is critical for both projects. How much space is needed for the activities? Which spaces need to be conditioned? Is it possible to eliminate or reduce parts of the program? Simple yet thoughtful formal strategies are used to zone, and in some cases even eliminate, the need for heating and cooling. Renewable energy strategies that integrate passive design and active systems are used where the need for heating and cooling cannot be eliminated.

As Jim Merkel reminds us in *Radical Simplicity*, modesty and humility are key to finding our place within the global community of species: "...'Share the Earth' is an easy enough phrase to say... I find it helpful to remind myself: 'I am one of six billion humans. My species shares paradise with 25 million other species. Each of these species has many thousands, or even billions in their population. How do I want to share the Earth with all of this life?'..."[12] The Government Canyon Visitor Center and SOLTAG Energy Housing demonstrate that architecture can embrace the limits of our planet, teach us ecological values, and demonstrate more resourceful ways of living on Earth. These projects also demonstrate that a more modest architecture can make living with less not a burden, but rather an opportunity.

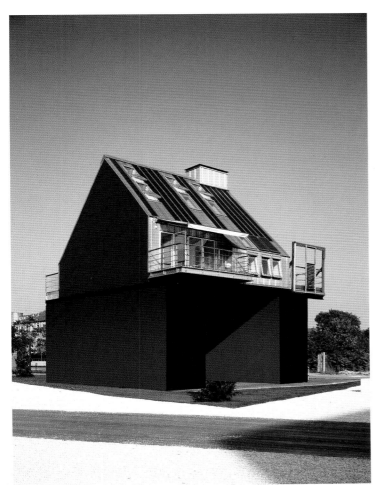

Endnotes:

1   Jim Merkel, *Radical Simplicity: Small Footprints on a Finite Earth* (Gabriola Island, BC: New Society Publishers, 2003), 16.
2   David Orr, *The Nature of Design: Ecology, Culture, and Human Intention* (Oxford: Oxford University Press, 2002), 27–28.
3   E.F. Schumacher, *Small is Beautiful: Economics as if People Mattered* (New York: Harper & Row Publishers, 1973), 25.
4   William Rees, professor at the University of British Columbia, and co-author of the ecological footprint analysis method, defines the Earth's "carrying capacity" in the following way: "We can now redefine human carrying capacity as the maximum rates of resource harvesting and waste generation (the maximum load) that can be sustained indefinitely without progressively impairing the productivity and functional integrity of relevant ecosystems wherever the latter may be located. The size of the corresponding population would be a function of technological sophistication and mean per capita material standards (Rees, 1988). This definition reminds us that regardless of the state of technology, humankind depends on a variety of ecological goods and services provided by nature and that for sustainability, these must be available in increasing quantities from somewhere on the planet as population and mean per capita resource consumption increase..." William Rees, "Revisiting Carrying Capacity: Area-Based Indicators of Sustainability." *Population and Environment: A Journal of Interdisciplinary Studies.* v. 17, no. 3 (1996 Human Sciences Press, Inc., January 1996); http://www.dieoff.org/page110.htm.
5   Ibid.
6   David Orr, 27–28.
7   Ibid.
8   William McDonough and Michael Braungart, *Cradle to Cradle: Remaking the Way We Make Things* (New York: North Point Press, 2002), 78.
9   Ibid, 61–62, 65.
10 Ibid, 81–82.
11 Paul Hawken, *Blessed Unrest: How the Largest Movement in the World Came into Being and Why No One Saw it Coming* (New York: Penguin Group, 2007), 181.
12 Jim Merkel, 52.

Tim and Karen Hixon (Government Canyon) Visitor Center
Helotes, Texas, USA
Lake|Flato Architects

"The design at Government Canyon considers the fundamental relation of people to the natural environment. The sun drives the ecosystem, from the wind to plants to landform to climate. The approach is to fit into the natural environment. To fit together humans, nature, and climate in simple and elegant ways. This is the basis of the design thinking."
Bob Harris, *Lake|Flato Architects*

View from the central gathering space looking toward the eastern entry. Drawing on the vernacular traditions of the region, the facility celebrates a modest and honest use of local materials and building forms. Simple design strategies for natural ventilation and daylighting give shape to the plan and section.

Design intentions
Shaped by the forces of water, sun, and wind, the Tim and Karen Hixon (Government Canyon) Visitor Center in Helotes, Texas, quietly teaches that people, nature, and climate can work together to promote ecological goals. The center was designed by Lake|Flato of San Antonio, Texas, as an educational hub for the recently established Government Canyon State Natural Area. The facility embodies the primary mission of the natural area, which is to preserve the land and ecosystem overlying the recharge zone for the Edwards Aquifer, the drinking-water source for San Antonio. The Government Canyon Visitor Center is a modest building, elegant in its simplicity, which models a new level of sustainability. It demonstrates how architecture that is restrained and humble, with a small ecological footprint, can protect the landscape, help us live within ecological and economic constraints, and achieve aesthetic integrity and beauty.

Climate and site
The moods, qualities, and characters of place, climate, and landscape deeply inform the work of Lake|Flato. Six essential design factors imbue their work: the land, light, craft, community, "spaces between," and sustainability. In their firm profile, Lake|Flato explain how these interrelated factors are tied to specific climates and sites: "Our work grows from the land—enhancing, connecting to, and at times repairing the natural landscape. Our buildings create a heightened awareness of the land and a strong connection to the environment. We consistently explore how the light of a specific region enlivens a space, brushes a wall, and animates materials. Our design process seeks contextual cues at many levels, from a neighborhood to the region. Our buildings blur the line between indoors and out through spaces that expand beyond their walls to form outdoor rooms. Spaces between buildings are as important as the buildings themselves."[1]

Lake|Flato's inherently sensitive approach to ecological design was vital for the Government Canyon site. The natural area of more than 3,480 ha (8,600 acres) protects the aquifer recharge area, preserves wildlife habitat and native ecology, provides educational venues, and hosts scenic recreational trails. The Texas Parks and Wildlife Department describes the special features of the ecosystem: "Steep slopes provide scenic overlooks of the surrounding Bexar County and glimpses of San Antonio. Rare birds such as the Golden-cheeked Warbler can be found. Geologically, the Natural Area lies on the Balcones Escarpment, an area of deeply entrenched canyons that defines the eastern boundary of the Edwards Plateau. Approximately 88 percent of the Natural Area overlays the Edwards Aquifer recharge zone. The remaining acreage overlies the transition zone for water recharge."[2] In the hot, arid climate, water is a particularly valuable resource and is scarce

during the dry season. With the rainy season lasting from May to September, an average low temperature of 10.5°C (51°F) in January and an average high of 29°C (84°F) in July, Government Canyon experiences seasonal flooding and distinct variations in climate.

The visitor center is sited at the mouth of a canyon in a field of native grasses surrounded by restored oaks. It serves as a gateway to the natural area, which contains a rich diversity of native flora, including mountain laurel, Ashe juniper, mesquite and live oak, as well as Mexican buckeye, Lindheimer's silk-tassel, and escarpment black cherry.[3] As an American Institute of Architect's Committee on the Environment (AIA COTE) award-winning project, the design is lauded for its thoughtful approach to preserving the aquifer recharge area as well as integrating comprehensive water-conservation strategies at the site and into building scales. In their project description, Lake|Flato explain how the facility was shaped by water: "… the building demonstrates sustainable water-use practices by conserving water, collecting rainwater, minimizing run-off and contaminants, and reducing the use of ground water."[4] On the integration of water at the visitor center, architectural writer Russell Fortmeyer commends the design team for their thoughtful solution: "Has another building ever so carefully deferred, in both section and plan, to the needs of a natural water system?"[5] The

forces of water are expressed at multiple scales, from the site design, which includes earthen berms, limestone walls, and native plantings that collect water, to the design of the roofs, which also collect water through gutters, rain chains, and channels that supply cisterns and water towers; and to the component scale with the use of low-flow fixtures.

Though shaped to harness and preserve water, the visitor center is equally compelling in the modest yet effective ways in which it addresses the forces of the sun and wind. In an interview architect Bob Harris explained that the sun was an essential ecological force that gave form to the architecture: "The design at Government Canyon considers the fundamental relation of people to the natural environment. The sun drives the ecosystem, from the wind to plants to landform to climate. The approach is to fit into the natural environment. To fit together humans, nature, and climate in simple and elegant ways. This is the basis of the design thinking." The site was designed to reveal and protect the underlying aquifer recharge zone and to educate visitors on the ecology of the natural area. Lake|Flato explain in their AIA COTE award submission: "All development occurs on nonsensitive land downhill from the recharge zone. The long walls of the Visitor Center, located in a highly impacted field, stretch out to parallel the recharge line, forming a visible edge between the developed land and the heart of the preserve

South facade of the centrally located exhibit space. The screened and adjustable envelope of the exhibition pavilion contrasts with the massive materials and deep overhangs of the walkways found on the entry and the classroom wings.

to the north. This delineation is the first clue visitors see as they begin to understand the often hidden structure of the Balcones Fault and the endangered-species habitat beyond."[6]

The Government Canyon facility includes three connected buildings, comprised of a central pavilion linked to staff wings that are joined by covered walkways and porches. A central courtyard with native landscaping weaves between the buildings to create outdoor spaces used for educational programs. The landscaped spaces were carefully designed to connect visitors to the natural area and to provide hands-on contact with the ecology of the site. Low limestone walls lead visitors from the parking and entry areas on the northeast side of the center through the building compound and out to a series of trails and picnic areas on the southwest. Bob Harris explains Lake|Flato's approach to Government Canyon: "We seek the cultural identity of the place to reveal what is peculiar and particular of the natural climate and culture. This is a fundamental part of design. We are not trying to 'announce' this in a boisterous voice, but rather as a subtle result."

Daylighting and thermal design
The buildings at Government Canyon are oriented on a northeast to southwest axis, with a central exhibition pavilion serving as the heart of the facility. Offices and a gift store bracket the pavilion to the northeast, while classrooms and restrooms

are located in the western wing. Lake|Flato explain how the building and landscape are interconnected: "The exhibit space, the Visitor Center's main focal point, is an open-air, screened room perched amid the native-grass landscape, providing visitors with a greater sensory connection to the land than can be provided indoors. The Visitor Center has two wings that form portions of long, low stone walls. The porch of the administrative wing forms a welcoming approach overlooking a native plant court, which serves as a collection point for rainwater storage. The elevated central exhibit space opens up beyond the court to views of the restored savanna and the canyon beyond. This elevated structure allows for uninterrupted surface water flow and cooling breezes. The classroom wing porch opens up to an outdoor gathering area adjacent to the rainwater collection tower, forming the heart of the group educational zone."[7]

Lake|Flato used a thin building profile to optimize airflow and natural daylight. Drawing on the language of regional vernacular architecture, metal roofs with large overhangs shelter the simple buildings. The screened exhibit pavilion is an unconditioned space that responds to diurnal and seasonal changes in temperature and climate. Large wooden doors roll open and allow the staff to modify exposure to light and air for differing educational and exhibition needs throughout the year. The metal roof acts as a visor to gather water for the cisterns and also to protect the envelope of the

pavilion from direct sunlight. Asymmetric in form, the varied roof overhangs are adapted to the sun angles of each orientation.

As Lake|Flato explain, daylighting was a key strategy in creating high-quality spaces that respond to the hot arid climate of Helotes, where the cooling load and heat gain are the primary concerns: "The building's narrow footprint allows for maximum use of indirect daylight from both the south and the north in all occupied spaces. Approximately 90 percent of occupied spaces enjoy effective daylight and views, and 100 percent of spaces have ventilation control. Dimming controls in the exhibit space balance electric light levels against available daylight. All windows are operable, oriented to catch both direct light and cooling breezes. Extensive use of conventional double-hung windows maximizes the open area and minimizes interference with work surfaces and flow paths, ensuring optimal usability."[8]

Simple bilateral sidelighting is used throughout the facility, with large asymmetric overhangs sheltering the southern facades of the two wings. Operable windows are precisely located to provide cross ventilation, and solar control is ensured by large overhangs and covered walkways that protect the windows. While the heating loads at Government Canyon are modest, the two wings adjacent to the exhibit pavilion do require occasional heating. The

passive heating strategies are simple and straightforward, making use of concrete slabs in the staff and classroom wings to absorb and store direct solar gains. Bob Harris explains the seasonal transformations of the visitor center: "There are sudden shifts in temperatures. The building is open to accept most sun except the harsh west sun. Offices are sheltered and open to the north and summer wind and winter sun. Porches on the south admit wind as the prevailing breeze is from the south in summer and the north in winter. The buildings convert in different months by opening to the breeze and shielding sun in summer. In winter there is solar access and deep wind barriers."

A characteristic of Lake|Flato's architecture is the use of abundant daylight, connections to the site, and carefully framed views coupled with a loving attention to detail, quality craft, and the use of local materials to create elegant and welcoming spaces. At Government Canyon, the play of light and shadows on horizontal and vertical surfaces is further animated by diverse textures such as the limestone walls, red-cedar cladding, copper screens, steel structures, and corrugated metal roofs. The late architect William Turnbull, whose sensitivity to the qualities of place is legendary, described the enduring contributions of Lake|Flato's approach: "Lake|Flato's architecture can serve as a lesson for us all: how a building stands to the sun, how it welcomes the cooling breeze,

West facade of the unconditioned centrally located exhibition area. This pavilion houses a variety of educational activities and displays. Adjustable exhibit walls enable the space to be easily reconfigured and the expansive views open onto a restored savannah and the canyon beyond. The elevated structure allows for uninterrupted surface water flow and cooling breezes. Sheltered walkways link the exhibit space to the conditioned educational and staff wings.

how it partners with plant materials. Nothing sensational or exotic, no visual fireworks of fashion, just architecture that intrigues the mind, delights the soul, and refreshes the eye with its elegant detail and simplicity. Timeless architecture needn't shout…"[9]

Energy systems

In framing the Government Canyon project, the design team set a goal of reducing energy and resource consumption, operating costs, and maintenance requirements by moving a significant portion of the interior circulation, exhibits, and classroom spaces to the outdoors. This is an example of "reduced sizing," in lieu of "right sizing." By reconsidering programmatic needs, the need for airconditioning was eliminated and the total size of the space to be cooled was reduced by 35 percent, thereby reducing downstream energy consumption and ecological impacts. A commitment to harvesting daylighting and natural ventilation helped to shape the overall site design, massing, and form of the project. Architectural critic Russell Fortmeyer discusses the energy strategies used for Government Canyon: "The project's tight budget was stretched by some key decisions: making the exhibition pavilion naturally ventilated, which shaved 35 percent off the center's mechanical system demands, and moving all circulation space to the exterior. The two conventionally enclosed buildings each have standard split systems for heating and cooling,

with the compressor outside, the fan inside… A comprehensive lighting control system—with photocells, occupancy sensors, and a solar photovoltaic power source for the water tower's pumping system—further reduces energy use."[10]

Lake|Flato took a decidedly low-tech approach to the energy design at Government Canyon. With the exception of a small photovoltaic array to power the water tower pump, and high-performance systems for heating and cooling, simple passive design strategies provide most of the daylighting, natural ventilation, and shading for solar control. Bob Harris explains that design came first, while active systems played a secondary role: "We fit in the environment and climate in the most passive way possible as the departure point. Then we determine when we are deviating from the comfort zone and look at the least expensive and energy-efficient ways. Active is used where appropriate and affordable. If design can't make people happy with the place they're in, we can't do it with technology. This is a bias and a departure point." In their project description for the AIA, Lake|Flato describe how, "The building's narrow floor plate, combined with deep porches, large overhang roofs, high-performance glazing, and reflective roofing, minimizes cooling loads while allowing daylight to penetrate deep into the interior. Radiant barriers, foam-in-place insulation, and daytime operating hours further minimize energy use. The lighting system uses effective daylighting

combined with efficient fixtures and photosensor and occupancy-sensor controls. The gravity-flow water systems, coupled with solar-powered water pumps, efficiently convey water while demonstrating renewable-energy technology. Natural ventilation, efficient equipment, fabric ducts, and accessible user controls increase comfort while providing further energy savings."[11]

The annual purchased energy for electricity at Government Canyon is only 80.8 kWh/m² (25.5 kBtu/sq ft). The building energy load is 34m²/ton (369 sq ft/ton) for cooling and 19 W/m² (1.8 W/sq ft) for connected lighting. The annual carbon footprint is estimated at 57 kg CO_2/m² (12lb CO_2/sq ft).[12]

Next-generation thinking

The Government Canyon Visitor Center successfully demonstrates the approach of "doing more with less" by putting reduced consumption at the center of the design solution. This strategy shaped the initial programming, in which the size of the conditioned space was reduced by 35 percent, and guided the design and detailing to optimize natural ventilation and daylighting while preserving the site, connecting to the environment, and providing beautiful views. The straightforward approach to the building form, extensive use of sidelighting, large overhangs and solar controls, exterior porches, and an adjustable layered envelope (including rolling doors and operable windows) creates a modest and thoughtful complex that

is uncompromising in its environmental quality, performance, and design excellence.

Bob Harris explains how the design team approached the delicate balance of responding to a program while meeting the ecological challenges of our day: "We formulated a philosophy of nature, place, craft, and restraint. We have a willingness to embrace restraint and the real conditions of place. If we do too much we diminish nature, if we do too little we diminish humans. We want to reduce the burden of building over time. It bothers me to overdesign; even with good intentions. We provide something with value over time and that has flexible use and growth to reduce the maintenance, upkeep, and energy. Providing more than they need is a burden and a cost-liability over time. We provide 'just enough,' with quality in relation to place, well-being, and comfort. We try not to upstage nature... The beautiful strikes a balance—nothing to add or subtract to diminish the whole. Just do enough." Mahatma Gandhi said, "There is enough for everyone's need, but not for everyone's greed." To take on the serious issues of energy, resources, and waste, the design professions must challenge the current standards of consumption in all aspects of design and operations. Although it has not yet achieved the goal of zero energy and zero carbon, the Government Canyon Visitor Center nevertheless takes a leadership role in defining an ethic of responsible consumption.

Above
View of the exhibition pavilion north facade looking back toward the stone walls of the entry and classroom wings on the south. A large southern overhang acts as a visor to protect the pavilion from direct sunlight, while generously sized overhangs on the east, west, and north mitigate solar gains during summer mornings and evenings.

Opposite
Rainwater and native gardens are found in the outdoor educational spaces. The corrugated metal roof of the exhibition pavilion acts as both a sunshade and a rain umbrella, depending on the weather. Water, a precious resource in this hot climate, is celebrated acoustically and visually through the choice of materials and integration of the landscape.

Plans, sections, drawings

Defining an ethic of enough: Tim and Karen Hixon (Government Canyon) Visitor Center

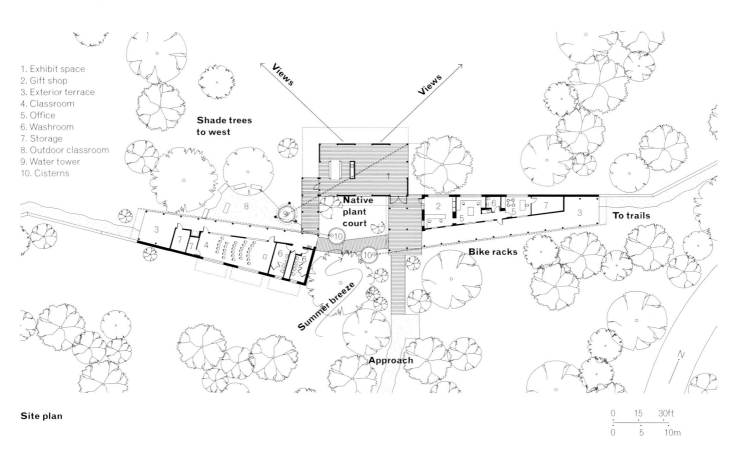

1. Exhibit space
2. Gift shop
3. Exterior terrace
4. Classroom
5. Office
6. Washroom
7. Storage
8. Outdoor classroom
9. Water tower
10. Cisterns

Shade trees
to west

Views

Views

Native
plant
court

To trails

Bike racks

Summer breeze

Approach

Site plan

| 0 | 15 | 30ft |
| 0 | 5 | 10m |

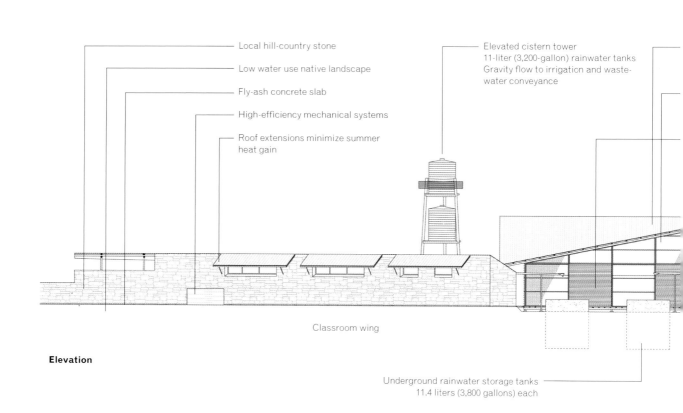

Local hill-country stone

Low water use native landscape

Fly-ash concrete slab

High-efficiency mechanical systems

Roof extensions minimize summer
heat gain

Elevated cistern tower
11-liter (3,200-gallon) rainwater tanks
Gravity flow to irrigation and wastewater conveyance

Classroom wing

Elevation

Underground rainwater storage tanks
11.4 liters (3,800 gallons) each

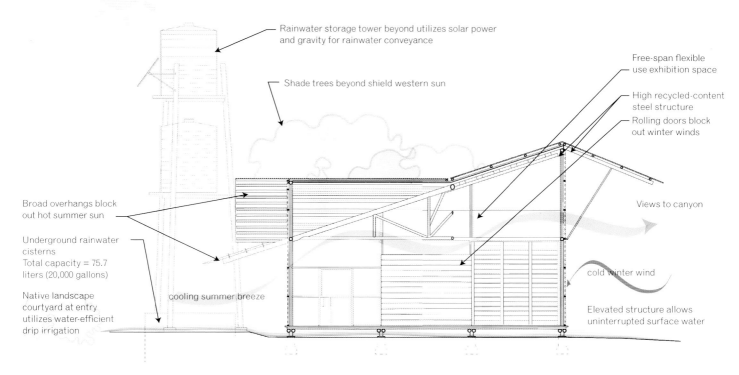

Summer sun

Rainwater storage tower beyond utilizes solar power and gravity for rainwater conveyance

Shade trees beyond shield western sun

Free-span flexible use exhibition space

High recycled-content steel structure

Rolling doors block out winter winds

Broad overhangs block out hot summer sun

Views to canyon

Underground rainwater cisterns
Total capacity = 75.7 liters (20,000 gallons)

cold winter wind

cooling summer breeze

Native landscape courtyard at entry utilizes water-efficient drip irrigation

Elevated structure allows uninterrupted surface water

Section through exhibition space looking west

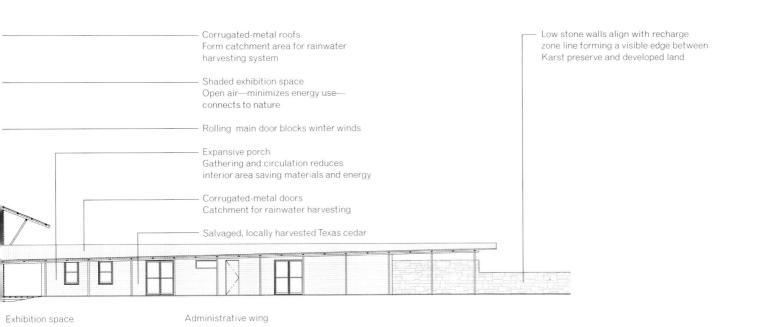

Corrugated-metal roofs
Form catchment area for rainwater harvesting system

Low stone walls align with recharge zone line forming a visible edge between Karst preserve and developed land

Shaded exhibition space
Open air—minimizes energy use—connects to nature

Rolling main door blocks winter winds

Expansive porch
Gathering and circulation reduces interior area saving materials and energy

Corrugated-metal doors
Catchment for rainwater harvesting

Salvaged, locally harvested Texas cedar

Exhibition space

Administrative wing

Wind studies

Project location:
Helotes, TX, USA

Wind data location:
San Antonio, TX, USA

Prevailing winds
March
Wind frequency (hours)
Location: San Antonio, USA (29.5°, -98.5°)
Time: 00:00–24:00

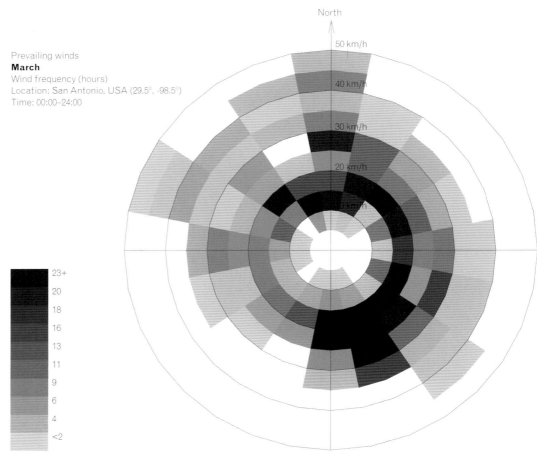

Prevailing winds
September
Wind frequency (hours)
Location: San Antonio, USA (29.5°, -98.5°)
Time: 00:00–24:00

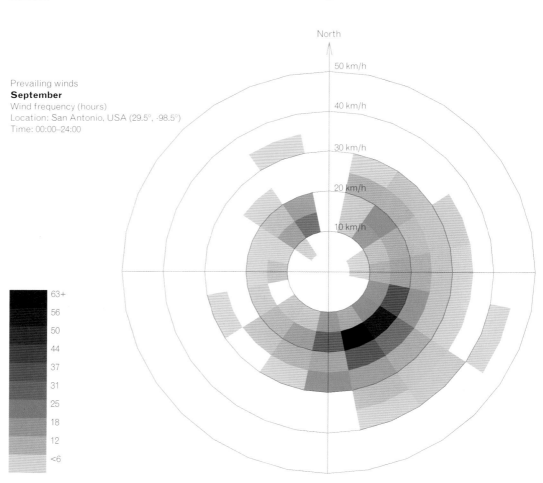

North

50 km/h

40 km/h

30 km/h

20 km/h

10 km/h

Prevailing winds
June
Wind frequency (hours)
Location: San Antonio, USA (29.5°, -98.5°)
Time: 00:00–24:00

54+
48
43
37
32
27
21
16
10
<5

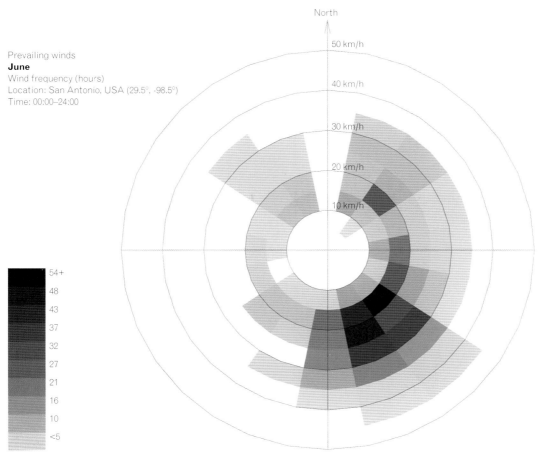

North

50 km/h

40 km/h

30 km/h

20 km/h

0 km/h

Prevailing winds
December
Wind frequency (hours)
Location: San Antonio, USA (29.5°, -98.5°)
Time: 00:00–24:00

38+
34
30
26
22
19
15
11
7
<3

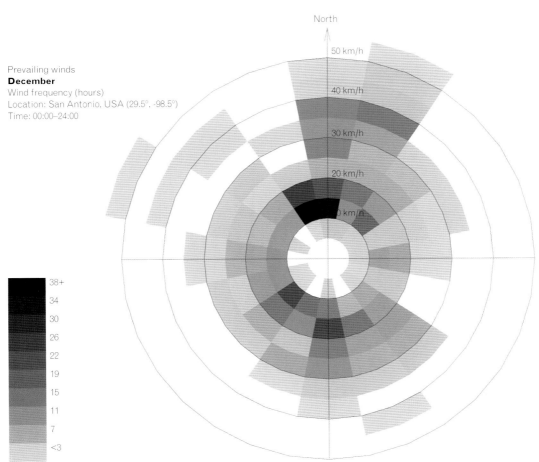

Sunpath case studies

Defining an ethic of enough: Tim and Karen Hixon (Government Canyon) Visitor Center

Project location:
Helotes, TX, USA
Latitude: 29° NL

December

09:00

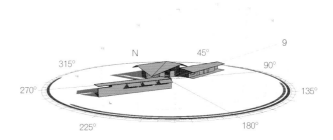

March/September

09:00

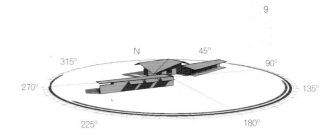

June

09:00

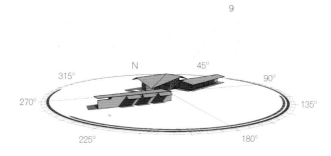

12:00

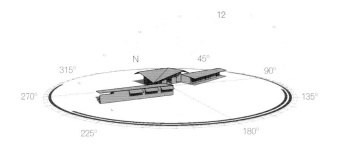

15:00

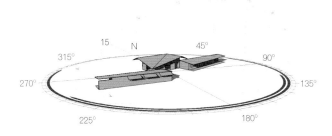

12:00

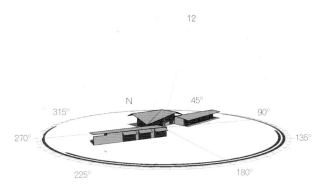

15:00

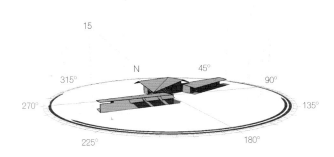

12:00

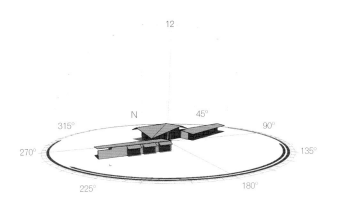

15:00

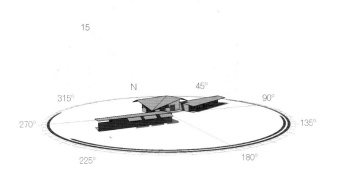

Climate data

Defining an ethic of enough: Tim and Karen Hixon (Government Canyon) Visitor Center

Project location:
Helotes, TX, USA

Climate data location:
San Antonio, TX, USA

Diurnal average temperatures

Maximum

Minimum

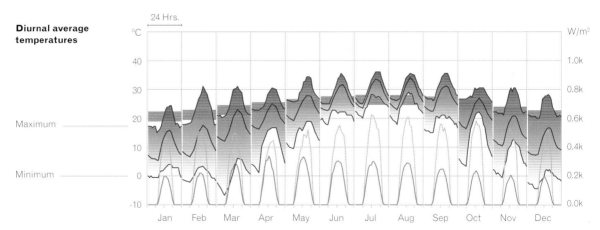

**Dry bulb temperatures
1 Jan to 31 Dec**

Maximum

Minimum

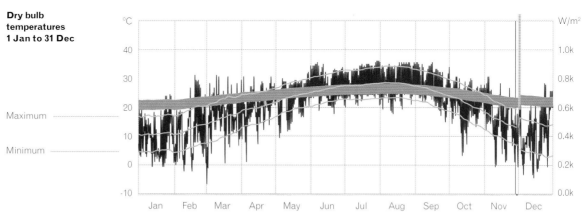

**Direct radiation
1 Jan to 31 Dec**

Maximum

Minimum

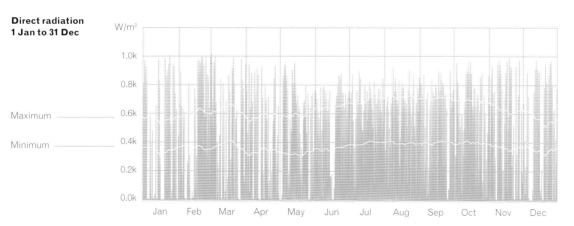

**Relative humidity
1 Jan to 31 Dec**

Maximum

Minimum

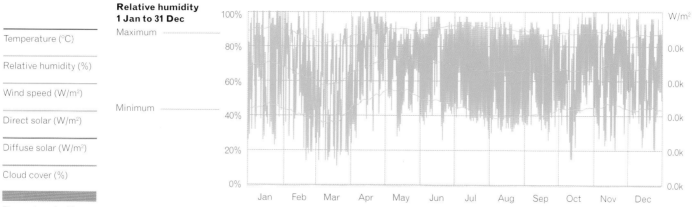

Temperature (°C)

Relative humidity (%)

Wind speed (W/m²)

Direct solar (W/m²)

Diffuse solar (W/m²)

Cloud cover (%)

Thermal neutrality

Design profile

Building profile	Building name:	**Tim and Karen Hixon (Government Canyon) Visitor Center**
	Architect:	Lake|Flato Architects, San Antonio, Texas, USA; www.lakeflato.com/
	Location:	Helotes, Texas, USA
	Building type:	Educational
	Square footage:	392 m² (4,224 sq ft)
Solar design profile	Latitude:	29° NL
	Heating Degree Days:	841 heating degree days °C (1,587 heating degree days °F) (18°C and 65°F base temperature; average 5 years)
	Cooling Degree Days:	1,974 cooling degree days °C (3,406 cooling degree days °F)
	Conservation strategies:	Reduce sizing of building, move select activities outside, reduce amount of conditioned floor space
	Passive solar strategies:	Narrow footprint, daylighting, direct-gain passive solar, exterior shading, open floor plan, natural ventilation, operable windows, thermal mass storage
	Active solar strategies:	None
	Other renewable energy strategies:	Photovoltaic-powered pump for the water tower
	High-performance strategies:	Daylighting photosensors, occupancy sensors, high-performance electric lighting, water-efficient faucets, radiant barriers in the roof
Performance profile [13] [14]	Total annual building energy consumption:	Electricity: 31,700 kWh (108 MMBtu); 80.8 kWh/m² (25.5 kBtu/sq ft) Cooling load: 11.5 tons, 34 m²/ton (369 sq ft/ton) Connected lighting load: 7.64 kW, 19 W/m² (1.8 W/sq ft)
	Total annual on-site energy produced:	None
	Size of photovoltaic system:	Not available (pump)
	Size of solar thermal system:	None
	Carbon dioxide emissions:	57 kg CO_2/m² (12 lb CO_2/sq ft)[15]

Endnotes:
Tim and Karen Hixon (Government Canyon) Visitor Center

1 Lake\|Flato Architects, profile, www.lakeflato.com.
2 Texas Parks and Wildlife Department, State of Texas, Government Canyon State Natural Area.
3 Ibid.
4 Lake\|Flato Architects, Government Canyon Visitor Center, www.lakeflato.com.
5 Russell Fortmeyer, "Case Study: Tim and Karen Hixon Visitor Center, Helotes, Texas,"
Greensource (January, 2008), 77.
6 American Institute of Architects Committee on the Environment, Top Ten Projects, American Institute of Architects; http://www.aiatopten.org/hpb/energy.cfm?ProjectID=796.
7 Ibid.
8 Ibid.
9 Lake\|Flato Architects, profile, www.lakeflato.com.
10 Russell Fortmeyer, 78.
11 American Institute of Architects
Committee on the Environment.
12 Russell Fortmeyer, 75.
13 American Institute of Architects Committee on the Environment.
14 Russell Fortmeyer, 74–79.
15 Ibid.

Project:
Location:

SOLTAG Energy Housing
Hørsholm, Denmark
(prototype designed for northern Europe)

Architect:

Nielsen and Rubow, Cenergia, Kuben Byfornyelse Danmark, and Velux Danmark

"The daylight is amazing. The reason is that instead of a flat ceiling, we sloped the roof. The room feels larger than it is. All windows are positioned to optimize daylight and view. This makes a difference in how people feel in the house."[1]
Kurt Emil Eriksen and Per Arnold Andersen,
Velux Danmark

View of the south facade including balcony, rooftop photovoltaic arrays, operable skylights, and adjustable external shading devices. The prototype house is designed as an infill project to be sited on the roof of an existing building or as an independent single-family home or row house.

Design intentions

Part of the Demohouse project for the European Union's Sixth Framework Program, SOLTAG, or "sun roof", is a prefabricated, solar based, energy-autonomous housing unit that can be added to existing building stock. The ambitious carbon-neutral performance goals of the project were inspired by new EU legislation and directives intended to reduce the carbon emissions and energy consumption of buildings. The house can be transported by truck in two pieces and assembled onsite. While it is designed for installation on the roof of an existing building with optimal access to the sun and wind, SOLTAG can also be configured as an independent single-family unit or assembled into row house and multifamily housing configurations.

SOLTAG is a collaborative effort of Nielsen and Rubow, Cenergia, Kuben Byfornyelse Danmark, and Velux Danmark; the team included design professionals and experts in energy, daylighting, building product manufacturing, and research. Velux explain the team's design intentions: "SOLTAG produces energy and a healthy indoor climate for houses and residents without 'polluting' its surroundings. The house is self-sufficient in terms of energy for heating, and creates carbon-neutral heating through solar energy. The home interacts with nature's upper air strata via strategically positioned windows, solar panels, solar cells, and air ducts. Sun, daylight, and fresh air are brought into the home

and transformed into electricity, heat, natural lighting, and ventilation."[2] In an interview, Velux team members Anna Dvarsater, Kurt Emil Eriksen, and Per Arnold Andersen explained that: "In SOLTAG we focused on optimizing passive solar and active systems, including strategies such as the building and window orientation, passive solar heating, daylighting, reducing cooling, and external shading. We reduce energy consumption by design. The energy that is needed can be from passive design for heat and light and active systems for electricity and hot water."

In addition to demonstrating new innovations in prefabricated housing design and construction, the prototype also seeks to improve the health and well-being of building occupants: "SOLTAG is based on the latest know-how in sustainable construction. The architecture exploits the best energy-optimizing building components and incorporates the prefabricated elements so that the construction technology is correctly applied and the elements speak the same design language. The various building components, each with its own energy function, are used to strengthen and contribute to a holistic solution featuring a healthy indoor climate in contemporary energy-balanced architecture built to respond to people."[3]

Climate and site

SOLTAG is a proposed design solution for northern temperate climates where there is little

need for cooling beyond natural ventilation and solar can be designed to optimize passive gains and daylight. The prototype is located at the Velux corporate office in Hørsholm, Denmark, a region that experiences temperate seasonal shifts, with an average low temperature of -0.4°C (31°F) in January and an average high of 18°C (71°F) in July. The relatively mild winter temperatures are accompanied by overcast skies and the sunniest part of the year is midsummer. Velux explain that: "The purpose of the project is to demonstrate energy-efficient refurbishment of existing buildings and provide examples of future housing standards. SOLTAG is basically intended as a roof refurbishment solution—a housing unit that can be attached to existing 1960s and 1970s multistory housing without needing to be connected to the building's existing energy systems. The flat roofs can then be used as 'new' building plots with upgraded roof and housing areas. However, SOLTAG is also ideal for new buildings such as terraced [row] housing units, single-family housing in towns, out in the country, and even on water as houseboats."[4]

Daylighting and thermal design

SOLTAG uses the roof to gather sun and air: the home is comprised of two rectangular prefabricated modules with living spaces, kitchen, and loft in the west module and a bedroom and bathroom in the east. Daylighting is used to create a sense of openness and spaciousness in the modest 84 m² (904 sq ft)

home. "In SOLTAG, high-level roof windows are installed to let in as much daylight as possible. A sloping surface lets in twice as much light as a vertical frontage—so the sloping roof areas are ideal sources of light. The roof windows reach right up to the ridge – like bands of light sending daylight down through the house. The roof windows, which run along the inner end walls, send reflections down across the walls, which in turn act as one large reflector in the room. The light is passed and reflected out into the room and in under the open loft space, down to the kitchen and dining area, erasing any shadows from the loft space above."[5]

The amount of glazing used for sidelighting and toplighting is equivalent to 28 percent of the floor area, which is a much higher percentage than in standard daylighting design. The loft is set back from the south facade to avoid blocking daylight and air, while light-colored surfaces throughout the home optimize daylight reflection. Skylights include automated blinds that control solar gains during the overheated period of the year and a simple retractable awning covers the southern balcony. Kurt Emil Eriksen and Per Arnold Andersen from Velux emphasize that the team paid great attention to the quality of daylight in the house: "The daylight is amazing. The reason is that instead of a flat ceiling, we sloped the roof. The room feels larger than it is. All windows are positioned to optimize daylight and view. This makes a difference in how people feel in

Above
Detail of the south roof and facade including skylights, windows, and shading devices.

Opposite
Interior view of the prototype house looking south. Direct sunlight is allowed to animate the spaces on a seasonally appropriate basis. Inhabitants control light, air, and solar gain by adjusting the interior and exterior shading devices, operable windows, and skylights.

the house." Daylighting studies used to analyze the daylight factors in the living spaces revealed an average daylight factor of 12.7 percent in the living space, 8.7 percent in the bedroom, and 9.7 percent in the bathroom.[6] Luminance studies were also used to evaluate potential problems with glare and excessive contrast, and to optimize the quantity and quality of daylight on diurnal and seasonal bases.

The SOLTAG design team approached daylighting as a series of dynamic forces that change with the seasons. As Per Arnold Andersen explains: "A window is not just a window. It has to perform in winter, summer, and during the night and day. The role of the windows is to control parameters and not compromise daylight quality. We used dynamic solutions." With solid walls on the east and west (which form party walls in the multi-unit configuration), the steeply pitched roof and vertical south and north facades contain of the windows and skylights and present distinct luminous and thermal design opportunities. The vertical slices of operable skylights and windows on the south provide daylighting, natural ventilation, passive solar gains, and site views. The north-facing windows and skylights balance daylight throughout the space and provide supplemental views to the north over the site. Automated shades are integrated into the window envelopes to control heat and light. Velux summarize the placement of the windows: "The largest window areas in the home face south. These south-facing roof windows are standard products that provide maximum access for sunlight. They provide heat as well as light. The low-energy windows used let energy into the home, but also limit heat loss. Facing north, the passive heat from the sun is limited, so the roof windows are designed to bring light in and retain energy. The north-facing roof windows in the ridge are super low-energy windows—passive house windows with minimum heat loss. Passive house windows consist of an external single glass unit with a low-insulation pane in the inner sashes. The sash is embedded deep in the frame."[7]

Energy systems

The integrated energy system at SOLTAG includes a heat pump, ventilation unit, hot-water tank, solar thermal panels (to heat water for underfloor heating and domestic hot water), and a double roof and solar cells. The roof is particularly important in meeting the comfort and energy needs of the house; it supports systems for heating, lighting, ventilation, hot-water heating, and electricity. The double-layer roof comprises a zinc surface with photovoltaic cells, an air space, and the interior roof structure. The air space is used to preheat air for the heat pump, which produces domestic hot water, and floor and air heating. Airflow beneath the photovoltaic cells also helps cool the cells to optimize performance. This system enables the house to meet zero-energy and

View of north facade including operable skylights, ventilation stack, and exterior balcony.

Exterior view of the west and south facades. Operable windows and skylights provide cross and stack ventilation. The south-facing awning can be extended to provide shading for the balcony and living areas. Photovoltaic cells and solar panels (for underfloor heating and hot water) are integrated into the double-layered roof, which also preheats air for the heat pump.

carbon-neutral goals for heating. Amorphous thin-film photovoltaic solar cells covering an area of 17.5m² (188 sq ft) produce an annual net zero-energy consumption for heating and hot water (0 kWh/m² / 0 Btu/sq ft). The house uses 60 kWh/m² (19 kBtu/sq ft) for heating and hot water when photovoltaic cells are not used. A solar thermal system (2 m²/21.5 sq ft) heats domestic hot water. Velux explain how the systems are integrated: "SOLTAG is devised as a home that runs itself and is independent of external heating systems. The independent heating production and maintenance are achieved by harnessing solar energy, which is generated by the windows' natural propensity to heat up, and by the solar panels that produce domestic hot water and underfloor heating. Solar cells produce the electricity to operate the pumps and ventilators." A compact, built-in heat-recovery ventilation unit and a mechanical ventilator transfer the heat from the 'spent,' heated air to new fresh air taken from outside. Ninety percent of the heat is recycled."[8]

The building envelope is described as a "solid climate screen," using airtight construction, 350 mm (14 in) insulation in the walls, and 400 mm (16 in) in the roof. An automated solar control system helps keep the house cool in the summer and eliminates the need for air conditioning. The system uses io-homecontrol®, which operates windows, lights, and other components manually, by remote control, or as preprogrammed

functions. Airflow and light are regulated by indoor Venetian blinds and ventilation is enhanced by the exchange of air through skylights. Roller shutters on the exterior can also be operated by the control system. The design and integration of the energy systems at SOLTAG demonstrate a simple, straightforward, and off-the-shelf solution to zero-energy and carbon-neutral heating for a northern temperate climate.

Next-generation thinking

SOLTAG strives to provide a zero-energy, carbon-neutral prefabricated housing prototype that can be replicated for northern climates. The project highlights the importance of integrating architectural design with uncomplicated off-the-shelf systems. The modesty and simplicity of the design are two of its greatest strengths. Daylighting is a focal point, celebrating the experience of changing light through thoughtful construction and finishes, while adhering to the strictest of energy and environmental standards. The modest form and section illustrate that each element of the design solution can address more than one challenge. As part of the European Union's Sixth Framework Program, SOLTAG also models new design approaches and collaborations between the building industry and design professions. Anna Dvarsater, Kurt Emil Eriksen, and Per Arnold Andersen of Velux explain: "This EU project required us to bring together research institutes, industry, and

Opposite
Interior view of the kitchen, dining area, and mezzanine. The south-facing windows and skylights have adjustable shading devices that enable inhabitants to respond to varying diurnal and seasonal needs for passive heating, daylighting, and natural ventilation. Daylight is balanced bilaterally by skylights and windows on the north facade.

Right
Detail of the reading niche on the south side of the bedroom. Operable windows and skylights integrate natural ventilation, thermal comfort, and daylighting. Dynamic shading devices are provided in the windows and skylights.

engineers and architects. With SOLTAG we were all partners. It was a dialog about indoor comfort, daylight, and energy. We considered how to use the sun to accumulate energy. It was inspirational how we worked." The project underscores the importance of forming alliances to meet the challenges of new design thinking: "SOLTAG is a holistic project conceived in cooperation between urban planners, architects, and energy and daylight experts. The project was designed to optimize homes on every scale and parameter recognized by these professionals. They inspired each other and injected their synergies into the project."[9]

Above left
The house is fabricated offsite and transported by truck in two pieces. View of one half of the prototype house en route to the demonstration site.

Above right
On-site construction of the prototype house. The living room unit and bedroom unit are fabricated off site, with the exterior cladding, finishes, and solar and mechanical systems completed on site.

Opposite
Interior view looking southwest from the bedroom toward the dining area. Double-height ceilings and light-colored surfaces enhance the reflection of daylight from the skylights and windows. The simplicity of the spaces allows flexibility of use.

Plans, sections, drawings

Floor plan illustrating the side-by-side relationship of the living room unit and the bedroom unit when joined together. The section reveals how bilateral daylighting from windows and skylights fully illuminates the spaces during daylight hours.

Defining an ethic of enough: SOLTAG Energy Housing

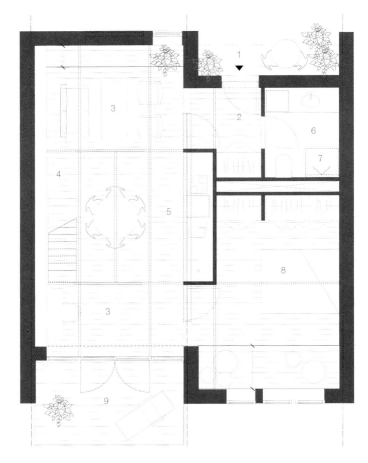

Plan

1. Entrance/roof terrace
2. Entrance hall
3. Living room
4. Built-in shelves with stairs to the loft space
5. Kitchen
6. Bathroom
7. Shower
8. Bedroom
9. Roof terrace

N

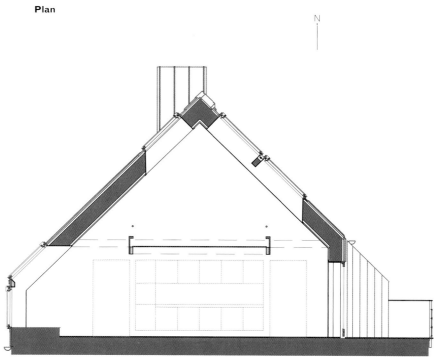

Section looking east

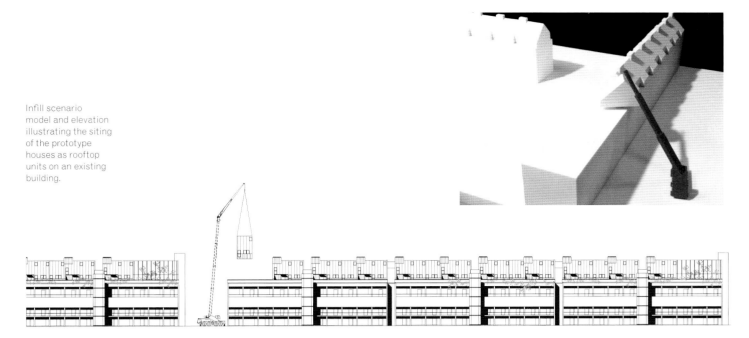

Infill scenario model and elevation illustrating the siting of the prototype houses as rooftop units on an existing building.

Elevation

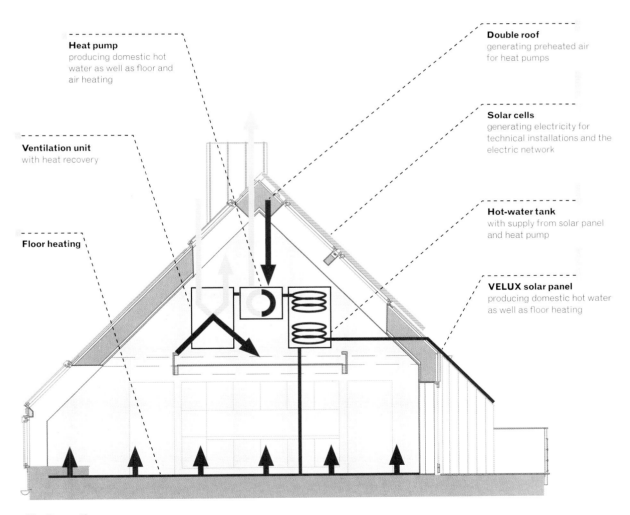

Heat pump
producing domestic hot water as well as floor and air heating

Ventilation unit
with heat recovery

Floor heating

Double roof
generating preheated air for heat pumps

Solar cells
generating electricity for technical installations and the electric network

Hot-water tank
with supply from solar panel and heat pump

VELUX solar panel
producing domestic hot water as well as floor heating

Heating section

Wind studies

Defining an ethic of enough: SOLTAG Energy Housing

Project location:
Hørsholm, Denmark

Wind data location:
Copenhagen, Denmark

Prevailing winds
March
Wind frequency (hours)
Location: Copenhagen, Denmark (55.6°, 12.7°)
Time: 00:00–24:00

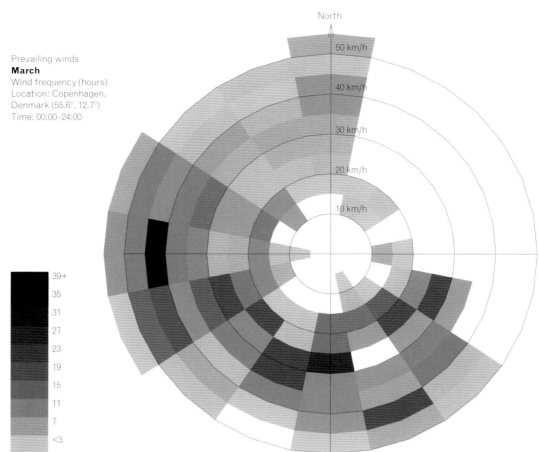

Prevailing winds
September
Wind frequency (hours)
Location: Copenhagen, Denmark (55.6°, 12.7°)
Time: 00:00–24:00

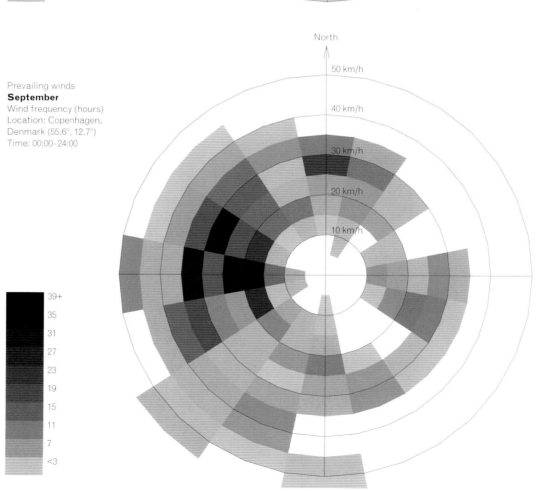

North

50 km/h
40 km/h
30 km/h
20 km/h
10 km/h

Prevailing winds
June
Wind frequency (hours)
Location: Copenhagen,
Denmark (55.6°, 12.7°)
Time: 00:00–24:00

47+
42
37
32
28
23
18
14
9
<4

North

50 km/h
40 km/h
30 km/h
20 km/h
10 km/h

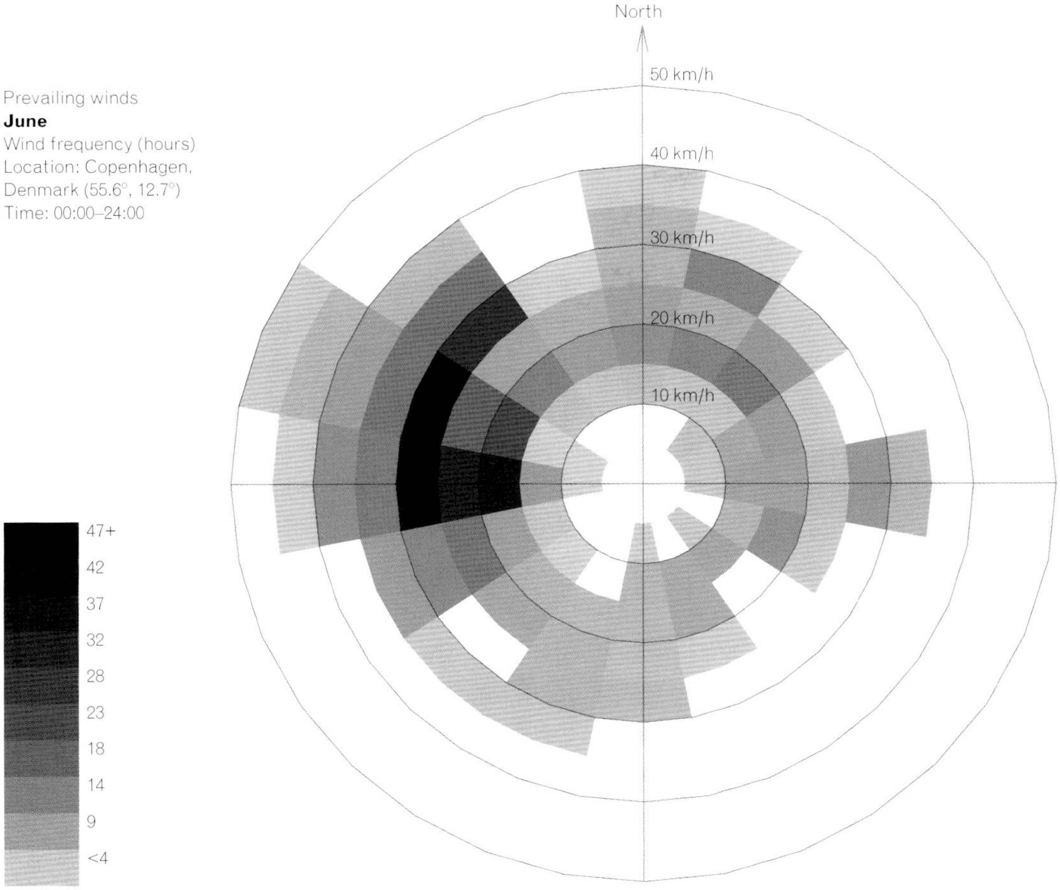

Prevailing winds
December
Wind frequency (hours)
Location: Copenhagen,
Denmark (55.6°, 12.7°)
Time: 00:00–24:00

32+
28
25
22
19
16
12
9
6
<3

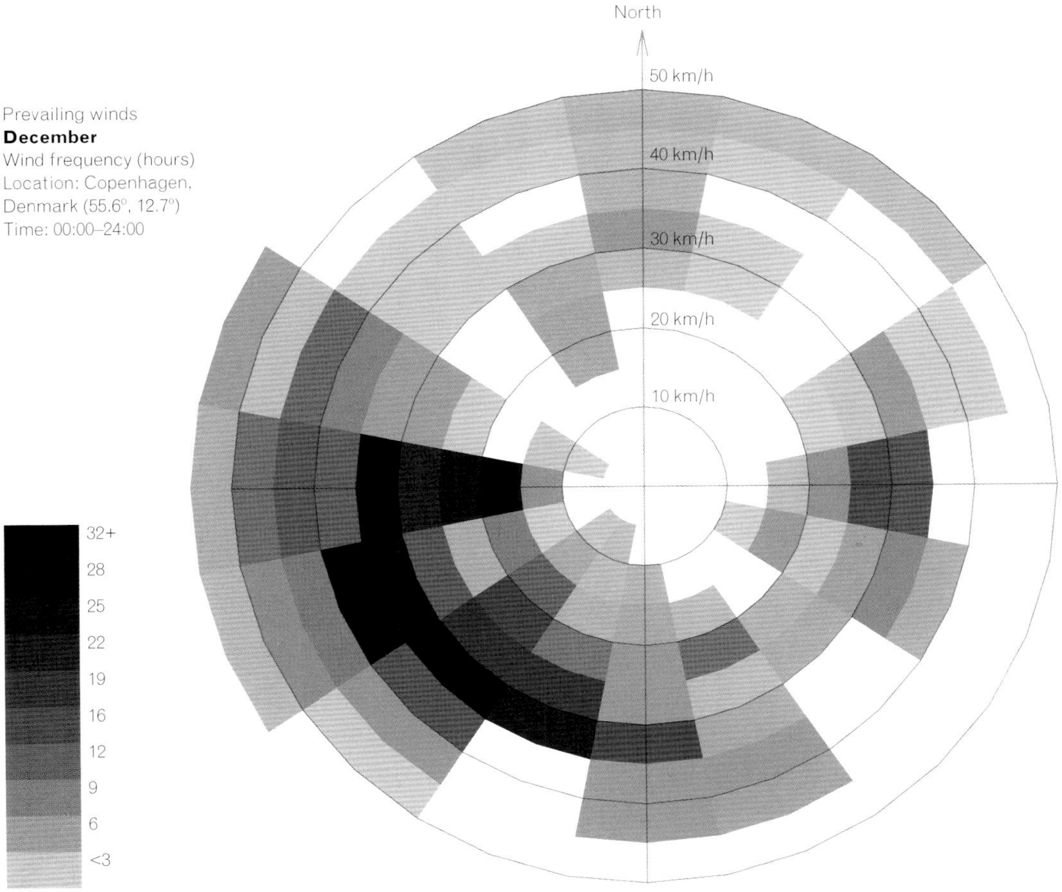

Sunpath case studies

Defining an ethic of enough: SOLTAG Energy Housing

Project location:
Hørsholm, Denmark
Latitude: 55° NL

December

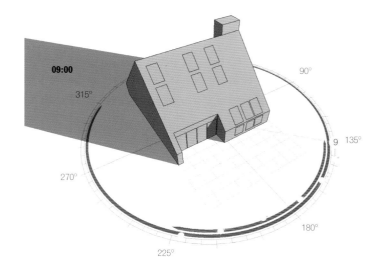

March/September

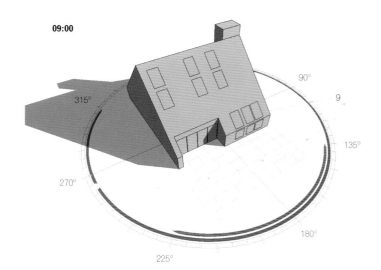

June

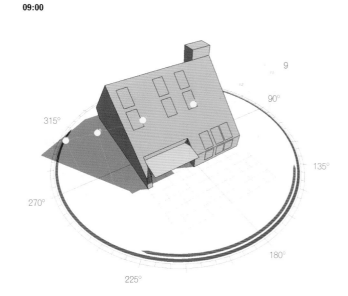

12:00

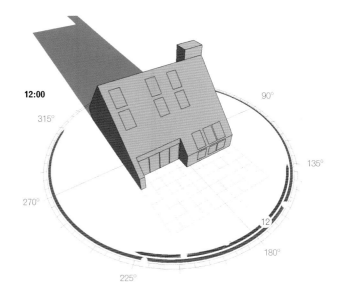

15:00

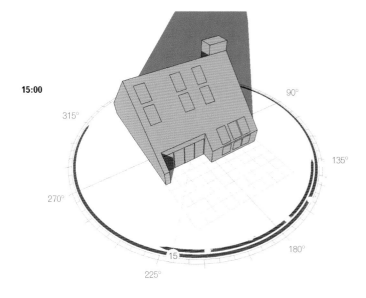

12:00

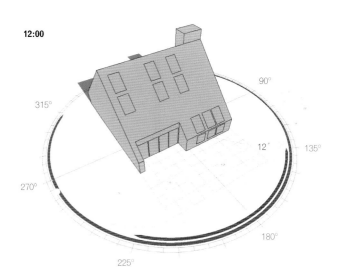

15:00

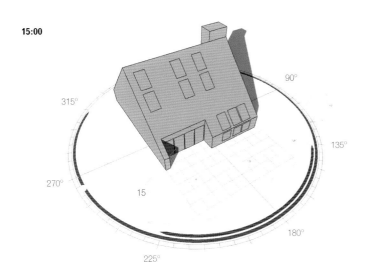

12:00

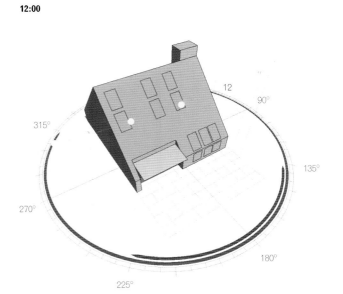

15:00

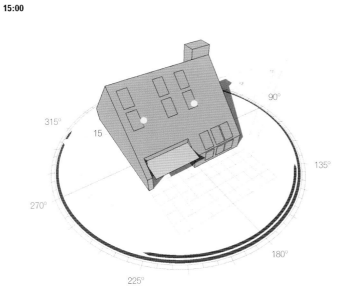

Climate data

Project location:
Hørsholm, Denmark

Climate data location:
Copenhagen, Denmark

Diurnal average temperatures

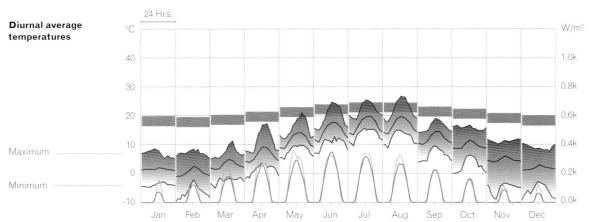

24 Hrs.

°C / W/m²

Maximum / Minimum

Jan Feb Mar Apr May Jun Jul Aug Sep Oct Nov Dec

Dry bulb temperatures 1 Jan to 31 Dec

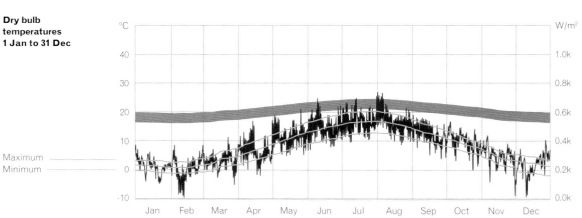

Maximum / Minimum

Jan Feb Mar Apr May Jun Jul Aug Sep Oct Nov Dec

Direct radiation 1 Jan to 31 Dec

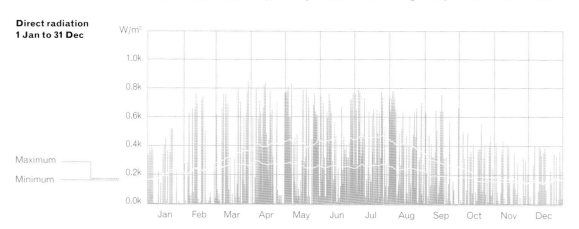

W/m²

Maximum / Minimum

Jan Feb Mar Apr May Jun Jul Aug Sep Oct Nov Dec

Relative humidity 1 Jan to 31 Dec

Maximum / Minimum

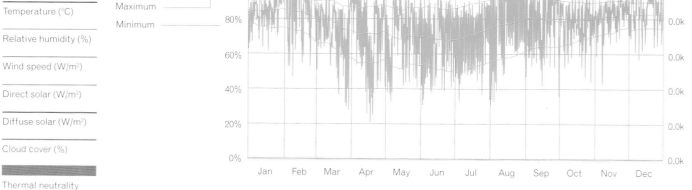

Jan Feb Mar Apr May Jun Jul Aug Sep Oct Nov Dec

Temperature (°C)

Relative humidity (%)

Wind speed (W/m²)

Direct solar (W/m²)

Diffuse solar (W/m²)

Cloud cover (%)

Thermal neutrality

Design profile

Building profile	Building name:	**SOLTAG Energy Housing**
	Architect:	Nielsen and Rubow, Cenergia, Kuben Byfornyelse Danmark, and Velux Danmark; www.soltag.net
	Location:	Hørsholm, Denmark
	Building type:	Residential
	Square footage:	84 m² (904 sq ft)
Solar design profile	Latitude:	55° NL
	Heating Degree Days:	3,286 heating degree days °C (6,109 heating degree days °F) (18°C and 65°F base temperature; average 5 years)
	Cooling Degree Days:	126 cooling degree days °C (199 cooling degree days °F)
	Conservation strategies:	Modest-sized spaces with low overall area
	Passive solar strategies:	Daylighting, cross ventilation, direct passive solar
	Active solar strategies:	Photovoltaic system, solar hot-water thermal system
	Other renewable energy strategies:	Not applicable
	High-performance strategies:	Heat recovery ventilation unit and mechanical ventilation; high-performance appliances, systems, and lighting; high-performance envelope; 350 mm (14 in) insulation in walls and 400 mm (16 in) in roof; airtight construction; double roof (generating preheated air for heat pump)
Performance profile [10] [11]	Total annual building energy consumption:	Energy consumption for heating and hot water: 60 kWh/m² without solar cells; 48 kWh/m² with 3.5m² solar cells; 0 kWh/m² with 17.5 m² solar cells (19 kBtu/sq ft without solar cells; 15 KBtu/sq ft with 3.5 m²/37.6 sq ft solar cells; 0 kBtu/sq ft with 17.5 m²/188 sq ft solar cells)
	Total annual on-site energy produced:	See above
	Size of photovoltaic system:	See above: from 3.5 m² (37.6 sq ft) solar cells to 17.5 m² (188 sq ft) solar cells (photovoltaic panels to run the pumps and ventilators throughout the year with an additional 14 m²/150 sq ft photovoltaic panels to meet energy demand for heating for winter; excluding energy for appliances and lighting, which is met by the external electric grid)
	Size of solar thermal system:	2 m² (21.5 sq ft); thermal hot water for domestic hot water and underfloor heating
	Carbon dioxide emissions:	Net carbon neutral for heating; 0 kgCO$_2$/yr (0 kBtu) with 17.5m² (188 sq ft) solar cells

Endnotes:
SOLTAG Energy Housing

1 Velux "SOLTAG [energy housing] brochure," (Hørsholm, Denmark: Velux A/S), 4.
2 Ibid.
3 Velux, "Professional Case Studies: Architecture," http://www.velux.co.uk/Professionals/Architects/Cases_domestic/SOLTAG/Architecture/
4 Velux, 6.
5 Velux, "Professional Case Studies: Daylight," http://www.velux.co.uk/Professionals/Architects/Cases_domestic/SOLTAG/Daylight/.
6 Ibid.
7 Ibid.
8 Velux, "SOLTAG [energy housing] brochure, 13.
9 Velux, "Professional Case Studies: The Project" http://www.velux.co.uk/Professionals/Architects/Cases_domestic/SOLTAG/The_Project/.
10 Soltag, www.soltag.net.
11 Velux, "Soltag Energy Housing," http://www.velux.co.uk/Professionals/Architects/Cases_domestic/SOLTAG/Energy/.

Chapter 4

Using responsive envelopes

"The intelligent fabric of the building envelope becomes a flexible, adaptive, and dynamic membrane, rather than a statically inert envelope."[1]
MICHAEL WIGGINTON AND JUDE HARRIS, *Intelligent Skins*

"Whether facades and roofs are 'more intelligent'... is another issue. What is clear, however, is that the transformation of the building skin into a climate modulator and polyvalent membrane enables it to react to changing weather conditions with increasing flexibility... the goal must be to achieve the highest possible level of architectural quality in the built environment."[2]
ROLAND KRIPPNER, *Solar Architecture*

The building envelope provides comfort and protection, it shapes the character of our living spaces, and it gives form to an aesthetic of design. With mounting concerns over global climate change and resource depletion, many architects are also looking at the building envelope as a key to reducing energy consumption throughout the lifetime of the building. As architects Michael Wigginton and Jude Harris explain: "The facade of a building can account for between 15 and 40 percent of the total building budget, and may be a significant contributor to the cost of up to 40 percent more through its impact on the cost of building services."[3] The growing interest in using architecture as a means to respond to environmental, economic, and programmatic concerns is leading designers around the world to treat the envelope as a dynamic skin that can change with the seasons, adapt to the weather, and respond to the varying needs of the occupants.

Thomas Herzog, an architect and professor at the Technical University in Munich, uses the metaphor of "living skin" to clarify the ecological role of the building envelope: "If we see the facade as the human body's 'third skin' (after that of the body itself and our clothing), the analogy of the design objective becomes clear: the fluctuations of the external climatic conditions on our bodies have to be reduced by each of these functional layers in turn in order to guarantee a constant body temperature…"[4] For greater ecological responsiveness, Herzog recommends a multilayered approach to the building envelope: "… the developments of recent decades, with the enormous increase in the requirements placed on the building envelope, have resulted in multiple-layer constructions in which every single layer has to perform specific functions."[5] Christian Schittich, editor of *DETAIL*, elaborates on the ecological promise of multilayered and dynamic building envelopes: "It isn't always easy to draw the line between a useful skin and ornamental packaging… As technical requirements grow ever more complex and challenging and insulation guidelines increasingly rigid, nearly every external skin becomes a multi-layered system… the building skin as a responsive skin, as one component of a sustainable low-energy concept. This begins with simple folding and sliding shutters or with the popular moveable louvers and culminates in multi-layered glass facades equipped with a multitude of devices for shading and glare protection, light deflection, heat and energy gain. Today, in the face of diminishing raw materials and growing CO_2 emissions, this approach is increasingly important. It seems to offer the best of both worlds: contemporary facade design without running the risk of superficial ornamentation…"[6]

The functions of the building envelope must be clearly defined in relation to specifics of climate, program, and users, as architect Werner Lang underscores in his essay "Is it All 'Just' a Facade": "When the options for construction are taken into consideration as well, we are presented with a tremendous variety of different skin systems, which can be conceived in correspondence to the desired functional requirements. At the same time, one has a clear sense of the enormous creative freedom that results

Exterior view of the Rozak House living wing at Lake Bennett in Northern Territory, Australia. The envelope provides varying degrees of enclosure, from the outermost screened living area with open floorboards to the more protected kitchen and dining spaces at the rear of the living wing. The mild yet humid climate guided the architect in creating an adjustable envelope that fosters connection to the landscape.

from using vastly different materials, surface structures, colors, formats, and propositions… the aim should be to develop a building skin that fully satisfies all the aspects relating to function, design, and ecology. To this end, it is indispensable to establish a clear profile of the requirements, which the building skin must fulfill."[7] When integrating passive and active solar, architects must balance daylighting, ventilation, passive heating, solar control, and renewable energy generation. Each of these needs informs design decisions such as the orientation and size of apertures and the choice of interior and exterior materials, layers, and detailing. Depending on the climate and thermal loads, the size and placement of apertures, ventilation, and solar control can vary dramatically. Manfred Hegger, architect and professor at the Technical University of Darmstadt, emphasizes the complex dynamics of solar design: "The utilization of solar energy further expands the already complex functional spectrum of the envelope. The interface between interior and exterior must be understood as a dynamic system, which responds to the permanent variability in external radiation, climate conditions, and internal requirements."[8]

A responsive building envelope also allows designers to accommodate the changing needs of users by giving them the ability to modify interior conditions during the day and as the seasons change. By adjusting interior and exterior layers, a responsive building envelope can be tuned to provide specific levels and qualities of daylighting, solar heating, shading, ventilation, views, and connections to site. These dynamic outcomes require a level of thoughtfulness and design integration that goes beyond technology, as architect Roland Krippner explains: "… [an] intelligent building is not necessarily just a matter of technical systems. The tremendous variety in regional approaches to building exemplifies what intelligent, that is, efficient, use of material and energy can be, because they combine rational thinking and craftsmanship with conclusive forms of expression. More technology is, clearly, not the only answer. Avoiding unnecessary technology, especially when it becomes an end in itself, can be just as innovative and intelligent."[9] An adjustable envelope responds to environmental forces, internal loads, and varying luminous and thermal demands in much the same way that an organism responds to external and internal stimuli. The metaphor of the building "skin" as a biological entity is particularly helpful in reminding architects to think of "responding" to the environment through design rather than of "controlling" the environment through technology.

Many terms are used to describe the responsive envelope—"dynamic," "living," and "intelligent" for example—yet all ecologically responsive building envelopes have in common a reliance more on design than on technology. Regardless of the approach, manual or automated, low tech or high, when occupants have the ability to control their sense of comfort, quality of space, relationship to the site, and consumption of energy, the quality of life and the ecological health of the planet are improved. The role of building occupants is paramount in the successful utilization of a responsive envelope, as Wigginton and Harris underscore:

Exterior detail of the operable photovoltaic louvers on the envelope of the Year 2015 Prototype Home, winner of the 2007 Solar Decathlon. Exhibited on the Mall in Washington, DC, in 2007, the house is now located in Darmstadt, Germany, where it is a hands-on demonstration project for design students, researchers, and practitioners.

"Of course, the building skin is not the envelope of a single living being: it accommodates many people, each with a different set of requirements, varying from time to time, and each in a different location… It is well established that building occupants should be offered maximum personal control over their immediate environment. Although the variable building fabric can still be effective with manual control, this places unsustainable demands on the predictive capability of occupants, and requires their continuous or very frequent presence… Involving building users in the decision making associated with their environmental comfort provides a sense of participation as well as an ability to control and vary the local environment…"[10]

The forces of sun, wind, and site also provide aesthetic opportunities that shape the architectural language and expression of the building envelope. New materials and components are expanding the design palette, as editor Frank Kaltenbach explains: "… now architects, and interior and other designers, have new building materials at their disposal, ranging from completely transparent to almost opaquely translucent. These products do not just meet increasingly complex requirements and regulations, but provide a design potential that is still far from exhausted… Functions like solar screening, glare protection, sight screening, or creative requirements can be fulfilled by membranes or perforated metal sheeting. Composite products, exploiting the positive properties of several materials, are also becoming more common."[11]

The following case studies illustrate ways in which the building envelope can help to achieve zero-energy and zero-emission architecture. The projects use contrasting design approaches to achieve similar ecological goals: the Rozak House, by Troppo Architects, uses a low-tech envelope while the Year 2015 Prototype Home for the 2007 Solar Decathlon by the Technische Universität Darmstadt is distinctly high tech. Both projects illustrate that a new level of ecological performance can be achieved by integrating environmental, programmatic, technological, and aesthetic considerations. Located in a temperate climate, the Rozak House envelope can be described as a filter that creates a minimal boundary between inside and out. Porches, screened walls and floors, operable jalousie windows, solar louvers, and extensive shading enclose spaces while creating dynamic and adjustable connections. The Year 2015 Prototype Home, designed for a northern cold climate, uses a layered envelope to integrate passive and active solar systems along with natural ventilation. An elegant system of operable external photovoltaic louvers (lamellae) provides the outer layer of thermal protection while also generating electricity. High-performance glazing, insulation, and interior shading complete the envelope. Both homes are interactive; the occupants are able to adjust the envelopes to optimize performance and comfort. Whether by simple manual adjustment or through sophisticated automated controls, the homes demonstrate that new levels of ecological response, user comfort, and aesthetically pleasing design can be achieved by dynamic and responsive building envelopes.

Interior view of the Year 2015 Prototype Home looking to the northeast. The retractable sleeping area is partially open to reveal the hidden bed, which stows in a cavity beneath the floor. The extension of the east facade accentuates the distinction between the glazed north facade and the solar envelopes in other orientations. Simple interior drapes provide privacy and luminous control on the north.

Endnotes:

1 Michael Wigginton and Jude Harris, *Intelligent Skins* (Oxford: Butterworth-Heinemann, 2002), 27.
2 Roland Krippner, "Solar Technology—From Innovative Building Skin to Energy-Efficient Renovation," *Solar Architecture*, edited by Christian Schittich (Basel: Birkhäuser, 2003), 35.
3 Michael Wigginton and Jude Harris, 3.
4 Thomas Herzog, Roland Krippner, and Werner Lang, *Facade Construction Manual* (Munich: Birkhäuser, 2004), 19.
5 Ibid, 7.
6 Christian Schittich, "Shell, Skin, Materials," *Building Skins: Concepts Layers Materials* (Basel: Birkhäuser, 2001), 9.
7 Werner Lang, "Is it All 'Just' a Facade: The Functional, Energetic and Structural Aspects of the Building Skin," *Building Skins: Concepts Layers Materials*, edited by Christian Schittich (Basel: Birkhäuser, 2001), 44.
8 Manfred Hegger, "From Passive Utilization to Smart Solar Architecture," *Solar Architecture*, edited by Christian Schittich (Basel: Birkhäuser, 2003), 19.
9 Roland Krippner, 28.
10 Michael Wigginton and Jude Harris, 31.
11 Frank Kaltenbach, ed., *Translucent Materials: Glass Plastic Metals* (Basel: Birkhäuser, 2004), 7.

Project:
Location:
Architect:

Rozak House
Lake Bennett, Northern Territory, Australia
Adrian Welke, Troppo Architects

"This remarkable project demonstrates that houses do not need large amounts of supplied energy. The principles of good tropical design are employed here with rigor: there is ample cross ventilation, relief from rising heat, employment of lightweight heat-reflective materials, and shading and sheltering of walls and openings. The building is self-sufficient in power and water use and all wastewater is treated on site."[1]
Jury Citation, *Royal Australian Institute of Architecture Awards*

Exterior view looking northeast towards the dual bedroom pavilions and centrally located living–kitchen pavilion. Hovering on the edge of a high outcrop, the living pavilion provides panoramic views to the dramatic landscape below. The building section is essentially the shape of a "lean-to", with screened verandahs opening to the south and sheltering roof overhangs on the north.

Design intentions
The lessons of Aboriginal structures and vernacular dwellings of the nineteenth and early twentieth centuries inspired Troppo Architects to create contemporary architecture that is grounded in the traditions of place while also reaching to the future in pursuit of environmental sustainability. Troppo Architects aspire to: "… promote a sense of place: through an architecture that responds to climate and the local setting: a dynamic architecture of adjustable skins; that connects the indoors with the out: a non-constant architecture that responds to the morning, the evening, the season, the heat, the cold, the sun, the rain, the moment that will never pass again."[2] The Rozak House is shaped by the sun and wind in response to ever-changing cycles of time, season, and weather. It is located in the harsh, rugged, and seemingly inhospitable landscape of the Top End in Northern Territory, Australia, where it is believed that people have lived for at least 40,000 years.[3] In the tradition of indigenous dwellings, the house has two essential design components: a roof to shade the sun and block the rain, and an elevated platform to capture the movement of air. The architect, Adrian Welke, explained his design intentions in an interview: "We designed the compound to be like camping; to be minimalist; almost a tent. The experience is like sitting on a platform. You're not behind a wall, you're inside and outside." The dwelling uses passive design and a permeable envelope to connect occupants to place while minimizing energy loads so that renewable energy systems are able to achieve zero-energy status.

Climate and site
The Rozak House is a regionally responsive and self-sufficient dwelling located in a remote and sparsely developed region 80 km (50 miles) south of Darwin, Australia. Perched like a tree house on the steep ridge of a spectacular rock outcrop, Rozak is exposed to the seasonal extremes of weather, including monsoons, cyclones, thunderstorms, and wind. The spectacular setting overlooks the expansive and primordial landscape of Lake Bennett and the winding Adelaide River. As Professor Philip Goad explains in his book on Troppo Architects: "The house appears delicate, almost fragile: a bird temporarily at rest. Another reading may be that the Rozak House was designed as a willfully organic humpy [a temporary Aboriginal structure], but it created an eagle's prospect for its proud keeper."[4]

The architectural challenge for a tropical dwelling is to provide shelter from the relentless heat of the sun in the dry season and relief from the torrential rains and humidity of the monsoon season. As owner Mike Rozak explains: "There are basically two seasons, the 'Dry' season from April through September, and the 'Wet' season from October through March. The dry season has highs of 32°C (90°F), lows of 17°C (63°F) at night, and no rain for six months; it's very comfortable during the day

and a bit chilly at night. All of Darwin's rain (about 2 meters of it) is saved up for the wet season, with highs of 36°C (97°F) and lows of 22°C (72°F), compounded by 90 percent humidity. This makes it very hot and humid during the day, but mostly comfortable at night."[5] The passive strategies focus on creating shade and catching the movement of air to mitigate humidity. The design also requires lifestyle changes for the occupants, especially a willingness to live without mechanical air conditioning. Both the dwelling and the occupants are tuned to the diurnal and seasonal rhythms, slowing down during the hottest parts of the day and accommodating the cycles of sunshine and rain.

The "house" is actually a compound of three pavilions woven together by boardwalks. The pavilions are elevated high above the ground to minimize heat gain and maximize airflow beneath and around the buildings. Their thin profiles and separate living spaces also increase exposure to breezes and views. The compound is organized along an east–west axis, with two bedroom–bathroom pavilions flanking a living space. Each pavilion provides distinctive views and changing qualities of light and air from morning to night. The centrally located living–kitchen pavilion appears to float over the edge of the outcrop, providing an expansive panorama of the land below and the ever-changing sky above. An observation tower, located at the heart of the three pavilions, provides a true bird's-eye view

of the environs. As Mike Rozak explains: "In the center of the house, joining all three sections together, is a tower that people can climb to get a 360-degree view of the territory. Or just to get away, or even sleep under the stars. The tower doubles as a platform for a lightning rod; Darwin has many immense lightning storms, and I feel safer with a lightning rod overhead when I'm living in a house on top of a hill."[6]

Daylighting and thermal design

Rozak House is located in the southern hemisphere, close to the equator at 12° SL, and both the south and north facades receive direct sunlight as the seasons change throughout the year. The sun shines on the southern facade during the "dry seasons" of fall and winter, while the northern facade receives sunlight during the "wet seasons" of spring and summer. The building section is essentially the shape of a "lean-to," with screened verandahs opening to the south and sheltering roof overhangs on the north. Architectural critic Paul McGillich explains the inspiration for the pavilion design: "Effectively, the house is a continuous verandah, because the slatted decking extends from the front deep back into the rooms (pods) where the kitchen and bathrooms have slate flooring. It is an idea reinforced by the fact that the front sections of each pavilion are not solid walls but steel mesh… This ensures a constant flow of air, not just through the mesh, but also up through the slatted flooring. Likewise, in the wild storms

View of the bedroom pavilion's north facades. The roofs act as solar visors to prevent the admission of direct sunlight and solar gains. An observation tower with a lightning rod is centrally located while rainwater cisterns are sited strategically along the perimeters of the roofs.

typical of the area, the rain will penetrate but run off through the flooring. Its transparency adds to the sense of being on a floating verandah and part of the surrounding landscape."[7]

The narrow building profile, permeable elevations, and elevated floors of Cyprus pine slats are designed to optimize airflow. Interior walls are clad with plywood panels. Elevated walkways covered with translucent polycarbonate roofs provide rain protection yet allow daylight to reach the building envelopes. The rest of the structure is made of steel, to resist fire and termites. Adrian Welke emphasizes that tropical architecture must be permeable: "In the tropics, less is more: architecture should be lightweight and elevated. The less you have of the building the better. It has to breathe and provide airflow to optimize the cooling capacity." To eliminate the need for air conditioning and to optimize passive cooling and daylighting, Welke twisted the shed roofs to create shade and provide shelter from the seasonally alternating sun and rain: "The pitching of the roofs is principally a means of venting hot air out through the roof space by convection. The whole of the building is un-insulated. There is not much point in insulating it because you can use the heat transfer through those skins to actually convect air from underneath the roof. It's the air inside the building that you're actually trying to get rid of, which gets heated up and moisture laden. To maintain the ambient temperature outside is

the best you can do in Darwin. You can't make it any better than that. You certainly can't take the moisture out of the air unless you go into air conditioning."[8]

Indirect daylight and air movement shape all aspects of the Rozak House design, from the building massing, plan, and section to the material choices and details of the facades and interiors. Multilateral fenestration provides cool indirect daylight throughout the pavilions, each of which is oriented in a different direction to provide a unique view and exposure to the luminous and thermal environment. Occupants can follow the sunlight from pavilion to pavilion throughout the day, or seek refuge in the ever-present spaces of shadow. As Philip Goad notes, the Rozak House contains both "sunrise" and "sunset" rooms.[9] The permeable and adjustable envelopes of the Rozak House heighten the experience of climate and site. The envelope of the living–kitchen pavilion transitions from mesh walls on the verandah into floor-to-ceiling jalousie windows in the dining area, and then into a combination of clerestories, jalousie windows, and solid corrugated metal cladding in the kitchen on the north. The living pavilion is deep enough for occupants to escape rain that may pass through the mesh walls by moving into the dining area or kitchen. To provide protection during heavy rainstorms, Rozak added an adjustable canvas blind that covers the mesh verandah in the living pavilion. Clerestory windows above the operable jalousies reflect indirect light onto the undersides

of corrugated-metal ceilings in the living–kitchen pavilion and between the verandah and bedrooms. In contrast, the bedroom–bathroom pavilions are protected on the north by deep and sheltering roof overhangs that act as visors, while horizontal cedar louvers positioned inside the mesh envelope block direct sunlight, reduce heat gain, and create shade in the spring and summer months. Large roof overhangs shelter the inwardly canted stainless steel mesh walls of the verandahs south of the bedroom–bathroom pavilions. The two bathroom modules are enclosed by perforated metal cladding for increased privacy.

Energy systems

The Rozak House demonstrates that passive design, energy conservation, efficient appliances, and renewable energy systems must be combined to achieve energy self-sufficiency. In addition, an energy-conscious lifestyle is essential, as owner Mike Rozak explains on his website: "Because solar systems are expensive, I've had to get appliances and lights that are energy efficient. I have a gas oven and cooktop because solar can't produce enough energy to run them. I don't have a dishwasher because of the high energy and water usage. Although with the kitchen designed the way it is I don't really miss it. No air conditioning is allowed, and even fan usage must be rationed. I don't even have a clothes dryer… Lighting is kept dim, not only because of energy concerns, but because strong light attracts more insects inside… Fluorescents

are the most energy efficient. If anyone in the house wants to read they need to plug in a lamp or wait until the sun rises."[10] While this ecological lifestyle may seem like a burden to some, it is clear that Rozak finds his modest and intentional way of living to be a welcome challenge.

The dwelling employs two active solar systems: a roof-mounted photovoltaic system generates electrical power that is stored on site (11.5 kW with 28 BP 75-watt panels), while domestic hot water for cooking and bathing is provided by a solar hot-water system. Rainwater is harvested from the roofs and stored in tanks for the dry season. All energy, water, and waste is captured or processed on site. Adrian Welke emphasizes that passive design for daylighting, cooling, and heating is the primary means of reducing energy loads. Active systems are of secondary importance and are fully integrated into the passive design. Welke explains his approach: "The entire effort is passive design for cooling with little active solar or technology. We first look at design, planning, and detailing across scales. We're doing everything with design; and also participation with the occupant. This is an autonomous house that collects its own energy with photovoltaics, all its water, and treats its waste."

Next-generation thinking

The Rozak House breaks down literal and metaphorical barriers between inside and out. By actively engaging the dynamic thermal and

Preceding pages
Exterior view looking northwest.

Above
Roof view looking south at the solar hot-water collector and photovoltaic array. The expansive and undeveloped landscape can be seen beyond.

Opposite
Exterior view looking north between the eastern bedroom pavilion and the living pavilion. The structural armature of the walkways creates a dynamic play of light and shadow that provides a visual counterpoint to the three pavilions. Except for the storage area, the pavilions are elevated above the ground plane to facilitate natural ventilation, and air even enters between the floorboards of the living pavilion.

Left
Panoramic view from
the living pavilion.
The envelope of this
pavilion transitions
from mesh walls
on the verandah to
floor-to-ceiling jalousie
windows in the dining
area, and then to
a combination of
clerestories, jalousie
windows, and solid
corrugated-metal
cladding in the kitchen
on the north.

Above
Designed to optimize
indirect daylight and
natural ventilation, the
living pavilion is thin in
profile and abundantly
illuminated by
clerestory windows
and multilateral
sidelighting. Careful
to block the admission
of direct sunlight, the
living space turns its
back to the sun.

luminous forces of its site, it challenges the
standard notion of a narrow and static comfort
zone and encourages the occupants to tune their
lives and daily routines to the cycles of nature,
time, and seasons. Welke emphasizes that the
lifestyle of the client must be considered when
using passive strategies for daylighting and
thermal comfort: "The owner matters; you have
to look at the person living there." Rozak is a
special client, choosing to live in a house with
permeable walls and floors, to depend on passive
strategies for daylighting and natural ventilation,
and to harvest sunlight and water on site. Rozak
elaborates on his experience of living in the house
(which he calls Eagle Eye): "The house's walls are
mostly windows, either louvered windows or a
wall of insect screening… People feel much more
exposed to nature, especially when a downpour
is blown in through the screens… Most of the
floors are decking hardwood… Any rain blown
into the house drips out through the gaps…
Visitors not only have views all around them
through the louvers and insect screen, but they
can look through the floor at the ground several
meters below. Eagle Eye is not for people afraid
of heights."[11]

While it is designed specifically for a tropical
climate, the ecological and experiential lessons
of the Rozak House can certainly be more
widely applied. The project challenges designers
to reconsider current notions of luminous and
thermal comfort, and it encourages them to

provide greater luminous and thermal flexibility
for occupants. As Welke explains: "An occupant
can adapt to the climate. They understand
that this is what life is about. We can enjoy
fluctuations and extend the comfort zone."

As we move toward the next generation of
sustainable design, we need to consider the
implications of a low- or zero-energy lifestyle:
the need to redefine comfort, to appreciate
the benefits of greater engagement with the
environmental forces of place, and to accept an
adaptable architecture that requires occupant
input and engagement. At the same time, the
Rozak House awakens us to the unique design
possibilities that arise only when there is a deep
experiential knowledge of a region and place.
Welke explains the early design philosophy
of Troppo: "We were primarily designing
architecture to be responsive to the region, not
to 'save the world,' but to save the soul and enjoy
place." The Rozak House inspires us to focus on
the ways in which we live and it illustrates that
by actively engaging and celebrating a place, we
may come to care much more for the world.

Plans, sections, drawings

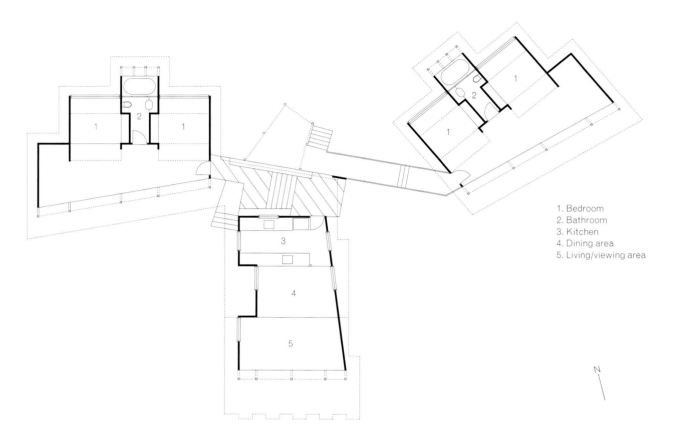

1. Bedroom
2. Bathroom
3. Kitchen
4. Dining area
5. Living/viewing area

Floor plan

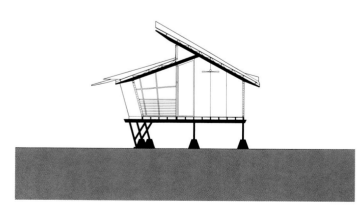

Section through bedroom wing looking west

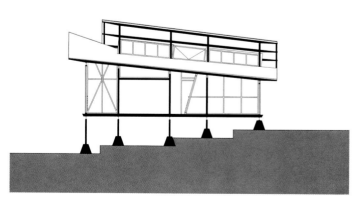

Section through bedroom wing looking north

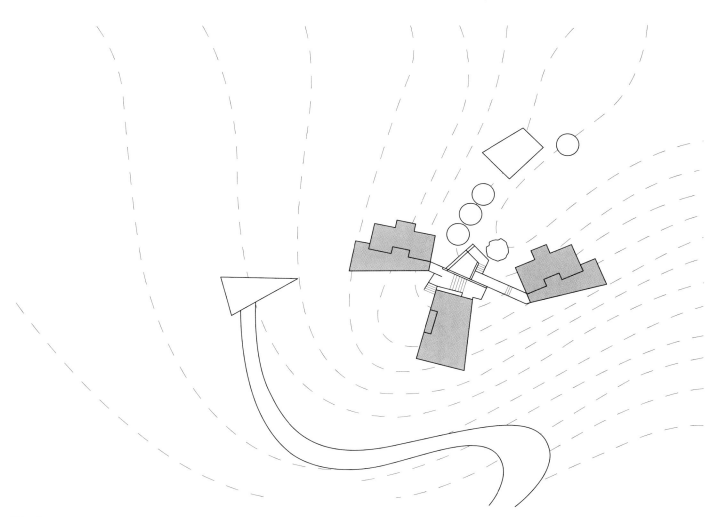

Site plan

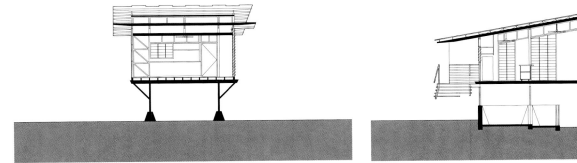

Section through living wing looking north

Section through living wing looking east

Wind studies

Project location:
**Lake Bennett, NT,
Australia**

Wind data location:
**Darwin, NT,
Australia**

Prevailing winds
March
Wind frequency (hours)
Location: Darwin, Australia (-12.4°, 130.9°)
Time: 00:00–24:00

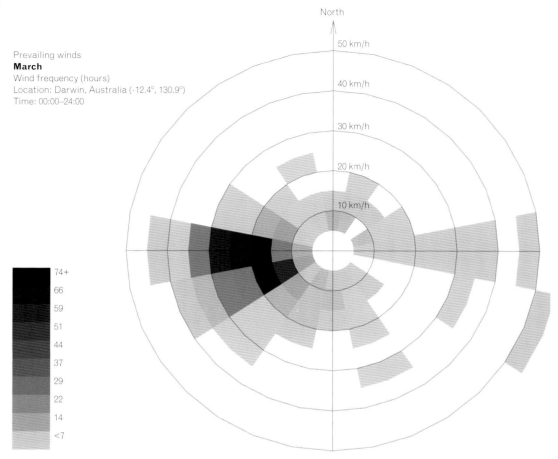

74+
66
59
51
44
37
29
22
14
<7

Prevailing winds
September
Wind frequency (hours)
Location: Darwin, Australia (-12.4°, 130.9°)
Time: 00:00–24:00

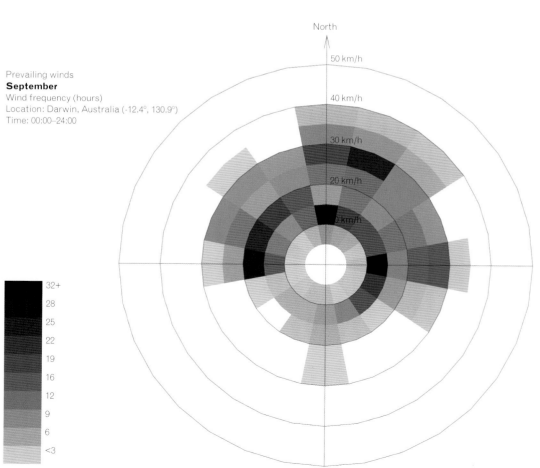

32+
28
25
22
19
16
12
9
6
<3

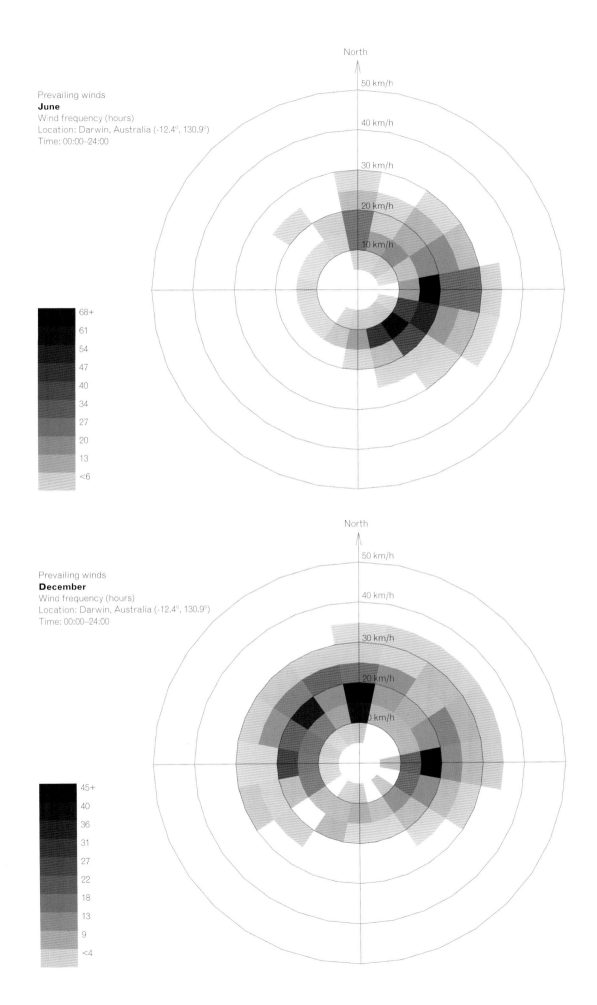

North

50 km/h
40 km/h
30 km/h
20 km/h
10 km/h

Prevailing winds
June
Wind frequency (hours)
Location: Darwin, Australia (-12.4°, 130.9°)
Time: 00:00–24:00

68+
61
54
47
40
34
27
20
13
<6

North

50 km/h
40 km/h
30 km/h
20 km/h
10 km/h

Prevailing winds
December
Wind frequency (hours)
Location: Darwin, Australia (-12.4°, 130.9°)
Time: 00:00–24:00

45+
40
36
31
27
22
18
13
9
<4

Sunpath case studies

Using responsive envelopes: Rozak House

Project location:
**Lake Bennett, NT,
Australia**
Latitude: 12° SL

December

09:00

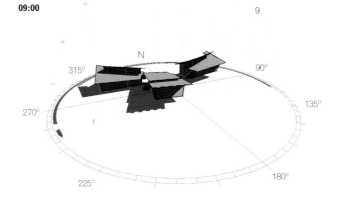

March/September

09:00

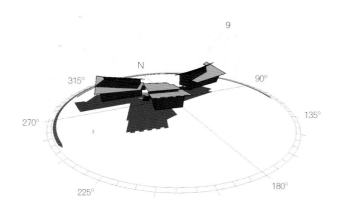

June

09:00

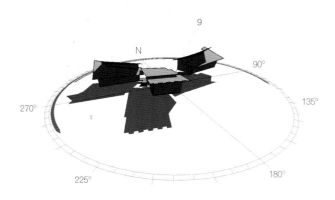

12:00

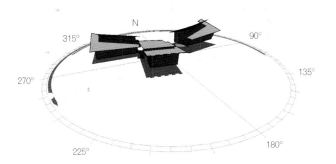

15:00

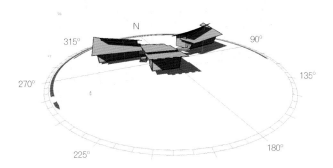

12:00

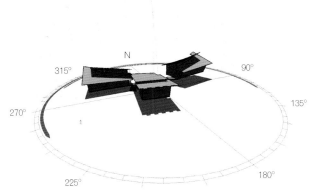

15:00

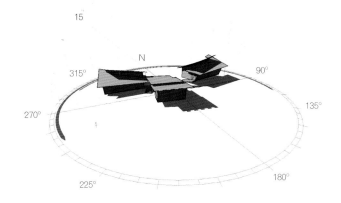

12:00

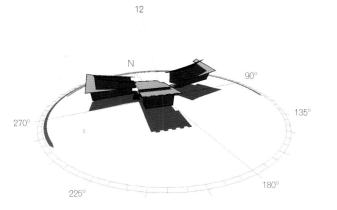

15:00

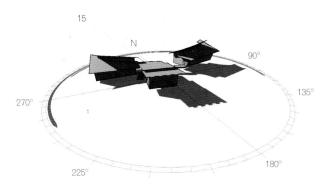

Climate data

Project location:
Lake Bennett, NT, Australia

Climate data location:
Darwin, NT, Australia

Diurnal average temperatures

Maximum

Minimum

24 Hrs.

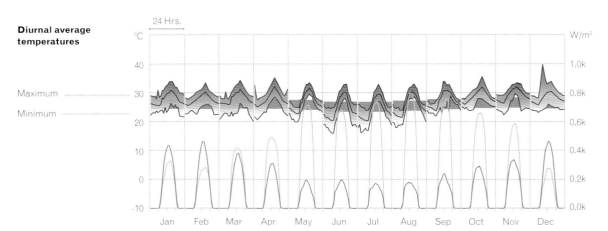

**Dry bulb temperatures
1 Jan to 31 Dec**

Maximum

Minimum

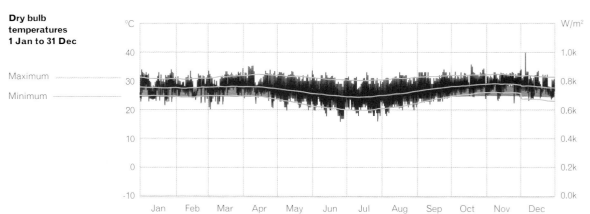

**Direct radiation
1 Jan to 31 Dec**

Maximum

Minimum

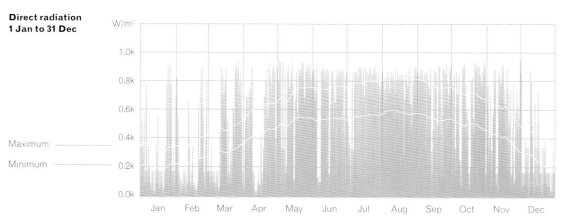

**Relative humidity
1 Jan to 31 Dec**

Maximum

Minimum

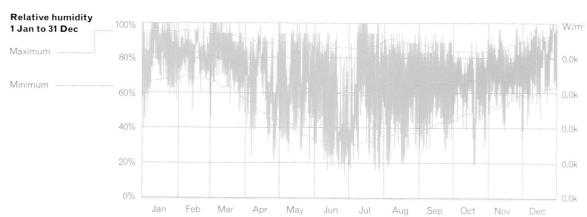

Temperature (°C)

Relative humidity (%)

Wind speed (W/m²)

Direct solar (W/m²)

Diffuse solar (W/m²)

Cloud cover (%)

Thermal neutrality

Design profile

Building profile	Building name:	**Rozak House**
	Architect:	Troppo Architects, Adrian Welke, assisted by Joanna Rees; www.troppoarchitects.com.au
	Location:	Lake Bennett, Northern Territory, Australia
	Building type:	Residential
	Square footage:	200 m² (2,153 sq ft)
Solar design profile	Latitude:	12° SL
	Heating Degree Days:	25 degree days °C (50 heating degree days °F) (18°C and 65°F base temperature; average 5 years)
	Cooling Degree Days:	3,374 cooling degree days °C (5,861 cooling degree days °F)
	Conservation strategies:	Separate living into three pavilions to facilitate airflow and cross ventilation at the site and building scales
	Passive solar strategies:	Daylighting, cross ventilation, operable jalousie windows, shading, louvers for solar control, screened envelope
	Active solar strategies:	Photovoltaic system, solar thermal hot water
	Other renewable energy strategies:	None
	High-performance strategies:	High-efficiency lighting, appliances, and fixtures
Energy profile[12]	Total annual building energy consumption:	Not available
	Total annual on-site energy produced:	Estimated 1,643 kWh (estimated 4.5 kWh per day; 2.5 kWh per day when on holiday for the refrigerator)
	Size of photovoltaic system:	11.5 kW (28 BP 75-watt panels)
	Size of solar thermal system:	Solahart Thermosiphon Roof Mounted System; 2.25 m² (24 sq ft)
	Carbon dioxide emissions:	Not available

Endnotes:
Rozak House

1 Jury Citation. "Award for Sustainable Architecture," *Architecture Australia* (November/December 2002), 62.
2 Troppo Architects, Firm website, http://www.troppoarchitects.com.au/.
3 Beth Gott, Aboriginal Trail, Department of Water, Environment, Heritage and the Arts, Australian Government; http://www.anbg.gov.au/anbg/aboriginal-trail.html.
4 Goad, Philip, *Troppo Architects* (Sydney: Pesaro Publishing, second edition, 2005), 88.
5 Mike Rozak, Eagle Eye website, http://www.mxac.com.au/EagleEye.
6 Ibid.
7 Paul McGillick, "Verandah House," *Steel Profile: Architectural Steel Innovation with BHP Steel*, no. 78 (March 2002).
8 Ibid.
9 Ibid.
10 Mike Rozak, Eagle Eye Website
11 Ibid.
12 Mike Rozak, Owner, Interview, September 2008.

Project: **Year 2015 Prototype Home—Made in Germany**
Location: **Darmstadt, Germany**
Architect: **Solar Decathlon Team, Technische Universität Darmstadt, Germany**

"Sustainability is a way of thinking. It tries to be in harmony with Gaia. We have to solve everything as a whole. The bottom line is all-inclusive thinking. There is a passive link to human consciousness and harmony. Solar architecture puts us back into touch with the outside and with sunlight. The basis of all architecture is harmony."[1]
Hannes Guddat, *Solar Decathlon Student Team Member and Staff Member of the Energy Efficiency Building Group, Technische Universität Darmstadt*

View of the side-lit loggia on the south facade of the structure. The shuttered bifold doors open to extend the living area onto the outdoor terrace and to provide a thermal buffer zone. Semi-transparent photovoltaic modules sandwiched between two panes of skylight glazing provide toplighting.

Design intentions

The Solar Decathlon, sponsored by the United States Department of Energy (DOE), challenges universities and student teams from around the world to design and build a net zero-energy home that is powered by the sun and renewable energy sources. Exhibited as a "solar village" of 20 houses on the Mall in Washington, DC, the competing teams come together to demonstrate the effectiveness of their designs during a three-week period. An elegant minimalist house by the Technische Universität Darmstadt Solar Decathlon Team won first prize in the 2007 competition. Promoted by the team as the "Year 2015 Prototype Home—Made in Germany," the name underscores Germany's place at the forefront of innovative solar architecture and technology. The 2007 contest categories included architectural design, engineering, systems integration (appliances, hot water, lighting), human comfort, and energy balance, along with communications, market viability, and even transportation using electric vehicles. Despite the competition's emphasis on active solar systems, the Darmstadt team prioritized passive solar design and then integrated state-of-the-art solar technologies. The Year 2015 Home expanded on the "Passivhaus" (passive house) design criteria of the Passivhaus Institut in Darmstadt. The team explains the importance of starting with passive design: "To provide high thermal comfort, with little use of energy, from the beginning our house was planned to be a

Passivhaus… In a 'Passivhaus,' a comfortable interior climate can be achieved, without a conventional HVAC [heating, ventilation, and air conditioning] system."[2] Hannes Guddat of the Energy Efficiency Building Group at Technische Universität Darmstadt, and a member of the student team, explained in an interview that the passive solar design intentions went far beyond energy performance to also embrace larger sustainable living goals: "Nothing influences life more than weather and the sun. We can't deny the sun; it has an influence on you. We wanted to do a building in harmony with what's going on outside, to do something that works like a tree, a house that is a machine in harmony with the environment." Guddat explains that the passive strategies of traditional Japanese dwellings also inspired the team to create an envelope that connects the house with the environment through a layered spatial sequence between the inside and outside.

Climate and site

Solar Decathlon teams faced the challenge of designing for a variety of climates around the world while also preparing to exhibit in Washington, DC, during the unpredictable weather of October. The Darmstadt team responded by creating a highly insulated structure with an envelope that can be adjusted to block or admit solar radiation and airflow for heating, shading, and passive cooling: "Our house has to provide comfort

and has to be optimized for the competition time period in Washington, DC, as well as for the subsequent use in Darmstadt, Germany… Therefore we used building simulation tools already in the early planning process to gain information about the complete system data and to inform design decisions… In this connection, possible weather scenarios such as rain, sun, or clouded sky, different sites of the house as well as specific material characteristics of the chosen building materials are incorporated. Based on these data we simulated heating, cooling, and electricity demands, shadowing, and not least the interior room climate of our house. That way we could adapt the integrated technical components to the specific demands."[3] Temperatures can vary greatly during the three-week competition, from an average high of 23°C (73°F) to an average low temperature of 5°C (41°F), and therefore the Decathlon houses have to be moderately heated and cooled. The 2015 home was also designed to function in the more extreme climatic conditions of Darmstadt, with temperatures that range from an average low of 1°C (34°F) in January, to an average high of 19°C (66°F) in July.

The most distinguished visual feature of the 2015 home is the shuttered envelope; part of a climate-responsive design that includes highly insulated walls, floors, and roof as well as the spatial layering of a loggia on the south facade,

perimeter living spaces, and a central service core. The house is built on a plinth that supports an oak deck with a ramp and garden space into which the interior rooms can be extended when the weather allows. As it is a prototype, the team emphasized the importance of adaptability and flexibility in configuring the envelope and rooms to accommodate a wide variety of sites and occupants. The target market for the 2015 home includes private owners at fixed sites, tenants, and those who might use the structure as a mobile home. After touring Germany, the 2015 home was returned to Technische Universität Darmstadt where it is on exhibit as part of the Solar Campus (Solare Lichtwiese) initiative at the university. The energy performance will be monitored over the next several years as the structure is used as a living laboratory and a solar-power plant.

Daylighting and thermal design

Inspired by the modest simplicity of traditional Japanese architecture, the 2015 Home is an elegant shuttered box made of oak that uses form, plan, and section to gather light, air, and views. Amorphous silicon photovoltaic cells on operable louvers (lamellae) cover the east, south, and west facades. The louvers adjust automatically to maintain optimal solar exposures for electrical generation, daylighting, and solar control. The loggia on the south facade of the structure is sidelit and has shuttered bifold doors that open to extend the living area

View of the multi-layered envelope, which includes adjustable bi-fold doors with photovoltiac shutters on the east, south, and west. The second layer includes vacuum-insulated walls on the east and west facades, high-performance quadruple glazing on the north, and triple glazing on the south. The third layer comprises the translucent and adjustable inner walls that enclose the service core in the kitchen–bathroom module.

onto the outdoor terrace. Semi-transparent photovoltaic modules sandwiched between two panes of skylight glazing provide toplighting. The loggia also acts a thermal buffer while allowing occupants to experience the dynamic and changing moods of the days and seasons. In plan, the structure is organized as a series of spatial layers, with a kitchen and bathroom service core located at the center. Adjustable translucent walls on the north side of the bathroom and a movable kitchen work-area allow occupants to modify the size and configuration of the core area. The adaptable living spaces along the perimeter, with fold-out seating and collapsible furniture, receive bilateral sidelighting through fully glazed and operable south and north facades. Solid walls on the east and west sides of the living spaces provide a quiet visual counterpoint to the highly articulated and shuttered facades.

The design team describes the envelope as being "like the skin of an onion," with the outer shuttered louvers serving a range of functions, including shading, passive cooling, daylighting, controlling passive solar gains, and generating electricity with photovoltaic cells.[4] The second layer of the envelope includes vacuum-insulated walls on the east and west facades, high-performance quadruple glazing on the north, and triple glazing on the south. The inner third layer comprises the translucent and adjustable walls that enclose the service core in the kitchen–

bathroom module. Each layer of the envelope was designed to integrate energy performance and thermal comfort, while also fostering a strong relationship to the site and the larger environment beyond.

Energy systems
With passive solar at the heart of the design concept for the 2015 home, the Darmstadt team explains their approach to energy system integration: "As a 'passive house,' the building features a highly insulated thermal envelope and relies mainly on the use of solar irradiation through the south-facing windows and interior gains for heating; it requires only 15 kWh/m^2/yr [4.7 kBtu/sq ft] for space heating (the average of the German building stock requires about 200 kWh/m^2 and new construction in Germany about 60 kWh/m^2/yr [19 kBtu/sq ft]). To prevent overheating, the building features a roof overhang in the south and is surrounded by an envelope of louvered shutters, allowing both cross ventilation and privacy. Thermal mass, which is provided through phase-change materials and is integrated in the east and west walls and the ceiling, buffers temperature swings. This system is complemented by a radiant-cooled ceiling (based on evaporative cooling of water that is pumped over the roof and collected at night). For extreme weather, when these systems may not be sufficient, there is a reversible heat pump, which can heat and cool the air, capture energy from the

waste air, ventilate the space, and use excess energy to heat water for household purposes and to heat the bathroom floor… flat-plate solar thermal collectors complement the heat pump by heating water in an integrated hot-water storage tank."[5]

Solar energy and mechanical systems are thoroughly integrated into the walls, roof, and floor of the 2015 home. The team used three types of photovoltaic systems: amorphous silicon photovoltaic cells on the shuttered louvers, translucent glass-embedded photovoltaic cells in the roof of the loggia, and high-efficiency monocrystalline silicon modules on the roof. The design team explains their decision to use a flat roof for the home: "We will earn the bulk of energy on our flat roof. Forty sunpower SPR-215 panels are installed. Twenty panels are oriented to the south and the other twenty are oriented to the north (slope = 3 degrees)—this creates a wave figure on our roof. The main reason to do so was the transportation issue. We had to save as much construction height as possible and we also wanted to show that a solar roof need not have such an enormous influence on architecture. Compared to the optimal slope and orientation we will only lose 8 percent of efficiency (result of simulations)."[6]

The flooring system is made of prefabricated insulated platforms that visually celebrate the integration and adjustability of the building systems and furniture. The unusual platform modules integrate fold-out furniture, storage, and mechanical systems, as the team explains: "Integrated into the platform are ducts for the electric system, water and ventilation pipes, and also the water tank for our cooling system. It also contains the living and sleeping areas which we call 'cavities.' This is a furniture which is designed and arranged following two principles: floor integration and flexibility."[7] Controls for the environmental systems are operated either manually or automatically. The design team intends the occupants to interact with, and tune, the building for light, air, thermal comfort, and relation to the site, as Hannes Guddat explains: "First of all do passive [start with passive design, so that occupants] operate and open doors and admit the natural light and air. The main feature is the passive design and then active solar in good measure. The second issue was to build a good house that is beautiful, uses good materials, responds to the bioclimate, and fulfills its purpose. The house takes care of you. We make visible how the house works to heat or ventilate and cool."

Next-generation thinking

Innovation and experimentation in solar design and the creative integration of technological systems are central to the mission of the Solar Decathlon. The DOE explains that the purpose of the event is to: "… demonstrate to the public the

Above left
Interior view of the bathroom. Indirect daylight is borrowed through translucent walls on the north. Adjustable walls and a movable kitchen work-area allow occupants to modify the size and configuration of the service core.

Above right
Interior view of the adjustable seating area in the living space. Daylighting and thermal comfort are controlled by the bifold louvered doors and loggia on the south facade, which provides a thermal and luminous buffer zone.

potential of Zero Energy Homes, which produce
as much energy from renewable sources, such
as the sun and wind, as they consume. Even
though the home might be connected to a utility
grid, it has net zero-energy consumption from
the utility provider."[8]

With 20 universities and student teams
competing, there are tremendous opportunities
for hands-on education at the competing
institutions as well as on the Mall in
Washington, DC. Home owners, educators,
members of the building industry, and designers
have an opportunity to see the solar designs
and experiments firsthand. More than 120,000
visitors toured the solar village in October 2007.
As Hannes Guddat explains: "With the Solar
Decathlon, we have to sell the house to people
on the Mall in Washington, DC. The public
dimension is a great challenge. The design has
to go all the way. This is not just a laboratory
house, it is not just performance, and the house
is not a spaceship. It has to be a good house."

During the 2007 award ceremony, US Secretary
of Energy Samuel Bodman concluded: "…
to our decathletes I say, this past week has
belonged to you. You have shown all of us how
the spirit of inventiveness, how inspiration and
knowledge can be put to use solving critical,
real-world problems."[9] The Solar Decathlon
provides an exceptional opportunity for students
of all ages to experience the process of design,
construction, and exhibition under the guidance
of the some of the world's most forward-looking
architects, educators, researchers, and industry
experts. The new generation of solar housing
developed for the Decathlon gives hope for
a future of high-quality housing that runs on
renewable energy and leads to ever-deeper
levels of sustainable living.

Plans, sections, drawings

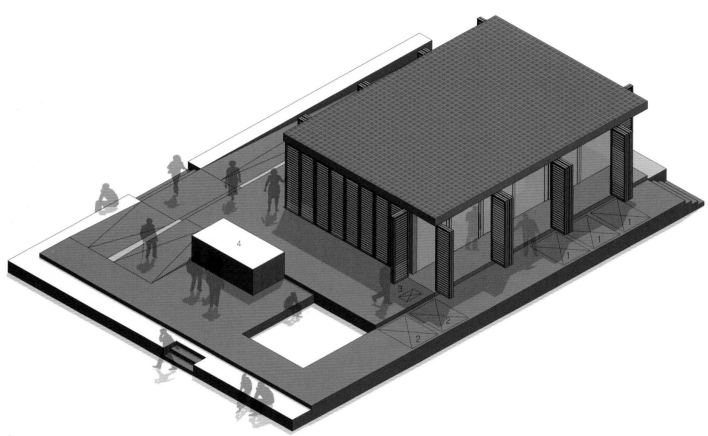

Axonometric view of west and south facades

Axonometric view of the site including the entrance ramp, outdoor landscaping, water feature, and podium.

1. Supported graywater tank beneath deck
2. Supported freshwater tank beneath deck
3. Supported booster station beneath deck
4. Supported podium including batteries and power inverter

1. Living area
2. Alternatively:
   small dining space
3. Expandable
   bathroom
4. Expandable kitchen
5. Bed/sleeping cavity
6. Alternatively:
   big dining space
   or workspace

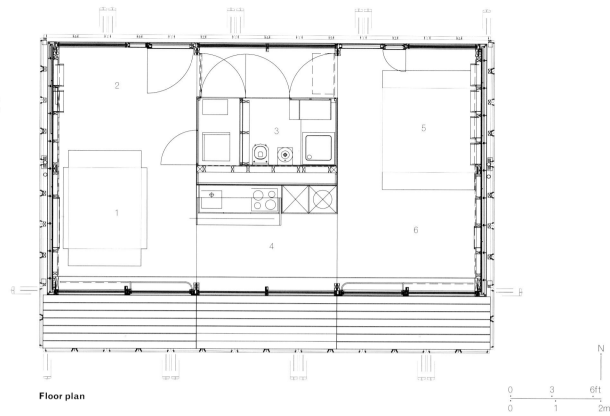

Floor plan

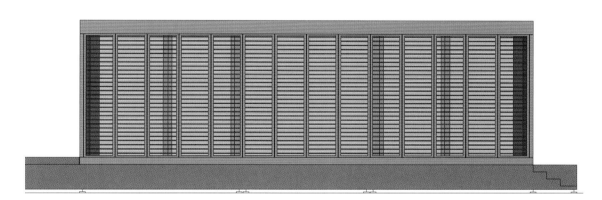

South elevation

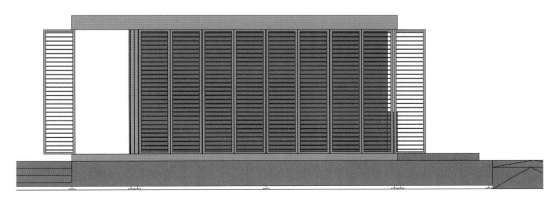

East elevation

Concept sections

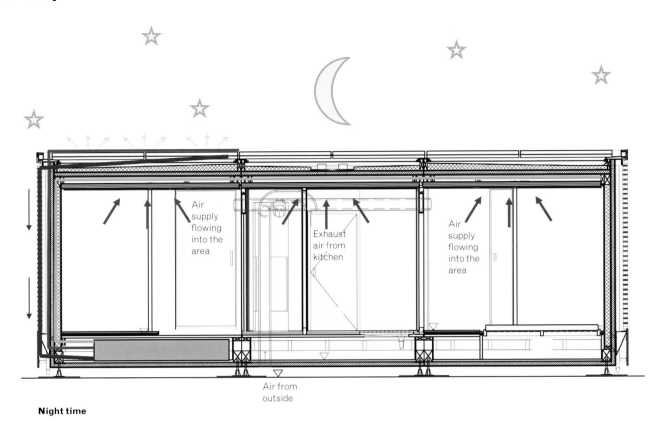

Air supply flowing into the area

Exhaust air from kitchen

Air supply flowing into the area

Air from outside

Night time

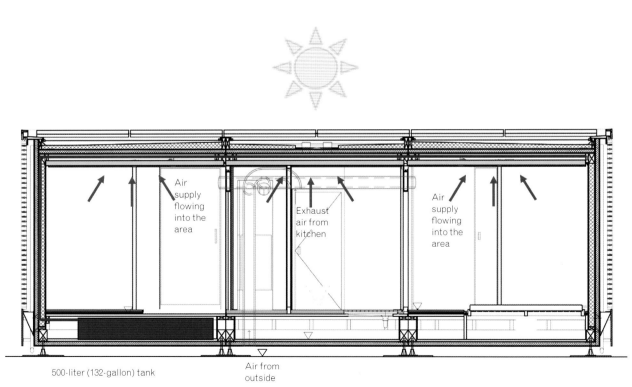

Air supply flowing into the area

Exhaust air from kitchen

Air supply flowing into the area

500-liter (132-gallon) tank

Air from outside

Daytime

Passive systems

- compact building
- highly insulated shell
- overheating protection
- daylight concept

- compact building
- highly insulated shell
- overheating protection
- daylight concept

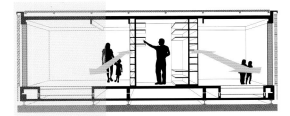

- compact building
- highly insulated shell
- overheating protection
- daylight concept

- compact building
- highly insulated shell
- overheating protection
- daylight concept

- compact building
- highly insulated shell
- overheating protection
- daylight concept

Active systems

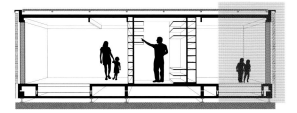

- compact building
- highly insulated shell
- overheating protection
- daylight concept

- photovoltaic modules

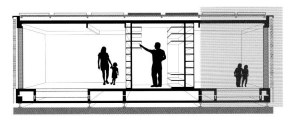

- photovoltaic modules
- solar thermal collectors

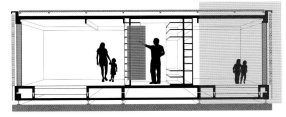

- photovoltaic modules
- solar thermal collectors
- compact device, heat pump, heat-storage tank, heat recovery

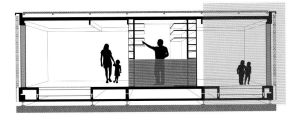

- photovoltaic modules
- solar thermal collectors
- compact device, heat pump, heat-storage tank, heat recovery
- energy-efficient appliances

Wind studies

Project location:
**Darmstadt,
Germany**

Wind data location:
**Frankfurt am Main,
Germany**

Prevailing winds
March
Wind frequency (hours)
Location: Frankfurt am Main,
Germany (50.0°, 8.6°)
Time: 00:00–24:00

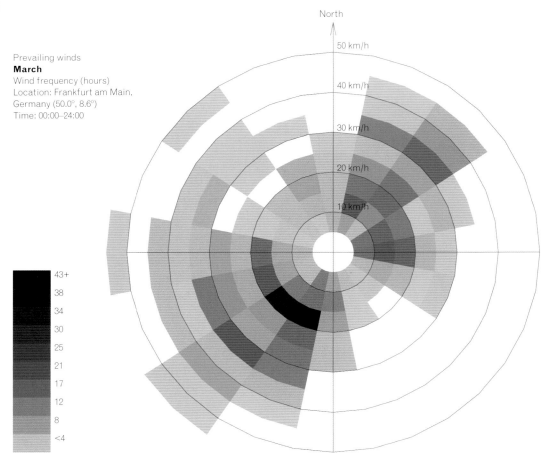

Prevailing winds
September
Wind frequency (hours)
Location: Frankfurt am Main,
Germany (50.0°, 8.6°)
Time: 00:00–24:00

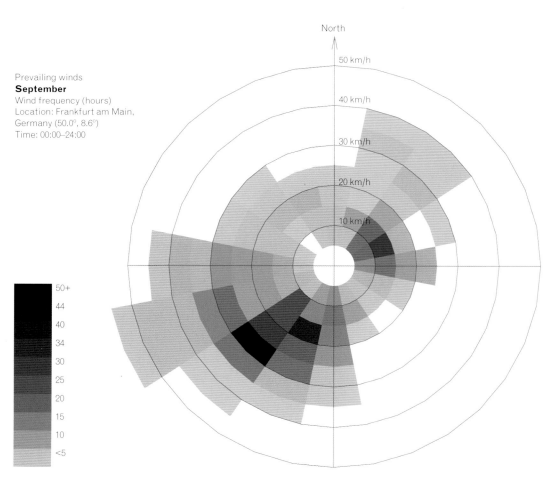

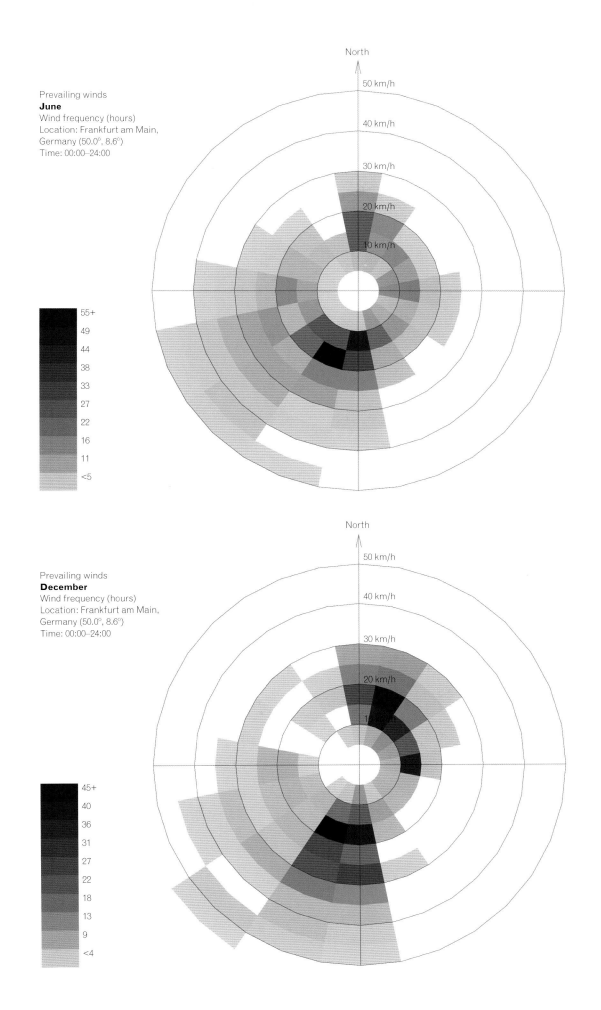

Prevailing winds
June
Wind frequency (hours)
Location: Frankfurt am Main,
Germany (50.0°, 8.6°)
Time: 00:00–24:00

North
50 km/h
40 km/h
30 km/h
20 km/h
10 km/h

55+
49
44
38
33
27
22
16
11
<5

Prevailing winds
December
Wind frequency (hours)
Location: Frankfurt am Main,
Germany (50.0°, 8.6°)
Time: 00:00–24:00

North
50 km/h
40 km/h
30 km/h
20 km/h

45+
40
36
31
27
22
18
13
9
<4

Sunpath case studies

Using responsive envelopes: Year 2015 Prototype Home—Made in Germany

Project location:
**Darmstadt,
Germany**

Latitude:
49° NL

December   **09:00**

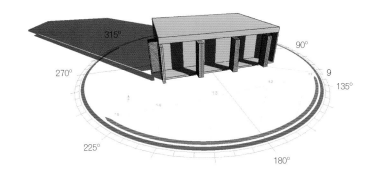

March/September   **09:00**

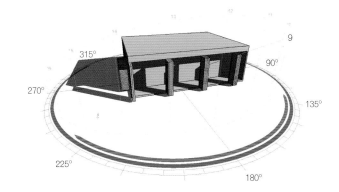

June   **09:00**

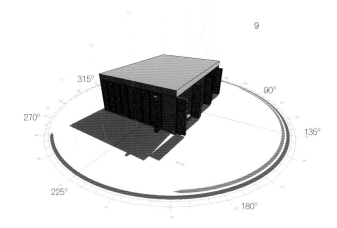

12:00

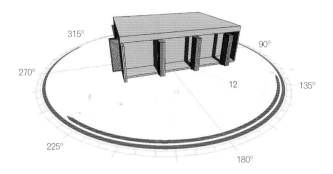

15:00

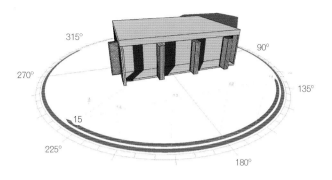

12:00

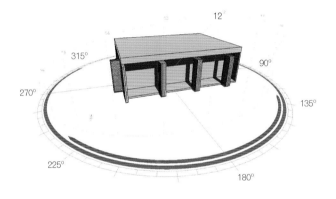

15:00

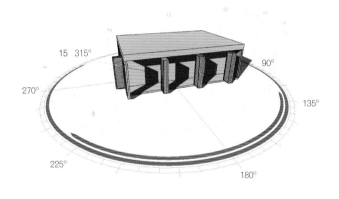

12:00

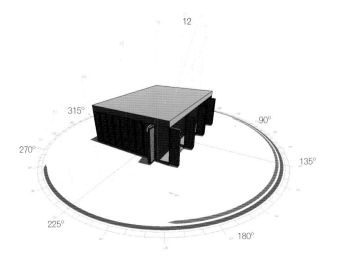

15:00

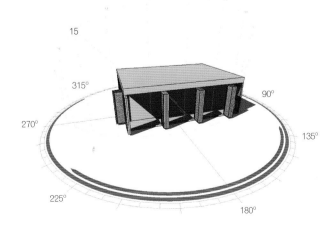

Climate data

Using responsive envelopes: Year 2015 Prototype Home—Made in Germany

Project location:
**Darmstadt,
Germany**

Climate data location:
**Frankfurt am Main,
Germany**

**Diurnal average
temperatures**

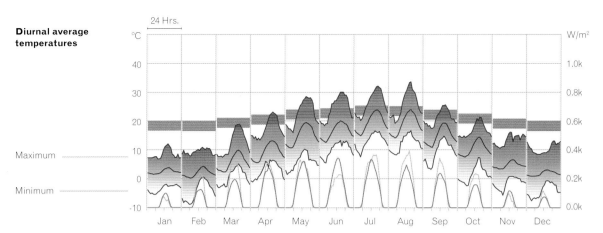

Maximum
Minimum

**Dry bulb
temperatures
1 Jan to 31 Dec**

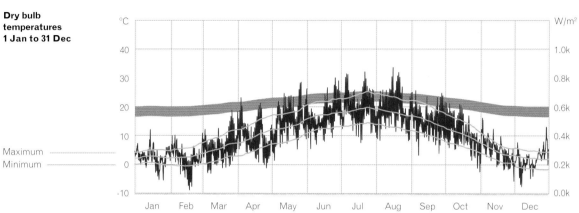

Maximum
Minimum

**Direct radiation
1 Jan to 31 Dec**

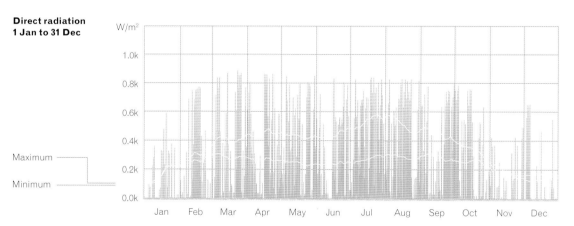

Maximum
Minimum

**Relative humidity
1 Jan to 31 Dec**

Maximum
Minimum

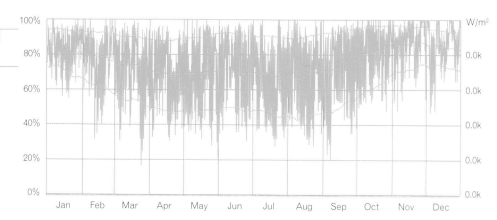

Temperature (°C)

Relative humidity (%)

Wind speed (W/m²)

Direct solar (W/m²)

Diffuse solar (W/m²)

Cloud cover (%)

Thermal neutrality

Design profile

Building profile	Building name:	**Year 2015 Prototype Home—Made in Germany**
	Architect:	Solar Decathlon Team, Technische Universität Darmstadt, www.solardecathlon.de
	Location:	Exhibited in Washington, DC; permanent location in Darmstadt, Germany
	Building type:	Residential
	Square footage:	74 m² (800 sq ft)
Solar design profile	Latitude:	38° NL at Washington, DC; 49° NL at Darmstadt
	Heating Degree Days:	2,847 heating degree days °C (5,301 heating degree days °F) (18°C and 65°F base temperature; average 5 years) at Darmstadt
	Cooling Degree Days:	347 cooling degree days °C (578 cooling degree days °F)
	Conservation strategies:	Reduced plan size, flexible space use and configuration
	Passive solar strategies:	Direct solar gain, daylighting, cross ventilation, solar shutters
	Active solar strategies:	Photovoltaic system, solar hot-water thermal system
	Other renewable energy strategies:	Radiant evaporative cooled ceiling (pumped over the roof and collected at night), thermal mass phase-change materials in east and west walls
	High-performance strategies:	High-performance systems and appliances; high-performance glazing and highly insulated envelope
Performance profile[10]	Total annual building energy consumption:	15 kWh/m² (4.7 kBtu/sq ft) for space heating Energy (heat) requirements (EnEV): 12 kWh/m² (3.824 kBtu/sq ft)
	Total annual on-site energy produced:	Not available
	Size of photovoltaic system:	Roof: 40 Sunpower SPR-215 photovoltaic panels; 9 kWp; Porch: 6 Scheuten glass modules with transparent PV cells; performance: 2 kWp Photovoltaic louvers: 34 frame elements with PV, including 1054 lamellae with PV; performance: east/west: 0.5 kWp, south 1 kWp; (there are a total of 48 frame elements and 1,488 lamellae; some without PV)
	Size of solar thermal system:	Flat-plate solar thermal collectors (size not available)
	Carbon dioxide emissions:	Not available

Endnotes:
Year 2015 Prototype Home–
Made in Germany

1 Technische Universität Darmstadt, "Talking Points," http://www.solardecathlon.org/pdfs/talking_points_07/2007_talking_points_darmstadt.pdf.
2 Solar Decathlon Team, Technische Universität Darmstadt, http://www.solardecathlon.de/index.ohp/home/mission-statement.
3 Solar Decathlon Team, Technische Universität Darmstadt, http://www.solardecathlon.de/index.php/our-house/simulation.
4 Technische Universität Darmstadt, "Talking Points"
5 Ibid.
6 Solar Decathlon Team, Technische Universität Darmstadt, http://www.solardecathlon.de/index.php/our-house/the-shell/.
7 Solar Decathlon Team, Technische Universität Darmstadt, http://www.solardecathlon.de/index.php/our-house/the-platform.
8 U.S. Department of Energy, Solar Decathlon, http://www.
solardecathlon.org/about.html.
9 U.S. Department of Energy, 2007 Solar Decathlon Closing Ceremony and Awards, http://www.energy.gov/news/5648.htm.
10 Technische Universität Darmstadt, "Talking Points"

Chapter 5

Expressing an ecological aesthetic

"How sense-luscious the world is. In summer, we can be decoyed out of bed by the sweet smell of the air soughing through our bedroom window. The sun playing across the tulle curtains gives them a moiré effect, and they seem to shudder with light… There is no way in which to understand the world without first detecting it through the radar-net of our senses… We need to return to feeling the textures of life."[1]
DIANE ACKERMAN, *A Natural History of the Senses*

"We do not need more economic growth as much as we need to relearn the ancient lessons of generosity, as trustees for a moment between those who preceded us and those who will follow. Our greatest needs have nothing to do with the possessions of things but rather with heart, wisdom, thankfulness, and generosity of spirit. And these virtues are part of larger ecologies that embrace spirit, body, and mind—the beginning of design."[2]
DAVID ORR, *The Nature of Design*

The integration of poetic and pragmatic considerations is a distinguishing feature of the most innovative and elegant design approaches to zero-energy and zero-carbon architecture; revealing that it is possible to respond to urgent ecological challenges while inspiring us through aesthetics to live more sustainably. Architect Lawrence Scarpa, of Pugh+Scarpa Architects, emphasized in an interview that aesthetic issues and the importance of good design should not be underestimated: "An energy hog is better than an energy-efficient building that no one loves. Don't worry about 'sustainable design,' focus on design." Aesthetics, beauty, human experience, health, and well-being are just as important as are a building's ecological footprint, energy profile, greenhouse gas emissions, and carbon reductions. Yet, given the urgency of current ecological concerns, why do aesthetics and beauty matter? The answer, as Scarpa suggests, is that people will be more likely to seek out and accept sustainable architecture when they love its beauty and good design.

Dated notions of a solar aesthetics and poor design are complicit in a resistance to the widespread adoption of solar design. Many architects, fearing narrow categorization, shy away from the idea of solar architecture given that it can still evoke images of the oftentimes experimental and occasionally outrageous solar buildings of the 1960s and 1970s. The new generation of solar architecture, however, transcends the narrow architectural expression of the past. These new designs integrate essential solar principles and precepts (such as attention to building orientation, appropriate room depth and height, methods of solar control, effective material characteristics and colors, and response to seasonal change) into formal expressions that remain diverse and open to creative interpretation.

In his paper on solar aesthetics, Ralph Knowles, professor emeritus at the University of Southern California, suggests that a true architecture of the sun (and wind) finds its inspirations in nature: "If we confront aesthetic questions of solar form, we must begin with nature."[3] Architect David Pearson agrees, suggesting that nature remains one of the architect's greatest teachers and sources for design inspiration: "Patterns and forms in nature, such as the spiral and fractal, are products of internal laws of growth and of the action of external forces, such as sun, wind, and water. Architects learn to use natural forms from observing living structures: trees, bones, shells, wings, webs, eyes, petals, scales, and microscopic creatures… They are the very forms of life and growth and have been key inspirations…"[4] This is not to suggest that the next generation of sustainable buildings will look like shells or wings (although they may), but rather that the forces of nature will deeply shape their designs.

Aesthetic experiences can have a profound impact on our understanding of nature and our place within the larger ecological web. Likewise, aesthetically pleasing architecture can enhance our relationship with the environment and foster ecological awareness. The movement of light in space, the textures and play of shadows, the weathering of materials all help us engage nature through time and place. How might we develop a design aesthetic that

View through a bamboo screen into the central courtyard of the Sino–Italian Ecological and Energy Efficient Building (SIEEB) at the Tsinghua University, Beijing, China.

honors basic ecological principles while celebrating the poetic and expressive qualities of the architecture, space, materials, and design elements? This is the question that faces designers as they go beyond the important emphasis on ecological performance and quantitative assessment to also face the challenge of balancing critical empirical data with more elusive and poetic design intentions concerning the ambiance of space and the sensuousness of luminous and thermal qualities at all scales of design.

It is through our senses of vision, touch, smell, hearing, and taste (as well as kinesthetic movement) that we intimately engage with architecture and the broader world. Author Diane Ackerman emphasizes these connections in *A Natural History of the Senses*: "There is no way in which to understand the world without first detecting it through the radar-net of our senses. We can extend our senses with the help of microscope, stethoscope, robot, satellite, hearing aid, eyeglasses, and such, but what is beyond our senses we cannot know. Our senses define the edge of consciousness…"[5] The next

generation of sustainable design delights the senses, elevates the spirit, and deeply reconnects us to the ecological world. We can look at all scales of design to reconsider how the building— through its orientation, massing, section, window size and detailing, envelope and layers, and material properties—can enhance our ecological connections and understanding. Choreographing the changing qualities of light, designing for seasonal migrations within spaces, adjusting our living patterns to diurnal cycles, framing special views, and enabling users to modify the building envelope are just a few ways in which to engage the body and senses in the experiential dimensions of ecological response. As we tune ourselves to the buildings we live in, we also tune ourselves to the rhythms of nature and the particular ecological moods and qualities of place. Experiential dimensions of architecture not only connect us to our world, but also help to reveal the ecological consequences of our actions. In *The Spell of the Sensuous*, author David Abram suggests that it is primarily through our senses that we notice and can begin

to change our behaviors on behalf of the Earth: "Only as we come close to our senses, and begin to trust, once again, the nuanced intelligence of our sensing bodies, do we begin to notice and respond to the subtle logos of the land. The senses, that is, are the primary way that the Earth has of informing our thoughts and of guiding our actions… it is only at the scale of our direct, sensory interactions with the land around us that we can appropriately notice and respond to the immediate needs of the living world."[6] How can architectural design encourage us to care for the Earth, to live more lightly, and to take actions which have positive ecological consequences? Greater ecological awareness may begin with simple design strategies that engage our senses to enhance our awareness of the rhythms of nature.

Living with the cycles of the sun, wind, seasons, and climate has compelling experiential implications and also helps us begin to understand the energy and resource implications of our lifestyles. Answers to our ecological challenges lie, to a great extent, in reframing

View of the south terraces and central courtyard at SIEEB. The building captures the eye and the imagination through the dynamic gestures of its multi-layered facades, adjustable glass louvers, photovoltaic shading devices, and staggered terraces.

the patterns of our behaviors and establishing more sustainable lifestyles. Architectural design can encourage us to care for the Earth, to live more lightly, and to take actions that have positive ecological consequences by framing our ecological relationships in positive ways. Awareness of these relationships may begin with simple design strategies that create new architectural rituals and enhance our connections to the rhythms of nature. Whether at the modest scale of the window, or through the overall building massing and form, architectural design provides unlimited opportunities to foster greater ecological awareness and concern.

The following case studies illustrate how the sun and wind can deeply shape architectural form, aesthetic expression, and human experience. The Steinhude Sea Recreational Facility by Randall Stout Architects and the Sino–Italian Ecological and Energy Efficient Building (SIEEB) by Mario Cucinella Architects reveal that the next generation of solar architecture embodies a "deep ecological aesthetic," which goes beyond surface and decorative expression to

inform all scales of design thinking. The projects suggest that an ecological aesthetic is not about style or architectural language, but rather about how architecture engages ecological and environmental forces. Both projects marry qualitative and quantitative design investigations; coupling state-of-the-art quantitative computer analyses with seemingly old-fashioned qualitative physical modeling, diagramming, and sketching. The distinct architectural expressions of Steinhude and SIEEB also show that an ecological aesthetic transcends style, revealing diversity as boundless as the human imagination.

Randall Stout and Mario Cucinella Architects first set out to design good architecture. Aesthetic experience and design quality are integrally woven into the ecological questions and goals of the projects. Stout and Cucinella demonstrate that a comprehensive approach to solar design is essential in marrying the ecological and technological needs of the projects while elevating the design and aesthetic opportunities. Architect and author Christian Schittich reflects

on the inspirational promise of the sun in forming a new architectural language: "If we do not succeed in bringing about a lasting change to our wasteful lifestyle and drastically diminish energy consumption, the only possible solution will be to rely overwhelmingly on renewable energy resources in the near future. True solar architecture, therefore, becomes a necessity. It will be far more than simply a new style. Its principles will become the basis for all building. It will change the face of architecture. Integrating the technical and functional requirements of solar architecture into an aesthetically satisfying comprehensive concept presents both a challenge and an opportunity for architecture."[7] The Steinhude Sea Recreational Facility and SIEEB projects demonstrate that response to the sun and wind are primary means of supporting design excellence while also engaging the senses, connecting to the environment, and meeting ecological goals. Both projects demonstrate how the sun and wind can give rise to new formal and expressive qualities in architectural design.

Left
Off-site fabrication of the roof structure for the Steinhude Sea Recreational Facility in Steinhude, Germany. To accommodate the sensitive ecology of the site and the limits on vehicle access, the facility was prefabricated in a factory on the mainland. The panelized system was transported to the island and erected by barge-mounted cranes.

Left
On-site construction of the Steinhude Sea Recreational Facility.

Endnotes:

1 Diane Ackerman, *A Natural History of the Senses* (New York: Vantage Books, 1990), xv, xviii.
2 David Orr, *The Nature of Design: Ecology, Culture, and Human Intention* (Oxford: Oxford University Press, 2002), 32.
3 Ralph Knowles, Solar Aesthetics (Ralph Knowles, 2008), 2; http://www-rcf.usc.edu/~rknowles/aesthetics/aesthetics.html.
4 David Pearson, *New Organic Architecture: The Breaking Wave* (London: Gaia Books Limited, 2001), 48.
5 Diane Ackerman, xv.
6 David Abram, *The Spell of the Sensuous* (New York: Vantage Books, 1997), 268.
7 Christian Schittich, "Shell, Skin, Materials," *Building Skins: Concepts Layers Materials* (Basel: Birkhäuser, 2001), 11.

Steinhude Sea Recreational Facility
Steinhude, Germany
Randall Stout Architects and Archimedes GmbH

"We did not 'bring' an architectural vocabulary to the project. The energy needs tell me what the building looks like. The end result is new to the world. It doesn't look like any other building. We let concepts of harvesting energy inform and inspire design. There are no boundaries to how far ideas of energy can go. It can help create your own signature architecture."[1]
Randall Stout, *Randall Stout Architects*

South-facing clerestory windows and east facade of the observation tower, which is the visual and physical highlight of the building for many visitors. The gently curved building is sited to minimize ecological impacts and to protect a neighboring bird sanctuary, while taking advantage of expansive northern views over the Steinhude Meer and harvesting on-site solar energy.

Design intentions
Designed as part of Expo 2000 in Hanover, Germany, the Steinhude Sea Recreational Facility is a model of energy independence and self-sufficiency that celebrates the exposition's ecological theme of "Humankind, Nature, and Technology." It is located 30 km (18.6 miles) northwest of Hanover on a 4.6-ha (11.4-acre) island (the Badeinsel) in the Naturpark Steinhuder Meer, and is surrounded by a nature preserve. The recreational facility consists of a lifeguard station, boathouse, and storage facility, and a public building with a café, restrooms and showers, exhibitions, and observation area.

Randall Stout Architects (RSA) of Los Angeles, California, and Archimedes GmbH of Bad Oeynhausen, Germany, designed the facility to be energy self-reliant and therefore all its energy needs are met on site through passive and active solar systems and other renewable energy technologies. In an interview, Randall Stout emphasized the importance of solar design in framing the intentions and goals for the project: "At Badeinsel, I treated the Steinhude building as an island sunbather. By carefully orienting the building on the site it was possible to maximize the solar potential; every south-facing surface is designed to harvest solar energy." With the sun and renewable energy at the heart of their design thinking, Randall Stout and the project team used passive heating, cooling, and lighting along with high-performance systems,

materials, and construction details. These features were integrated with renewable energy from a photovoltaic system, a co-generation microturbine, and solar hot-water heating. As RSA explain, the integration of design through multiple scales and systems enables the building to be energy independent: "These systems meet all of the lighting and power needs for the building, recharge a fleet of eight photovoltaic-powered boats, and also produce excess electricity that is sold back to the utility grid."[2] The recreational facility meets net zero-energy goals while preserving site ecology and enriching the experience of visitors. Although modest in scale, Steinhude demonstrates a new level of solar performance and design excellence in which architecture has the potential to meet the energy needs of buildings, the community, and even the world beyond.

Climate and site
The Steinhude Sea Recreational Facility is located on previously disturbed land on the island, which is at the south end of Steinhude Meer, a large lake of 8 by 4.5 km (4.9 by 2.7 miles). The facility was built on a jetty that was designed to reduce erosion from the wind and lake currents. It is on the northern side of the island with unobstructed access to the lake and deep water for boats. The gently curved building is sited to minimize ecological impacts and to protect a neighboring bird sanctuary, as well as to take advantage of expansive northern

views over the Steinhude Meer while harvesting on-site solar energy. The climate of the region is sufficiently moderate in the winter and summer to support passive and active solar strategies. The average low temperature in January is 0.7°C (33°F) and an average high temperature is 17°C (63°F) in July. Seasonal variations in sun, wind, and climate shaped the design and technological approaches to the facility.

Randall Stout explains the varied approaches to solar at the facility: "We are thinking of orientation (site plan), sun-angle altitudes (overhangs), materials (opacity, transparency, and translucency), and fenestration (daylighting) from the very first stages of design throughout the project. In order to be successful, sustainable strategies must be synthesized and incorporated from the beginning." Stout elaborated on his solar concept in an interview for Art and Architecture Online: "This building is rather interesting in the sense that every elevation is so dramatically different. It is hard sometimes when we talk about a project and its origins, to talk of any one imagery or characteristic, because it evolves from side to side as you move around the building. The overall gesture has something to do with a perhaps reclining sunbather, a kind of figure stretched out on the beach and getting a lot of south exposure there."[3] RSA explain that each activity area was carefully sited to take advantage of the unique programmatic concerns as well as the site conditions and views: "Element

locations are determined by their function. The café and lifeguard areas are positioned for beach and marina views. The observation deck, 9 m [30 ft] in height, allows unobstructed views with panoramic graphics panels which identify shoreline landmarks and the historic Wilhelmstein Island… Dramatic night-lighting effects are created by ambient spill light from the building, emphasizing the building form… The southern edge of the building roofline is held unusually low so that it appears to emerge from the landscape. The roof form is curved toward the earth berms to create harmonious lines between built and natural forms."[4]

While access to solar and renewable energy were site priorities, the designers also carefully managed water at the building and site scales through permeable landscaping and a graywater system that is integrated into the terraced landscape. The graywater is used for the restrooms, while a sewer system is connected back to the mainland to eliminate potential problems with the high water table. The project sought to minimize impacts on the native ecology and to celebrate the beauty and unique ecology of the site. The island presented other ecological challenges that influenced the design and construction of the building. RSA explain that the sensitive ecology of the site and the limits on vehicle access led them to prefabricate the facility on the mainland: "The low load capacity of the bridge to the mainland meant that getting

Exterior view of the north and west facades with the observation tower and public spaces. A walkway cuts through the center of the lower portion of the building, inviting views of the landscape to weave through the building. Translucent polycarbonate panels clad the western facade, providing diffused daylight and revealing the wood-frame structure beneath.

heavy equipment to the island would be difficult and the delicate nature of the island-edge condition suggested that the presence of such equipment would be very detrimental to the site. Therefore, the decision was made to fabricate the building in a factory on the mainland and bring it to the island as a panelized system that could be erected from barge-mounted cranes at the shore edge."[5]

Daylighting and thermal design

Steinhude is not a classic passive solar building. The facility is rotated 180 degrees from the standard southward orientation for solar and instead opens to the north. The northern views created distinct design opportunities in response to differing solar criteria in each orientation. The south facades and roofs are shaped to gather sun and wind, while the northern facade is designed as an overlook to the lake and surrounding landscape. On the south roof there are roof-integrated photovoltaic cells along with evacuated tube solar collectors to produce hot water. The south, west, and north facades have translucent polycarbonate envelopes that admit indirect daylight. Simple roof overhangs are designed to provide seasonal solar control. South skylights and extensive areas of north-facing transparent glazing are used on the observation tower to celebrate the panoramic views of the lake and surrounding nature preserve.

Although Steinhude operates year-round, there

is modest need for heating. Passive solar was not a heating priority; instead the facility uses a ground-source heat pump. The passive design favors natural ventilation and daylighting during the more popular cooling season. Active solar systems for electricity and hot water are well integrated, and daylight is admitted through sidelighting and skylights that provide abundant illumination throughout the building. Natural ventilation creates passive cooling through slots, operable windows, and the stack effect. In contrast to the expansive openings on the west and north glazing, the south facade is terraced to accommodate alternating layers of photovoltaic panels and clerestory windows that cascade to the south.

In plan, the building curves gently along an east–west axis. Visitor facilities and staff spaces are located in the lower linear portion of the two-story building and the three-story observation tower rises from the north corner. The observation tower is the visual and physical highlight of the building for many visitors. With floor-to-ceiling glazing, it is crowned with a curved roof and observation deck. For visitors and local residents, the tower provides a seasonal lookout to track the changing weather, bird migrations, and activities on the lake and in the nature preserve. Operable windows facilitate natural ventilation from the prevailing easterly and westerly breezes during the summer months. A walkway cuts through the center of the lower

portion of the building, inviting the landscape and views to weave through the building. Visitors typically approach the facility from the western side of the island, with the festive undulating roof and west walls of the visitor building providing a welcoming entry. Translucent polycarbonate panels clad the western facade, providing diffused daylight and revealing the wood-frame structure beneath. Acting as a beacon at night, the luminous envelope is electrically lit to celebrate the transition of light from day to night. An open plan and light-reflective surfaces at the entry create a visually dynamic space that changes with the weather and seasons.

Human experience is central to the design of Steinhude: "RSA takes great care in creating forms that are inviting and artistic without being static. Light, shadow, form, and materials all contribute to shaping a dynamic architecture that heightens one's awareness of space and sense of discovery: the sequence of rooms and views emphasizes the experience of the building rather than the display of form. Users are not a passive audience on a staged set but actors in their own unfolding space."[6] RSA were particularly aware of the seasonal qualities of the thermal and luminous environment at Steinhude: "An interior dominated by diffuse natural light and natural cross ventilation creates a healthy indoor environment, while the creative use of solar energy technologies contributes to visually striking patterns of light and shadow. The building

has spaces that provide soothing relief from the hot summer sun and other spaces that feel like the German tradition of 'wintergarten,' flooded with light and warmth in colder weather."[7] Surrounding the building is native landscaping, a dock, and sitting areas and terraces, which provide varied qualities and choices of outdoor space depending on whether a visitor seeks a watery outlook, direct sunlight, or a shady refuge.

Energy systems

Passive systems are used for natural ventilation and daylighting, while active renewable energy systems provide domestic hot water, space heating, and electricity via solar hot-water collectors, photovoltaic panels, a ground-source geothermal heat pump, and a seed-oil fueled co-generation microturbine. The 153-m² (1,646-sq ft) photovoltaic system produces 60,000 kWh of energy annually, with an equivalent 60,000 kg (132,277 lb) yearly reduction in carbon dioxide emissions.[8]

Randall Stout emphasizes that the energy performance benchmarks extended beyond the building: "This project is not only energy self-sufficient but also recharges a fleet of eight solar-powered boats and generates surplus power to sell back to the utility grid. The photovoltaic panels distribute cells within an insulated glazing unit, allowing the photovoltaic panels to serve as roof, daylight provider, and electricity generator in one application. The panels (with inverter and batteries) provide all of

Left
With floor-to-ceiling glazing, the observation tower is crowned by a curved roof and observation deck from which to observe the changing weather, bird migrations, and other activities on the lake and in the nature reserve.

Right
Detail of the curved roof of the observation tower and the south-facing clerestory windows, with a distant view of the lake and surrounding nature reserve and recreational park.

Left
Interior view of the public restroom showing the dynamic play of light and shadow cast by the glazed photovoltaic roof.

Right
Translucent polycarbonate panels provide diffused daylight and reveal the wood-frame structure beneath. Acting as a beacon at night, the luminous envelope is electrically lit to celebrate the transition of light from day to night.

the building's lighting needs. Domestic hot-water needs are met by a solar hot-water collection system (cylindrical glass-tube array within a dual glazed frame)… A co-generation microturbine fueled by rapeseed oil provides back-up power for extended cloudy days and supplemental power for peak loads associated with the café equipment. High standards of energy conservation, including natural ventilation, daylighting, thermal-mass storage, and building automation, reduce power consumption… Portions of the building are zoned primarily for summer use and are not mechanically climate controlled."[9] High-performance construction details, including insulated glazing and insulated polycarbonate panels, ensure optimal thermal performance. Fundamental to the project's success were a reduction in initial energy loads and the subsequent reduction in overall energy consumption achieved through programming, design, and efficient systems.

Although Steinhude is not a classic passive solar-heated building, it does successfully use the site, orientation, massing, and section to balance seasonal needs for daylight, natural ventilation, and active solar electric and water systems. The project accentuates creative responses to the potential challenges facing designers in the integration of passive solar design and renewable energy technologies, and also illustrates the expressive formal potential of architecture as a net energy producer.

Next-generation thinking

The Steinhude Sea Recreational Facility demonstrates that architecture—through its physical design strategies, spatial characteristics, systems integration, and expressive qualities—can meaningfully inform visitors about the forces of nature and the specific ecology of a region. The passive and active design strategies provide hands-on demonstrations and compelling architectural experiences that teach visitors how a building can generate its own energy and live in relation to the land. Randall Stout explains the unique design and technical opportunities at Steinhude: "Projects like Steinhude are rare, where the client and architect have equally high ambitions and priorities for solar energy. Our hope for future projects is to capture the essence of integrated solar design, so that it inspires the concept of a building and is a complete visual and technical response to climate and environment. In this way it becomes part of the architect's larger challenge, not just to build but to provide a meaningful translation of social and cultural issues in the time in which we work."

An interactive and inclusive design process is another important feature of Randall Stout's work. He explains how the team approaches design: "We listen intently to clients and ask numerous questions to understand their goals and philosophy, as well as their program and functional relationships. Finding the ideal functional diagram is basic to a successful project. Therefore, the firm

often generates several model studies that relate to program distribution on the site, functional adjacencies, contextual issues, and massing before the form studies are begun. Neither our formal solutions nor the design references are premeditated; rather, they are the result of a highly involved study technique that utilizes models, computers, sketches, analytic diagrams, and photography, while simultaneously engaging in an intensive dialog and relationship with the client and the site."[10]

In addition, the team uses a variety of physical and computer modeling techniques to understand both the quantitative and qualitative dimensions of the design: "A significant part of our design process relies upon the use of models at various scales to address everything from how the building fits within the neighborhood to full-size mock-ups of construction details... Integrating the clients and users as members of the design team results in an exciting aesthetic variety. The models often range from simple wood blocks that represent massing to refined assemblies including interiors and internal lighting to create nighttime images... These models, despite being 'process' models, serve well to build client support and community enthusiasm for projects. They also allow the engineer/consultant and contractor team to clearly visualize the project, thereby improving quality control in construction documents and clarifying bidders' understanding of the construction requirements. When possible,

we photograph the models, as we find the camera has a distinct way of forcing the eye to realistically evaluate visual compositions from the user's position on the ground plane."[11]

New computer tools and prefabrication processes enabled RSA to have the Steinhude Recreational Facility built without conventional construction documents: "... Instead, it was constructed as a panelized assembly in a factory from the three-dimensional computer databases that were created at the end of the design development phase. It was our first project for which the contractor submitted the entire building as something of a shop drawing. In the factory setting it was possible for portions of the project to be uniquely and economically fabricated by computer-/robotic-driven cutting and assembly devices in a process coming to be known as mass customization."[12] Innovative approaches to both the design and construction processes enabled the team to extend architectural, technical, and aesthetic boundaries.

Steinhude also reveals that there are new aesthetic and experiential opportunities for solar design. Randall Stout explains that there was no predetermined aesthetic when the team initiated the design: "We did not 'bring' an architectural vocabulary to the project. The energy needs tell me what the building looks like. The end result is new to the world. It doesn't look like any

Aerial view of the roof and south clerestory windows. The roof is made of photovoltaic panels that distribute cells within an insulated glazing unit, allowing the panels to serve as a roof, daylight provider, and electricity generator in one single structure.

The south facades and roofs are shaped to gather sun and wind. Roof-integrated photovoltaic cells and evacuated tube solar collectors produce hot water while simple roof overhangs are designed to provide seasonal solar control. The northern facade overlooks the lake and surrounding landscape. Expansive areas of transparent glazing celebrate the panoramic views of the lake and nature reserve.

other building. We let concepts of harvesting energy inform and inspire design. There are no boundaries to how far ideas of energy can go. It can help create your own signature architecture."

The Steinhude Sea Recreational Facility is a pioneering project on many fronts. As one of the first contemporary energy self-reliant buildings of the twenty-first century, it shows the design promise of a new solar architecture.

Plans, sections, model studies

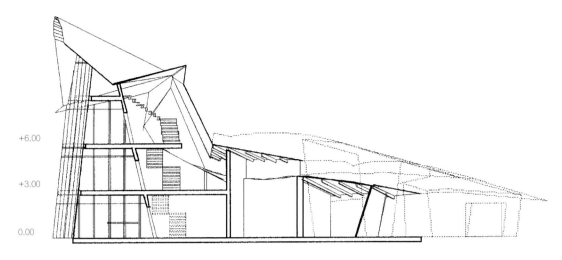

+6.00

+3.00

0.00

Section

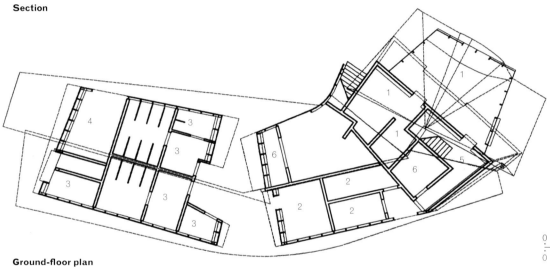

Ground-floor plan

1. Café
2. Lifeguard facilities
3. Public toilets and showers
4. Boathouse
5. Circulation corridor
6. Mechanical spaces

N

| 0 | | 15ft | | 30ft |
| 0 | | 5 | | 10m |

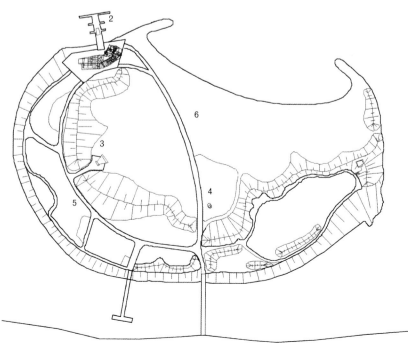

Site plan

N

| 0 | 150 | 300ft |
| 0 | 50 | 100m |

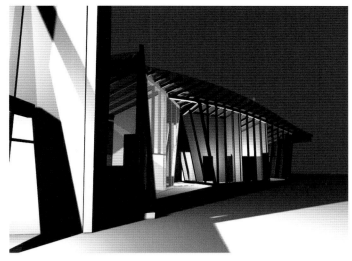

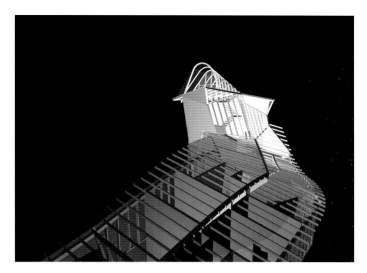

Computer models showing structural framing for **CNC** fabrication

Final design building model

Final design site model

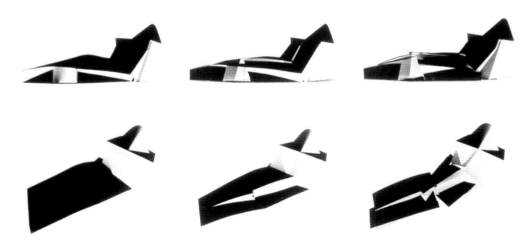

Enhanced photographs of physical models used to study solar access to roof surfaces

Wind studies

Project location:
**Steinhude,
Germany**

Wind data location:
Hanover, Germany

Prevailing winds
March
Wind frequency (hours)
Location: Hanover, Germany (52.5°, 9.7°)
Time: 00:00–24:00

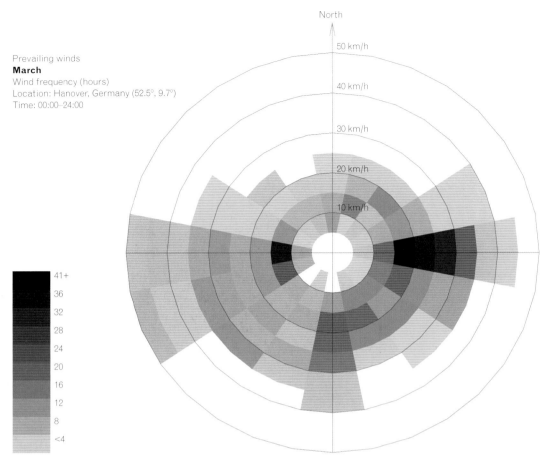

Prevailing winds
September
Wind frequency (hours)
Location: Hanover, Germany (52.5°, 9.7°)
Time: 00:00–24:00

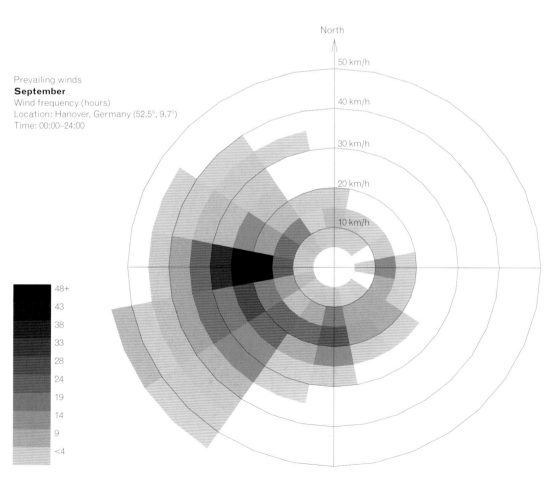

North

50 km/h

40 km/h

30 km/h

20 km/h

10 km/h

Prevailing winds
June
Wind frequency (hours)
Location: Hanover, Germany (52.5°, 9.7°)
Time: 00:00–24:00

39+
35
31
27
23
19
15
11
7
<3

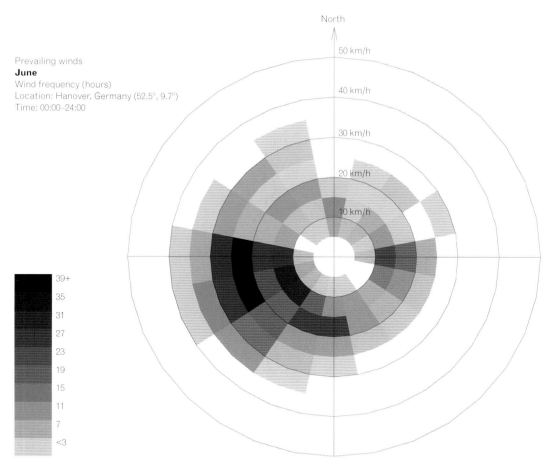

North

50 km/h

40 km/h

30 km/h

20 km/h

10 km/h

Prevailing winds
December
Wind frequency (hours)
Location: Hanover, Germany (52.5°, 9.7°)
Time: 00:00–24:00

42+
37
33
29
25
21
16
12
8
<4

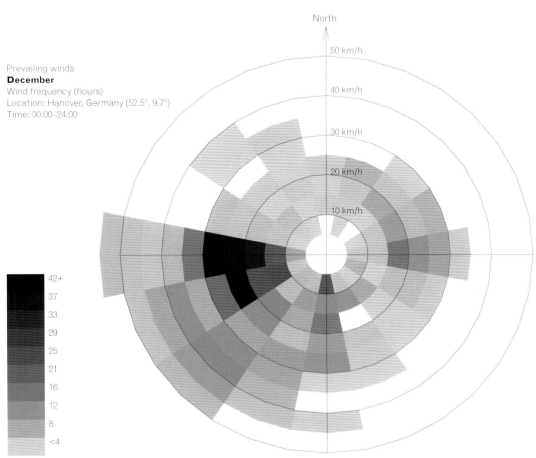

Sunpath case studies

Project location:
**Steinhude,
Germany**
Latitude: 52° NL

December

09:00

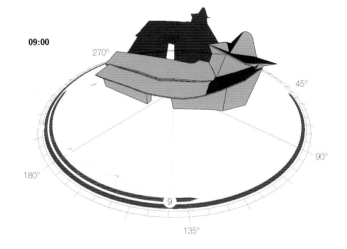

March/September

09:00

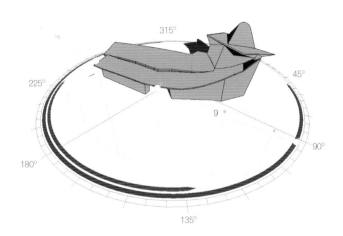

June

09:00

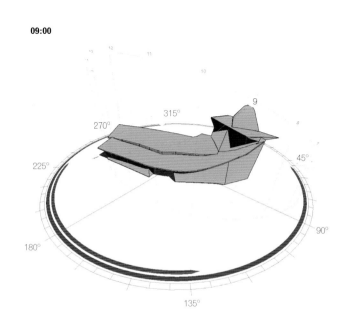

12:00

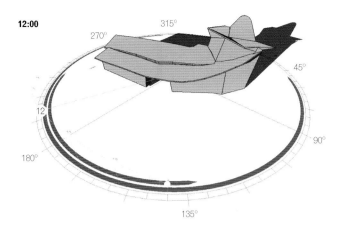

15:00

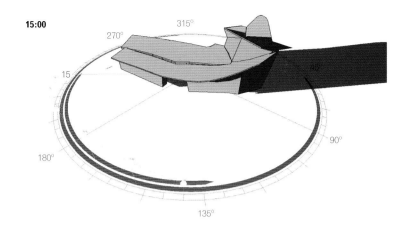

12:00

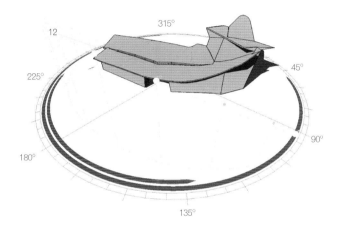

15:00

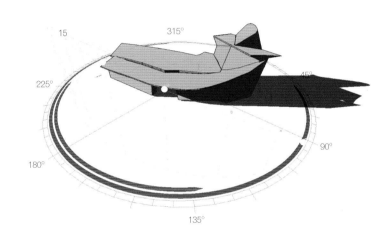

12:00

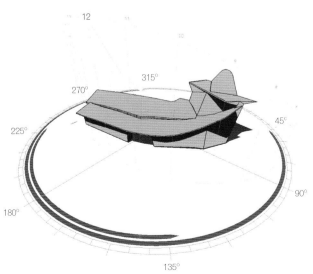

15:00

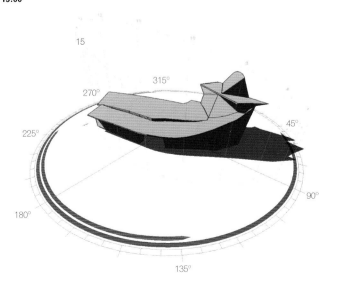

Climate data

Expressing an ecological aesthetic: Steinhude Sea Recreational Facility

Project location:
Steinhude, Germany

Climate data location:
Hanover, Germany

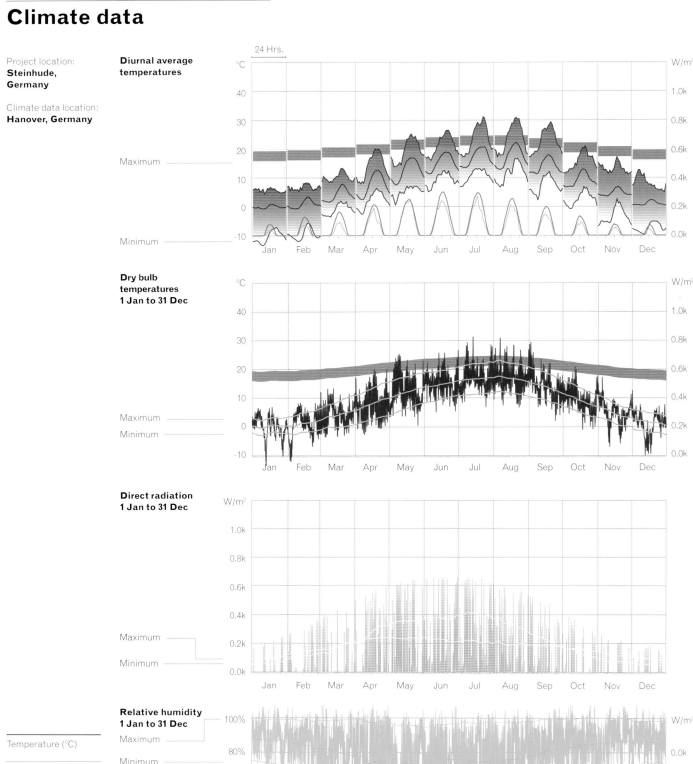

Diurnal average temperatures

Dry bulb temperatures
1 Jan to 31 Dec

Direct radiation
1 Jan to 31 Dec

Relative humidity
1 Jan to 31 Dec

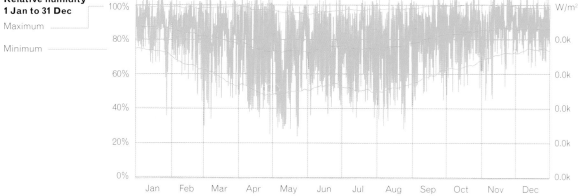

Temperature (°C)

Relative humidity (%)

Wind speed (W/m²)

Direct solar (W/m²)

Diffuse solar (W/m²)

Cloud cover (%)

Thermal neutrality

Design profile

Building profile	Building name:	**Steinhude Sea Recreational Facility**
	Architect:	Randall Stout Architects, Los Angeles, California, USA, www.stoutarc.com and Archimedes GmbH, Bad Oeynhausen, Germany
	Location:	Steinhude, Germany
	Building type:	Recreational
	Square footage:	296 m² (3,190 sq ft)

Solar design profile	Latitude:	52° NL
	Heating Degree Days:	3,095 heating degree days °C (5,758 heating degree days °F) (18 °C and 65 °F base temperature; average 5 years; Hanover, Germany)
	Cooling Degree Days:	216 cooling degree days °C (358 cooling degree days °F)
	Conservation strategies:	Modest size, thermal zoning, prefabricated off site
	Passive solar strategies:	Daylighting, natural ventilation, direct gain passive solar, exterior shading, thermal mass storage
	Active solar strategies:	Grid-tied photovoltaic system, solar hot-water thermal system for domestic hot water
	Other renewable energy strategies:	Ground-source geothermal heat pump, rapeseed-oil fueled co-generation microturbine
	High-performance strategies:	Building automation system, insulated glazing, insulated polycarbonate panels, mineral-fiber insulation, zoning for summer use (portions of building are not mechanically controlled)

Performance profile[13][14]	Total annual building energy consumption:	None (not including the co-generation microturbine fueled by rapeseed oil which provides back-up power for extended cloudy days and supplemental power for peak loads)
	Total annual on-site energy produced (from renewables):	203.8 kWh/m² (64.3 kBtu/sq ft)
	Size of photovoltaic system (wind and other renewable energy sources on site):	60,000 kWh/yr. photovoltaic system; 153 m² (1,646 sq ft). A co-generation microturbine fueled by rapeseed oil provides back-up power for extended cloudy days and supplemental power for peak loads
	Size of solar thermal system:	Evacuated tube solar hot-water heating for domestic hot water (size not available)
	Carbon dioxide emissions:	60,000 kg CO_2/yr (132,277 lb) reduction

Endnotes:
Steinhude Sea Recreational Facility

1 Randall Stout Architects, "Process," http://www.stoutarc.com/.
2 American Institute of Architects Committee on the Environment, AIA COTE Top Ten Green Projects, http://www.aiatopten.org/hpb/images.cfm?ProjectID=195.
3 Art and Architecture Online, Design Profiles, Volume 5: http://www.volume5.com/rstout/html/architect_randall_stout_interv1.html.

4 Randall Stout Architects, Steinhude Sea Ranch Facility, http://www.stoutarc.com.
5 AIA COTE Top Ten.
6 Randall Stout Architects, profile, http://www.stoutarc.com.
7 AIA COTE Top Ten.
8 US Department of Energy, Energy Efficiency & Renewable Energy (EERE) website, "Energy." http://www.eere.buildinggreen.com/energy.cfm?ProjectID=195.
9 AIA COTE Top Ten.

10 Randall Stout Architects, "Process," http://www.stoutarc.com/.
11 Ibid.
12 Ibid.
13 EERE website, "Energy."
14 AIA COTE Top Ten.

Project:

Sino–Italian Ecological and Energy Efficient Building (SIEEB)

Location:

Tsinghua University, Beijing, China

Architect:

Mario Cucinella Architects

"Beauty is relating to the environment. The concept of beauty changes in relation to time and culture. Early before the industrial revolution, the building related to the climate and more complex issues of culture and urban context. Beauty always related to climate and solar exposure. Beauty has many forms. In every era technology has had an impact on design. How can solar, photovoltaics, and shading be a new aesthetic of architecture?"

Mario Cucinella, *Interview*

View of the south and east facades. The stepped building section allows light and air to enter the lower level while also creating abundant visual and physical connections between interior and exterior spaces. The southern shading devices and outside gardens are designed to provide seasonally appropriate luminous and thermal qualities, while the double envelope on the east and west facilitates natural ventilation during the summer months.

Design intentions

The Sino–Italian Ecological and Energy Efficient Building (SIEEB) at Tsinghua University in Beijing captures the eye and the imagination through the dynamic gestures of its multilayered facades, adjustable glass louvers, photovoltaic shading devices, and staggered terraces. The SIEEB functions as both the symbolic and the physical expression of the collaboration between the Ministry of Science and Technology of the People's Republic of China and the Ministry for Environment and Territory of the Republic of Italy. The 20,000 m² (215,278 sq ft) multistory building houses a research center, laboratories, and educational facilities. It was designed as a hands-on case study for collaboration between ecological designers, researchers, and expert consultants from China and Italy, as Mario Cucinella Architects explain: "The SIEEB Project [is]… regarded as a platform to develop the bilateral long-term cooperation in the environment and energy fields and a model case for showing the CO_2 emission reduction potential in the building sector in China."[1]

Mario Cucinella Architects and the Sino–Italian team worked together to develop, test, and implement the design and construction of the facility, which is a model for low-energy and low-carbon architecture in China and throughout the world. Team member and energy expert Professor Federico Butera, along with colleagues at Energetica and the Department of Building

Environment Science and Technology, Politecnico di Milano in Italy, emphasizes that reducing greenhouse gas emissions is a high priority in China: "It is expected that the building stock, residential and commercial, will be doubled by year 2015 … The energy structure of China is coal-based, resulting in emission of large quantities of pollutants and greenhouse gases (GHGs). It is, therefore, strategically important to introduce advanced environmental and energy technologies into this field and to promote the construction of green, energy-saving buildings."[2]

Given the mission of the Sino–Italian Cooperation Program, low-energy and low-carbon design are primary considerations for the SIEEB project. The early collaboration of designers, researchers, and consultants with specialized expertise in related areas of site, architectural form, energy, and systems enabled the team to realize exceptional re-educations in energy consumption and carbon emissions. Mario Cucinella is also quick to underscore that design and human experience are at the heart of his ecological design. The sun, site, and wind are sources of inspiration, as Cucinella explained in an interview: "Beauty is relating to the environment. The concept of beauty changes in relation to time and culture. Early, before the Industrial Revolution, the building related to the climate and more complex issues of culture and urban context. Beauty always related to climate and solar exposure. Beauty has many forms. In every era technology

has had an impact on design. How can solar, photovoltaics, and shading be a new aesthetic of architecture?" The SIEEB project, which is deeply shaped by the forces of the site and climate, challenges architects to look beyond energy performance and also consider the aesthetic and experiential implications of a new architecture of the sun and wind.

Climate and site

Beijing is located on the northern China plain, sheltered by mountains to the west and north, with open agricultural plains to the south and east of the city. The continental climate brings monsoons with high temperatures and humidity in the summer months and cold, windy winters. The average low temperature of -4.6°C (23.7°F) occurs in January, while the average high temperature reaches 26°C (78.8°F) in July. The monsoon season persists through the summer months, with a peak average rainfall of 22 cm (8.6 in) in the month of July. Infamous for air pollution and dust storms due to erosion, the city of Beijing will greatly benefit from an increased pursuit of sustainable infrastructure and architecture.

The first priority for the site design was to minimize energy consumption through passive strategies and solar control for heating and cooling, while balancing larger contextual and cultural issues. In Beijing ancient structures are frequently juxtaposed with state-of-the-art buildings. The project team was therefore careful

to consider the urban setting, adjacent buildings, and cultural contexts when evaluating the varied design proposals. The SIEEB project used a rigorous and iterative site design process that included computer simulations to investigate these and other performance characteristics for many proposed building configurations. Professor Butera and colleagues explain that the integrated site design process for SIEEB was critical in reaching new levels of ecological performance: "In the preliminary design process, a number of appropriate shapes were considered and a feasibility analysis was carried out to check how the building was able to cope with all the requirements in terms of available area, specific building volume, and space distribution. The resulting shapes were then analyzed in terms of their solar performance. Using the shape analysis, best shape was developed with the aim of maximizing solar gains in winter and minimizing them in summer."[3]

A terraced building form was selected to block northern winter winds and admit winter sun, while providing solar control and shading to the south during the summer months. Mario Cucinella explains that the pragmatic and aesthetic considerations are weighed simultaneously: "We sought the best shapes and preliminary concept in the building due to the wind, the sun, terraces, and interior side of the offices. We did preliminary analyses of the site and shape. We approach the equilibrium between

The central courtyard facades include external safety-glass louvers with reflective solar coatings. The louvers pivot in front of double-glazed windows that house internal blinds.

The south facades and roofs are shaped to gather sun and wind. Roof-integrated photovoltaic cells and evacuated tube solar collectors produce hot water while simple roof overhangs are designed to provide seasonal solar control. The northern facade overlooks the lake and surrounding landscape. Expansive areas of transparent glazing celebrate the panoramic views of the lake and nature reserve.

other building. We let concepts of harvesting energy inform and inspire design. There are no boundaries to how far ideas of energy can go. It can help create your own signature architecture."

The Steinhude Sea Recreational Facility is a pioneering project on many fronts. As one of the first contemporary energy self-reliant buildings of the twenty-first century, it shows the design promise of a new solar architecture.

Plans, sections, model studies

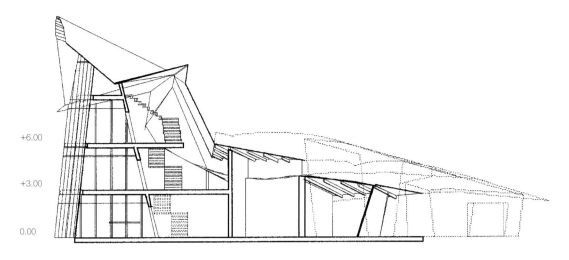

+6.00

+3.00

0.00

Section

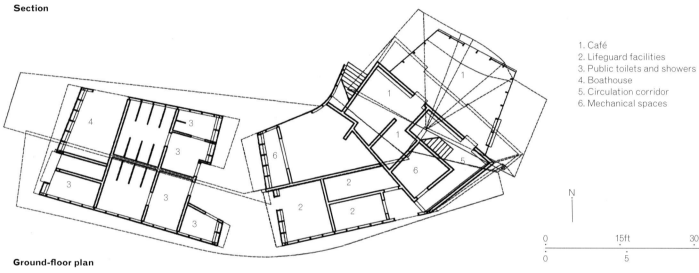

1. Café
2. Lifeguard facilities
3. Public toilets and showers
4. Boathouse
5. Circulation corridor
6. Mechanical spaces

N

0		15ft		30ft
0		5		10m

Ground-floor plan

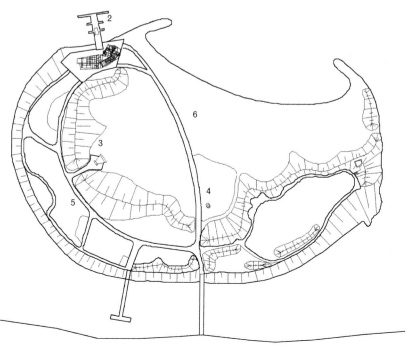

N

0		150	300ft
0		50	100m

Site plan

performance and shape for the site, urban context, and performance. The best performance is not always the best shape. The shape analysis is an important issue. The aesthetic comes through this process. Research and engineering help you to define the aesthetic." Cucinella underscores that both the sun and wind are critical ecological design issues in Beijing: "We studied the relation to the solar path and wind location. Our interest in the site at the first point is the climate data; not only technical sun and latitude; also better understanding where to put the building. In Beijing we need to understand the context of building. There is also the cold Gobi Desert, so we open to the south."

Daylighting and thermal design

Early computer simulations and concept diagrams demonstrated that the terraced building massing created very effective seasonal solar access and control. The U-shaped building is symmetrical along the north–south axis and has cascading southern terraces that wrap around a central courtyard tucked below the street level. The central courtyard is a public space that includes garden terraces, ramps, and walkways that draw people toward the heart of the building. Laboratories and offices are located on the upper levels overlooking the public gardens. The stepped building section allows light and air to enter the lower level while also creating abundant visual and physical connections between interior and

exterior spaces. The southern shading devices and outside gardens are designed to provide seasonally appropriate luminous and thermal qualities, while the double envelope on the east and west facilitates natural ventilation during the summer months. The form of the building optimizes passive strategies for daylighting, natural ventilation, and solar heat gains. SIEEB uses solar design to capture the imagination through a dynamic expression of state-of-the-art low-energy and low-carbon architecture.

Each facade of SIEEB features a different environmental response with a corresponding architectural expression. As Mario Cucinella Architects explain, Italian materials and systems were featured in the project: "The envelope components, as well as the control systems and the other technologies are the expression of the most updated Italian production, within the framework of a design philosophy in which proven components are integrated in innovative systems."[4] Glazing types were selected to optimize differing thermal and luminous characteristics based on orientation. On the northern facade, a massive blue insulated glazed wall provides an imposing presence at the main entry to the building. Distinguished by its color, opacity, and modestly sized windows, the north facade reads as a protective and sheltering buffer against the winter winds that move in from the Gobi Desert to the north. The two-story entry provides a glimpse through the north facade of

the building to the inner courtyard and expansive views and site connections on the south.

Comprised of a layered envelope, the east and west facades include external glazing (facade B) and an internal glazing (facade A). Facade B is an exterior layer of safety glazing that floats free of the double-wall envelope and uses horizontal silk-screen bands of varying density to mediate light and solar gains. An aluminum shading device is horizontally mounted between the exterior glazing (facade B) and the interior double-skin envelope (facade A). The insulated double-skin envelope (facade B) includes double glazing, operable windows, light shelves, and a simple manually operated interior blind. At the outer boundaries of the east and west facades, the silk-screened glass facades extend delicately beyond the double-skin envelope to visually reinforce the layered quality of the facades.

An animated cascade of terraces, gardens, and shading devices protects the extensive glazing of the south facade, with shading created by the projecting upper floors and the huge horizontal photovoltaic devices. To provide thermal and luminous control, the glazed facades of the interior court include operable windows and adjustable horizontal reflective glass louvers. The louvers are positioned to accommodate differing solar conditions during the changing seasons and times of day. The inner court facades include external safety glass louvers with reflective solar

coatings. The louvers pivot in front of double-glazed windows that house internal blinds. Extensive daylighting, solar control, and thermal studies were used to optimize luminous and thermal comfort and performance, taking into account seasonal concerns such as glare, solar control, luminance levels, and thermal loads.

Despite the high-tech envelope, Mario Cucinella stresses the importance of the non-technological aspects of the design. He explains that the building enhances human experience and ecological understanding: "The public spaces connect the outside and inside… The garden and quality of the park space (the terrace gardens) are friendly and domestic. The building can open the mind. You see the photovoltaic systems. They are integrated as part of the building. It is also educational… It has a positive message. You see that sustainable design is related to reality." The building teaches the users and visitors about renewable energy systems and more sustainable ways of living. Both the architectural design and the technological systems play important educational roles. The passive solar design for daylighting, cooling, natural ventilation, and heating are expressed in the overall building form and section, while the innovative systems and technologies are embodied in the details of the building envelope and shading devices.

Energy systems

A team of leading ecological designers and energy experts from Italy and China ensured

Left
View of the central courtyard garden terraces, ramps, and walkways. This public space welcomes people into the heart of the building. Laboratories and offices are located on the upper levels overlooking the public gardens.

Right
Detail of the south terrace gardens cascading over a facade that looks onto the central courtyard. Terraces, gardens, and shading devices protect the extensive glazing of the south facade, with shade created by the projecting upper floors and the huge horizontal photovoltaic devices.

that the SIEEB project hosts the latest in high-performance systems. Lighting and thermal systems were designed to complement and integrate with passive design strategies. Efficient lamps, fixtures, an electric-light dimming system, and occupancy sensors are integrated with the daylighting design to reduce lighting and cooling loads. Displacement ventilation and a radiant ceiling system are combined to provide thermal comfort. Mario Cucinella Architects explain that this integrated approach reduces the amount of electricity needed for pumps and fans: "Lightweight radiant ceilings allow for lower air temperature in winter and higher in summer, thus reducing energy consumption; moreover, the presence [occupancy] sensors, coupled with CO_2 sensors, can modulate either the airflow or the ceiling temperature when few or no people are in the room, thus avoiding useless energy consumption. In summer, night cooling takes place."[5] The waste heat from gas-fired electric generators is harvested to heat water throughout the year and to provide heat in the winter and cooling in the summer through the use of absorption chillers.

Professor Butera and research colleagues explain why they used combined heat and power (CHP) in the energy design: "The CHP system is the core of the energy system of the building. Since… China presently is not allowed to sell electricity to the grid, the system is controlled in such a way that neither the

electricity production exceeds the building's demand nor the waste heat produced exceeds the heating or cooling demand. This means that sometimes, when thermal loads are low, electricity production is not sufficient and some power has to be taken from the grid. Some other times the cooling loads—that are higher than the heating ones—are so high that too much electricity would be produced; in this case, the excess electricity is diverted to compression chillers, slightly reducing, at the same time, the power of the engines. A sophisticated, intelligent control system manages the plant."[6] The control system further reduces unnecessary energy consumption by adjusting the temperature and air changes in response to the actual, rather than hypothetical, occupant loads in the rooms.

Based on their energy study, Professor Butera and colleagues estimated significant energy savings from the high-performance equipment and the integrated CHP system: "The study shows that the energy demand for air-conditioning has a very high contribution in total energy loads of SIEEB. Cooling demand dominates the building energy loads (40 percent) and the heating demand is relatively lower (18 percent). The estimated annual energy loads for reference and optimized case are estimated as 2,415 MWh and 1,883 MWh, respectively. The peak loads for cooling, heating, and lighting and equipment in SIEEB are 963, 357, and 230 kW respectively. Further it was concluded that

Left
View of the west facade. An exterior layer of safety glazing floats free of the double-wall envelope and uses horizontal silk-screen bands of varying density to mediate light and solar gains. An aluminum shading device is mounted horizontally between the exterior glazing and the interior double-skin envelope which includes double glazing, operable windows, light shelves, and a simple manually operated interior blind.

Right
Detail showing a landscaped terrace, the building envelope, and photovoltaic shading. Visitors and occupants of the building have panoramic views of the city and distant mountains.

for the optimized case, the annual energy load reductions for cooling, heating, and lighting and equipment can be achieved up to 30 percent, 23 percent, and 20 percent respectively."[7]

Additional reductions in energy consumption are provided by the photovoltaic system, which is integrated into the south-facing horizontal shading devices on the terraces. The system comprises 190 modules of photovoltaic panels that cover an area of more than 1,000 m² (10,764 sq ft) and have a peak power capacity of 19.95 kW.[8] The Sino–Italian Cooperation Program estimates that SIEEB will produce 1,200 tons of CO_2 and five tons of SO_2 per year, which represents a significant reduction in greenhouse gas emissions compared to standard buildings of similar size in China.[9] In assessing the SIEEB project, Carmen Glorioso and colleagues at the Italian Ministry for the Environment, Land, and Sea suggest that zero emission is a reasonable target: "[In] a more or less near future the SIEEB could become a zero-emission building. This is possible by using biofuels instead of natural gas to power the engines, simply adapting or substituting them. A more long-term scenario includes the use of fuel cells powered by hydrogen produced from renewable energy.[10]

Next-generation thinking
In reflecting on the distinctions between solar architecture of the 1970s and today, Mario

Cucinella emphasized the current design innovations as well as new technological innovation: "The 1970s were more experimental and missing the capacity to make analysis. Today there is another level of complexity. With today's level of analysis we can see the invisible; we can see airflow, shadow, and invisible parts of design. Today solar is more scientific. Thinking about solar—zero-energy and carbon-neutral design—is deeply scientific." In addition to his appreciation of the scientific, analytical, and technological realms of solar design, Mario Cucinella is deeply grounded in principles of passive and climate-responsive architecture that reflect the discipline's earliest roots. It is not difficult to see SIEEB as having formal bonds with ancient indigenous architectures— for example, the tenth-century Anasazi site of Pueblo Bonito, in Chaco Canyon, Arizona, rebuilt with a high-technology wrapper for twenty-first-century China.

Cucinella argues that energy and carbon are at the heart of good design: "There is an aesthetic in carbon-neutral design, in beautiful buildings. I like the idea of discovering something that informs us about the shape of architecture. More and more we find new solutions, we're more competent and informed by other disciplines. The future of sustainable design is not about more photovoltaics. In the future of building, we need more work on the quality of space and integration of solar and carbon-neutral design so

Interior view of the lecture hall with a distant view to the central courtyard. Indirect daylight is admitted from above.

View of a ground-level
entry with bilateral
daylighting and a
view beyond to the
lower-level central
courtyard.

that it is part of the process—so that the shape
of the building solves the problem." He believes
that energy and design aesthetics are intimately
related: "Every building is a new possibility and
form. There is no preconception of shape…
The aesthetic comes through this process. The
aesthetic is the end, the beautiful building."

SIEEB demonstrates that new partnerships,
collaborations, and design processes are an
integral component in realizing new ecological
goals and aesthetic possibilities for solar
architecture in the twenty-first century.

Plans, sections, drawings

Expressing an ecological aesthetic: Sino-Italian Ecological and Energy Efficient Building (SIEEB)

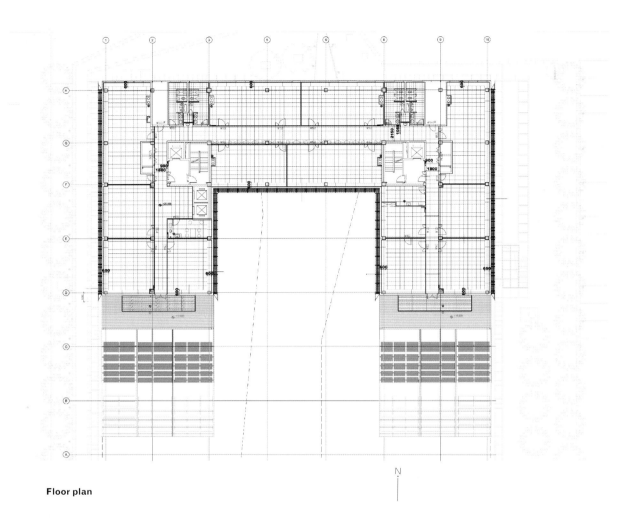

Floor plan

N

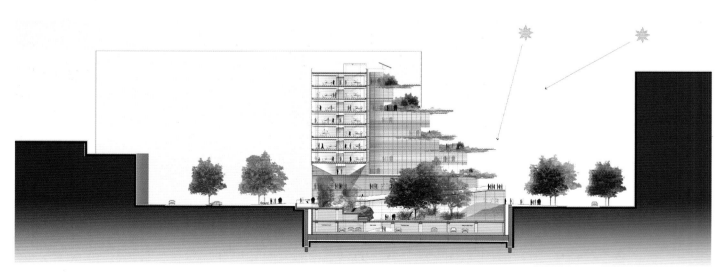

Section through courtyard

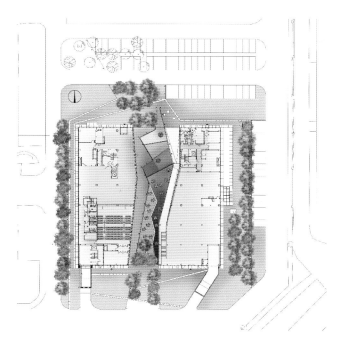

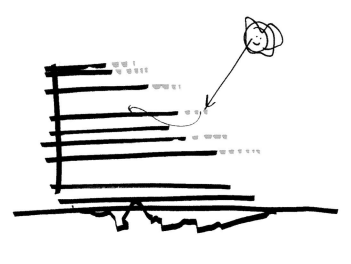

Site plan

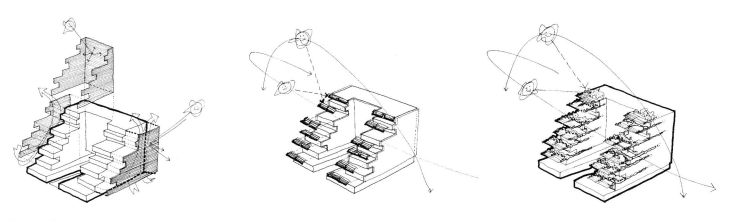

Concept diagrams

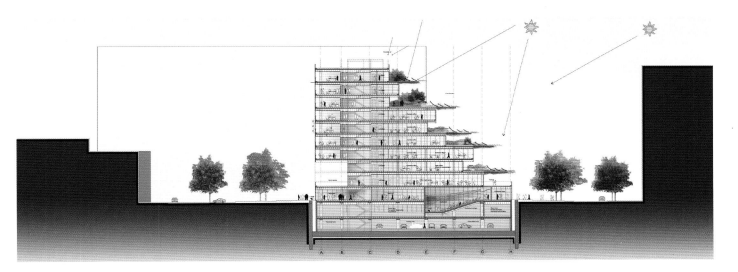

Section through offices

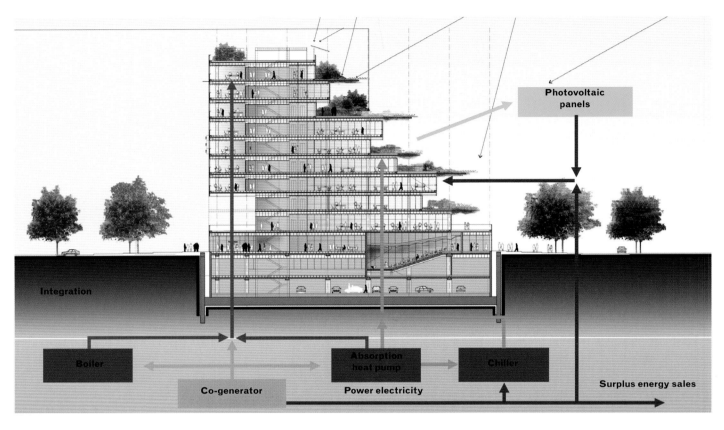

Systems diagram

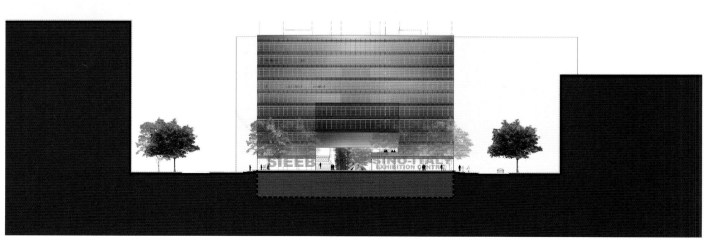

North facade

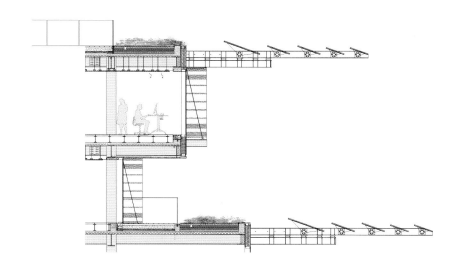

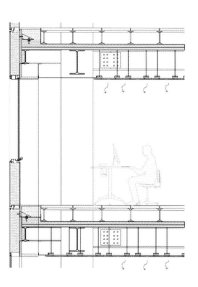

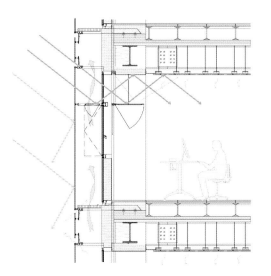

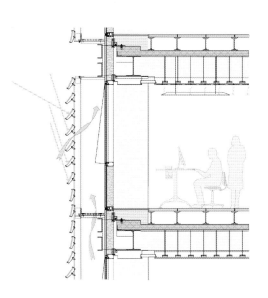

Section envelope details

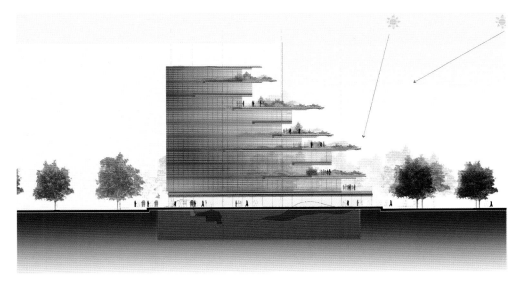

West facade

Wind studies

Project location:
Beijing, China

Wind data location:
Beijing, China

Prevailing winds
March
Wind frequency (hours)
Location: Beijing, China (39.8°, 116.5°)
Time: 00:00–24:00

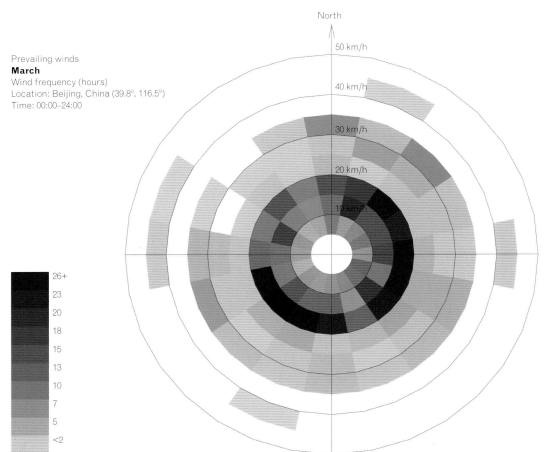

Prevailing winds
September
Wind frequency (hours)
Location: Beijing, China (39.8°, 116.5°)
Time: 00:00–24:00

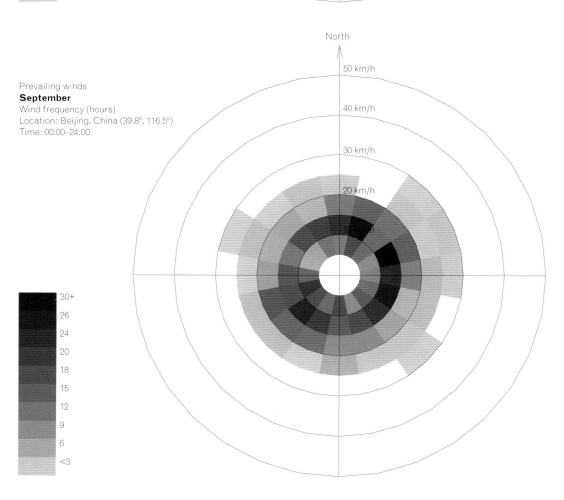

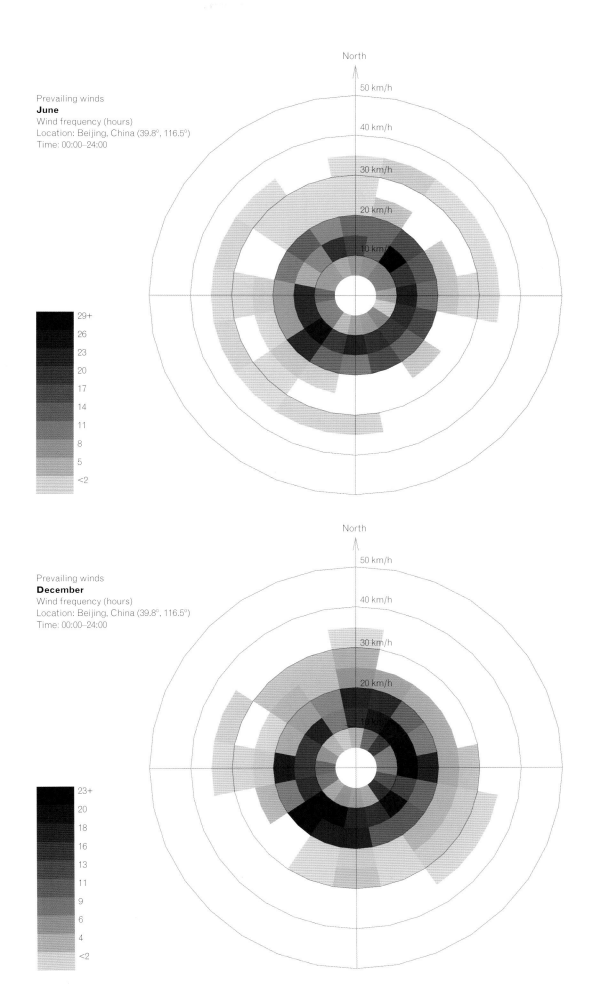

North

50 km/h

40 km/h

30 km/h

20 km/h

10 km/h

Prevailing winds
June
Wind frequency (hours)
Location: Beijing, China (39.8°, 116.5°)
Time: 00:00–24:00

29+
26
23
20
17
14
11
8
5
<2

North

50 km/h

40 km/h

30 km/h

20 km/h

10 km/h

Prevailing winds
December
Wind frequency (hours)
Location: Beijing, China (39.8°, 116.5°)
Time: 00:00–24:00

23+
20
18
16
13
11
9
6
4
<2

Sunpath case studies

Expressing an ecological aesthetic: Sino-Italian Ecological and Energy Efficient Building (SIEEB)

Project location:
Beijing, China
Latitude: 39° NL

December

09:00

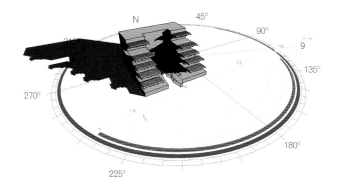

March/September

09:00

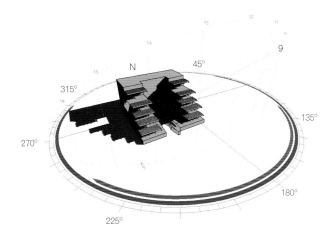

09:00

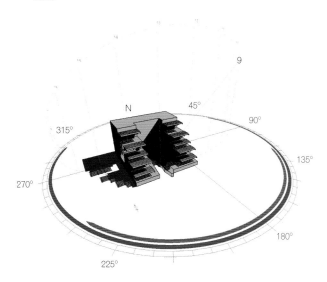

12:00

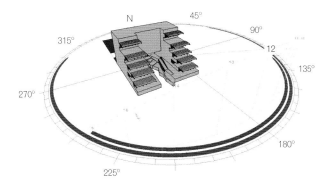

15:00

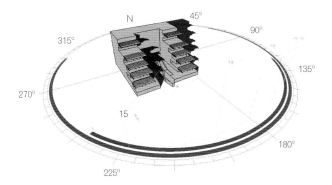

12:00

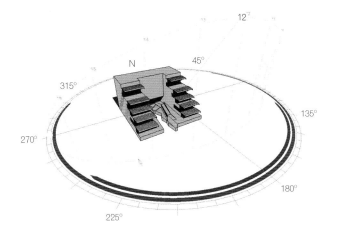

15:00

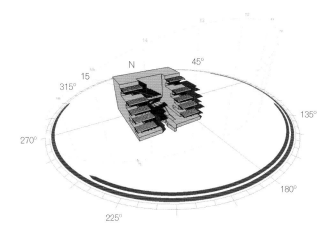

12:00

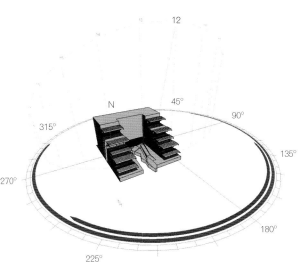

15:00

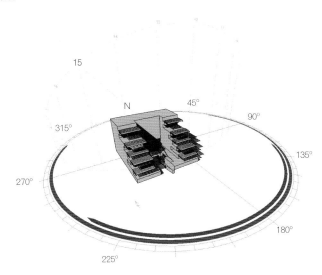

Climate data

Project location:
Beijing, China

Climate data location:
Beijing, China

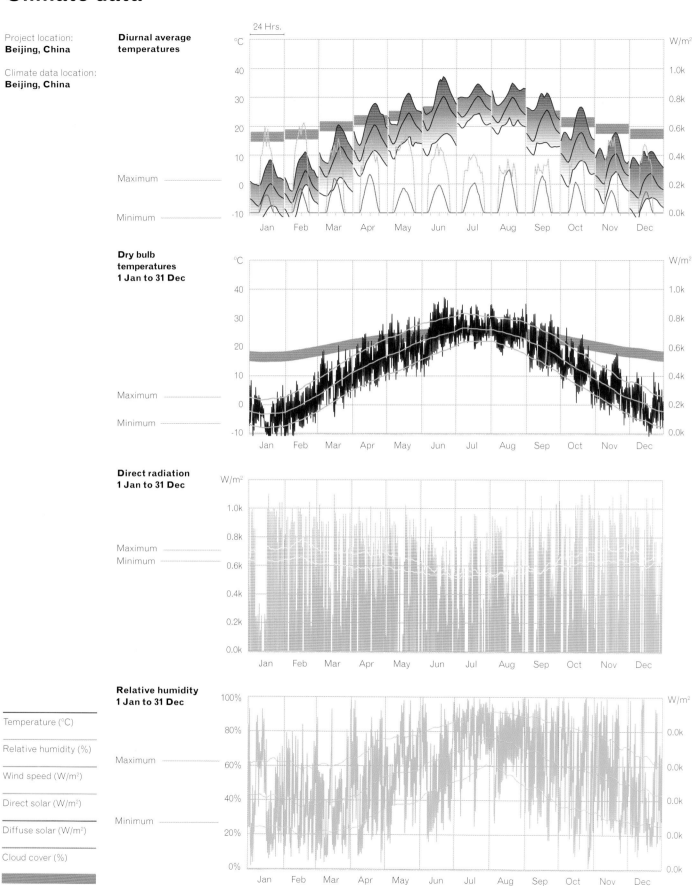

Diurnal average temperatures

24 Hrs.

Maximum

Minimum

Dry bulb temperatures 1 Jan to 31 Dec

Maximum

Minimum

Direct radiation 1 Jan to 31 Dec

Maximum
Minimum

Relative humidity 1 Jan to 31 Dec

Maximum

Minimum

Temperature (°C)

Relative humidity (%)

Wind speed (W/m²)

Direct solar (W/m²)

Diffuse solar (W/m²)

Cloud cover (%)

Thermal neutrality

Design profile

Building profile	Building name:	**Sino–Italian Ecological and Energy Efficient Building (SIEEB)**
	Architect:	Mario Cucinella Architects, Bologna, Italy; www.mcarchitects.it
	Location:	Tsinghua University, Beijing, China
	Building type:	Research
	Square footage:	20,000 m² (215,278 sq ft)

Solar design profile	Latitude:	39° NL
	Heating Degree Days:	2,848 heating degree days °C (5,251 heating degree days °F) (18°C and 65°F base temperature; average 5 years)
	Cooling Degree Days:	1,032 cooling degree days °C (1,766 cooling degree days °F)
	Conservation strategies:	Optimize building form and massing; luminous and thermal zoning
	Passive solar strategies:	Daylighting, direct gain passive solar, exterior shading, thermal mass storage, open floor plan, natural ventilation, operable windows
	Active solar strategies:	Photovoltaic system
	Other renewable energy strategies:	None
	High-performance strategies:	Daylight photosensors, occupancy sensors, high-performance electric lighting, combined heat and power, radiant ceilings, displacement ventilation, high-performance glazing and envelope

Performance profile[11] [12] [13]	Total annual building energy consumption:	Estimated 1,883 MWh (all values are from the optimized energy studies prior to construction)[14] Estimated cooling load: 963 kW Estimated lighting load: 357 kW Estimated heating load: 230 kW
	Total annual on-site energy produced:	Not available
	Size of photovoltaic system: (wind and other renewable energy sources on site):	19.95 kW photovoltaic system, 1,000 m² (10,764 sq ft)[15]
	Size of solar thermal system:	None
	Carbon dioxide emissions:	Estimated 1,200 tons CO_2 and 5 tons SO_2 emissions per year[16]

Endnotes:
Sino-Italian Ecological and Energy Efficient Building (SIEEB)

1 Mario Cucinella Architects, "Sino–Italy Environment & Energy Building (SIEEB)," www.mcarchitects.it.
2 F. Butera, R.S. Adhikari, P.Caputo, S. Ferrari and P. Oliaro, "The Sino–Italy Environment & Energy Building (SIEEB): A Model for a New Generation of Sustainable Buildings;" International Conference for Passive and Low Energy Cooling, Santorini, Greece (May 2005), 935.
3 Ibid.
4 Mario Cucinella Architects, www.mcarchitects.it.
5 Ibid.
6 F. Butera, et al, 937.
7 Ibid.
8 Carmen Glorioso, Mario Lionetti and Francesco Presicce, "Energy Efficiency and Renewable Energy Italy—National study," Mediterranean and National Strategies for Sustainable Development Priority Field of Action 2: Energy and Climate Change, Italian Ministry for the Environment Land and Sea, Plan Bleu Regional Activity Centre, Sophia Antipolis, (March 2007), 31.
9 Sino–Italian Cooperation Program, http://www.sinoitaenvironment.org/ReadNewsex1.asp?NewsID=1930.
10 Carmen Glorioso, et al, 30.
11 F. Butera, et al, 928.
12 Carmen Glorioso, et al, 31.
13 Sino–Italian Cooperation Program.
14 F. Butera, et al, 938.
15 Carmen Glorioso, et al, 31.
16 Sino–Italian Cooperation Program.

Bibliography

Abram, David, *The Spell of the Sensuous*, New York: Vantage Books, 1997

Ackerman, Diane, *A Natural History of the Senses*, New York: Vantage Books, 1990

Aldo Leopold Legacy Center, website: http://www.aldoleopold.org/legacycenter

Allenby, Guy, *Eight Great Houses,* Sydney: Pesaro Publishing, 2002

American Institute of Architects Committee on the Environment (AIA COTE), "Z6 House," *AIA COTE Top Ten Green Projects.* 2007 Awards Program, website: http://www.aiatopten.org

Art and Architecture Online, *Design Profiles*, vol. 5, website: http://www.volume5.com/rstout/html/architect_randall_stout_interv1.html

Behling, Sophia and Stefan, *Solar Power: The Evolution of Sustainable Architecture*, Munich: Prestel, 2000

Berry, Thomas, *The Great Work: Our Way into the Future*, New York: Bell Towers, 1999

Bordass, Bill, *Society of Building Science Educators Listserver*, December 4, 2008

Butera, F., R.S. Adhikari, P. Caputo, S. Ferrari, and P. Oliaro, "The Sino-Italy Environment & Energy Building (SIEEB): A Model for a New Generation of Sustainable Buildings," *International Conference for Passive and Low Energy Cooling*, Santorini, Greece (May 2005), p935

Department for Communities and Local Government, *Code for Sustainable Homes*, London: Department for Communities and Local Government, 2006

Fortmeyer, Russell, "Case Study: Tim and Karen Hixon Visitor Center, Helotes, Texas" in *Greensource* (January 2008), p77

Fuller, R. Buckminster, *Critical Path*, New York: St. Martin's Press, 1981

Gipe, Paul, "Freiburg's Solar Siedlung" in *Windworks* (April 7, 2007), website: www.windworks.org

Glorioso, Carmen, Mario Lionetti and Francesco Presicce, "Energy Efficiency and Renewable Energy Italy—National study," *Mediterranean and National Strategies for Sustainable Development Priority Field of Action 2: Energy and Climate Change*, Italian Ministry for the Environment Land and Sea, Plan Bleu Regional Activity Centre, Sophia Antipolis (March 2007)

Goad, Philip, "Top End Eyrie" in *Monument*, vol. 48 (June/July 2002), pp96–100

Goad, Philip, *Troppo Architects*, Sydney: Pesaro Publishing, second edition, 2005

Golden, Greg, "Kappe House" in *The Architect's Newspaper* (May 2, 2007), website: www.archpaper.com

Gott, Beth, *Aboriginal Trail*,

Department of Water, Environment, Heritage and the Arts, Australian Government, website: http://www.anbg.gov.au/anbg/aboriginal-trail.html

GreenBiz Staff, "USGBC Awards LivingHomes First-Ever Platinum Rating in Residential Design" in *GreenBiz* (August 16, 2006), website: http://www.greenerbuildings.com/news/2006/08/16/usgbc-awards-livinghomes-first-ever-platinum-rating-residential-design

Hagemann, Ingo B., "Solarsiedlung am Schlierberg, Freiburg (Breisgau), Germany" in *PV Upscale*, website: http://www.pvupscale.org/IMG/pdf/Schlierberg.pdf

Hawken, Paul, *Blessed Unrest: How the Largest Movement in the World Came into Being and Why No One Saw it Coming*, New York: Penguin Group, 2007

Hegger, Manfred, "From Passive Utilization to Smart Solar Architecture" in *Solar Architecture*, edited by Christian Schittich, Basel: Birkhäuser, 2003

Herzog, Thomas, Roland Krippner, and Werner Lang, *Façade Construction Manual*, Munich: Birkhäuser, 2004

Jury Citation, "Award for Sustainable Architecture" in *Architecture Australia* (November/December 2002), pp62–63

Kaltenbach, Frank, ed., *Translucent Materials: Glass Plastic Metals*, Basel: Birkhäuser, 2004

Kingspan, "Lighthouse," website:http://www.kingspanlighthouse.com

Kingspan Lighthouse, website: http://www.kingspanlighthouse.com/accomodating_climate_change.htm

Kingspan Lighthouse, website: www.kingspanlighthouse.com/energy.htm

Knowles, Ralph, *Ritual House*, Washington, DC: Island Press, 2006, website: http://islandpress.org/bookstore/details.php?isbn=9781597260503

Knowles, Ralph, *Solar Aesthetic*, Ralph Knowles, 2008, website: http://www-rcf.usc.edu/~rknowles/aesthetics/aesthetics.html

Krippner, Roland, "Solar Technology—From Innovative Building Skin to Energy-Efficient Renovation" in *Solar Architecture,* edited by Christian Schittich, Basel: Birkhäuser, 2003

Kubala Washatko Architects, website: http://www.tkwa.com

Kubala Washatko Architects, "The Greenest Building in the World?", *Living Futures* 2008 Conference, 2008

Lake | Flato Architects, *Firm Profile*, website: www.lakeflato.com

Lake | Flato Architects, *Government Canyon Visitor Center*, website: www.lakeflato.com

Lang, Werner, "Is it All 'Just' a Facade: The Functional, Energetic and Structural Aspects of the Building Skin" in *Building Skins: Concepts Layers Materials*, edited by Christian Schittich, Basel: Birkhäuser, 2001

Leopold, Aldo, *A Sand County Almanac*, London: Oxford University Press, 1949

LivingHomes, "Z6 House Brochure", Santa Monica, CA: no date, website: http://www.aia.org/SiteObjects/files/Z6House_12pg.pdf

Mario Cucinella Architects, "Sino-Italy Environment & Energy Building (SIEEB)," website: www.mcarchitects.it

Mau, Bruce, *Massive Change*, New York: Phaidon Press Limited, 2004

McDonough, William and Michael Braungart, *Cradle to Cradle: Remaking the Way We Make Things*, New York: North Point Press, 2002

McGillick, Paul, "Verandah House" in *Steel Profile: Architectural Steel Innovation with BHP Steel*, no. 78 (March 2002)

Merkel, Jim, *Radical Simplicity: Small Footprints on a Finite Earth*, Gabriola Island, BC: New Society Publishers, 2003

Miller, David E., *Toward a New Regionalism*, Seattle: University of Washington Press, 2005

O'Connell, Sandra Andrea, "Light Years Ahead—Kingspan Century's Lighthouse" in *Architecture Ireland* (Sept 2007), p89

Orr, David, *The Nature of Design: Ecology, Culture, and Human Intention*, Oxford: Oxford University Press, 2002

Passivhaus Institut, website: http://www.passivehouse.com

Pearson, David, *New Organic Architecture: The Breaking Wave*, London: Gaia Books Limited, 2001

Potton, "Lighthouse by Potton," website: http://www.lighthousebypotton.co.uk/Press/LighthouseBrochure.pdf

Purvis, Andrew, "Is This the Greenest City in the World?" in *The Observer* (Sunday, March 23, 2008), website: http://www.guardian.co.uk/environment/2008/mar/23/freiburg.germany.greenest.city

Randall Stout Architects, *Process and Steinhude Sea Ranch Facility*, website: http://www.stoutarc.com

RE News, "Built Green" in *Solar Today*, Nov/Dec. 2006, p38

Rees, William, "Revisiting Carrying Capacity: Area-Based Indicators of Sustainability" in *Population and Environment: A Journal of Interdisciplinary Studies*, v. 17, no. 3 (1996 Human Sciences Press, Inc., January 1996), website: http://www.dieoff.org/page110.htm

Rich, Sarah and Geoff Manaugh, "London Cooling" in *Dwell*, vol. 8,

no. 6 (May 2008), pp100–102, 104

Rolf Disch Architects, website: http://www.rolfdisch.de

Rothermel, Winfried, "A German City's Long Focus on the Sun," *ABC News*, July 19, 2007

Rozak, Mike, website: http://www.mxac.com.au/EagleEye

Schittich, Christian, "Shell, Skin, Materials" in *Building Skins: Concepts Layers Materials*, Basel: Birkhäuser, 2001

Schittich, Christian, ed., *Solar Architecture*, Basel: Birkhäuser, 2003

Schumacher, E.F., *Small is Beautiful: Economics as if People Mattered*, New York: Harper & Row Publishers, 1973

Sheppard Robson, "Kingspan Lighthouse," London: Sheppard Robson, no date

Sino-Italian Cooperation Program, "The Sino-Italy Environment & Energy Building (SIEEB)," website: http://www.sinoitaenvironment.org/ReadNewsex1.asp?NewsID=1930

Smith, Peter F., *Architecture in a Climate of Change: A Guide to Sustainable Design*, Oxford: Architectural Press, 2001

Solar Decathlon Team, Technische Universität Darmstadt, website: http://www.solardecathlon.de

Solarsiedlung GmbH, "Freiburg, Solar City" in *Ottagono Design, Architettura, Idee*, website: http://www.solarsiedlung.de/presse

Technische Universität Darmstadt, "Talking Points," website: http://www.solardecathlon.org/pdfs/talking_points_07/2007_talking_points_darmstadt.pdf

Texas Parks & Wildlife Department, *Government Canyon State Natural Area*, Texas: State of Texas, website: http://www.tpwd.state.tx.us/spdest/findadest/parks/government_canyon

Troppo Architects, website: http://www.troppoarchitects.com.au

Troppo Architects, *Punkahs and Pith Helmets*, Darwin: Troppo Architects, 1982

Turner, Chris, "Solar Settlement" in *Azure*, v. 23, issue 175 (May 2007), pp62–66

U.S. Department of Energy, "Steinhude Sea Recreational Facility," *Energy Efficiency and Renewable Energy (EERE) Program*, website: http://eere.buildinggreen.com/energy.cfm?ProjectID=195

U.S. Department of Energy, *Solar Decathlon*, website: http://www.solardecathlon.org/about.html

U.S. Department of Energy, *2007 Solar Decathlon Closing Ceremony and Awards*, http://www.energy.gov/news/5648.htm

Velux, "Professional Case Studies: Architecture," website: http://

Index

www.velux.co.uk/Professionals/
Architects/Cases_domestic/
SOLTAG/Architecture/
Velux, "Soltag Energy Housing,"
website: http://www.velux.co.uk/
Professionals/Architects/Cases_
domestic/SOLTAG/Energy/
Velux, "SOLTAG [energy housing]
Brochure," Hørsholm, Denmark:
Velux A/S, p4
Wigginton, Michael and Jude
Harris, *Intelligent Skins*, Oxford:
Butterworth-Heinemann, 2002
Wörner, Dieter, "Sustainable
City Freiburg," *Freiburg Fair*,
Madison, WI: Office of the
Mayor (August 2005), website:
http://www.madisonfreiburg.org/
sustainablecity.htm

Picture Credits

Acknowledgments

I would like to extend my sincere thanks and appreciation to my colleagues, students, friends, and family who have inspired and supported this project. I thank the College of Design and School of Architecture at the University of Minnesota for research support during the past year. I very much appreciate the always lively conversations with my colleagues from the Society of Building Science Educators who are exploring the emerging areas of zero-energy and carbon-neutral architecture and design education. Special thanks to my colleagues Loren Abraham, AIA, LEED AP, for his help in framing the quantitative assessments and for sharing his experience with zero-energy design, and to Ian McLellan, Associate AIA, for his solar studies, climate analyses, and assistance with graph materials. I greatly appreciate the insights and inspiration provided by the architects featured in this book who gave so generously of their time for interviews, as well as the architectural design firms and photographers who made accessible their beautiful photographs and drawings. A special thanks to James, Bert, Izzy, Pat, and my dear family and friends. Finally, I thank my editors Philip Cooper and Liz Faber at Laurence King Publishing Ltd for their support and commitment to this project and Jason Godfrey of Godfrey Design for his great attention to detail and his thoughtful design of the book.